IMAGES
of America

PITTSBURGH FILM AND TELEVISION

On the Cover: This image shows the cast and crew of *Mister Rogers' Neighborhood* in the early 1970s. (Courtesy of Sam Silberman, © The Fred Rogers Company, used with permission.)

IMAGES
of America

PITTSBURGH FILM AND TELEVISION

John Tiech

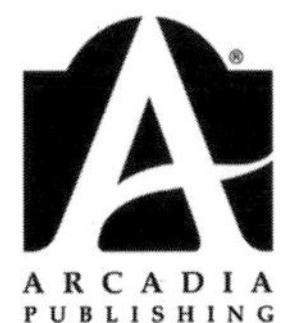

ISBN 978-1-4671-2088-3

Published by Arcadia Publishing
Charleston, South Carolina

Printed in the United States of America

Library of Congress Control Number: 2013943717

For all general information, please contact Arcadia Publishing:
Telephone 843-853-2070
Fax 843-853-0044
E-mail sales@arcadiapublishing.com
For customer service and orders:
Toll-Free 1-888-313-2665

Visit us on the Internet at www.arcadiapublishing.com

For the talented Pittsburgh film community.

Contents

Acknowledgments 6

Introduction 7

1. Establishing Film in Pittsburgh 9

2. Pioneering Pittsburgh Television 21

3. Location Filmmaking in Pittsburgh 37

4. Behind the Scenes of Modern Pittsburgh Filmmaking 75

ACKNOWLEDGMENTS

I would like to thank all of those who helped make this project possible. David Newell, Brittany Smith, Rick Sebak, and Sam Silberman are responsible for the wonderful collection of WQED, *Mister Rogers' Neighborhood*, and *The Children's Corner* pictures shared in this book. The representatives at WPXI Channel 11 graciously gave permission for the use of *Chiller Theater* and *Studio Wrestling* advertisements. Russ Streiner, Jim Cirronella, and the folks of Image Ten Inc. provided the use of behind-the-scenes images from their *Night of the Living Dead* collection. Bochy Fu, Vicki Tallon, Coleen Angel, Denise Merriman, and Tony Amen shared their own personal behind-the-scenes photographs, and I am honored to call these people my friends. Speaking of friends, my talented friend Kailyn Trainer-Walters is responsible for a few of the location photographs. Her great talent is also appreciated. To those who aren't mentioned, and there are many, their work and dedication to the Pittsburgh film community should not go without recognition. I also would like to take this opportunity to thank them for everything that they do.

All chapter one images from the *Pittsburgh Moving Picture Bulletin* are courtesy of the Library and Archives Division of the Western Pennsylvania Historical Society at the Senator John Heinz History Center. All chapter one images from *The Moving Picture World* are courtesy of the University of Pittsburgh Hillman Library Microforms. The images in chapter two are courtesy of Sam Silberman, the images in chapter three are part of the author's collection, and the images in chapter four are courtesy of actor Tony Amen.

Introduction

When *Pittsburgh Film History: On Set in the Steel City* was released, readers and film lovers were provided with the first book to explore the history of film and television in a single American city. The book provides the most comprehensive list and information on movies, television shows, casting agencies, businesses, schools, and organizations that make up the Pittsburgh film industry. *Pittsburgh Film and Television* tells more of the visual story along with the accompanying facts, providing a visual tour through time. This extended tour through Pittsburgh's film and television history begins in the early 20th century and ends in the present day. Despite the accolades and great success of *Pittsburgh Film History* and the publication of *Pittsburgh Film and Television*, this story will always be unfinished.

As film was being established as an entertainment commodity, Pittsburgh was at the forefront of the movement. Most notably, Pittsburgh was the home of the first nickelodeon in the United States, established by Harry Davis and John P. Harris. The Smithfield Street establishment was the first of its kind and paved the way for several more theaters to be built in Pittsburgh only a year later, with all of them under the ownership of Davis. However, the growth of the film community was nowhere near limited to the theaters. Film exchanges arrived in Pittsburgh to eventually establish "film row," an area of a city that comprises film-related businesses such as exchanges and supply houses. The first well-documented incarnation of film row was along the intersection of Fourth Avenue and Ferry Street (now Stanwix Street) in downtown Pittsburgh. During the first week of May 1916, film row migrated to Penn Avenue in order to secure space that was specifically tailored for film businesses. Most of those businesses were located in a single building called the Film Exchange Building at 938–940 Penn Avenue, while the others remained nearby. However, film row migrated once more to an area along the Boulevard of the Allies during the 1920s, becoming the final incarnation of film row in Pittsburgh. At these exchanges, films could be bought, rented, or traded by theater owners (known as exhibitors at the time) for the purpose of showing the motion pictures to the public at their theater. Miscellaneous film businesses also emerged. Some of these businesses represented part of film row, whereas others were not and were scattered around Pittsburgh. They provided equipment and supplies, such as projectors and ticket dispensers, for the theaters. Pittsburgh was even briefly used for the filming of *The Perils of Pauline* in 1914 and *Via Wireless* during the summer of 1915. The Pittsburgh film industry grew so large that it even had its own publication called the *Pittsburgh Moving Picture Bulletin*. Regardless of the great success, the ever-changing film industry eventually led to the collapse of the Pittsburgh film industry, rendering it virtually nonexistent for many years. A more complete look at Pittsburgh's early film industry can be found in Michael Aronson's *Nickelodeon City*.

The film industry in Pittsburgh essentially vanished with major motion pictures primarily being made in New York and California studios. However, the advent of television brought new life to Pittsburgh's film industry. The first television station established in Pittsburgh was KDKA in 1949, followed by several other stations over the next decade. One of the most active and educational stations was WQED, which was established in 1953 and went on the air a year later. Josie Carey and Fred Rogers signed onto the station in 1953 and were responsible for creating an educational and entertaining program for children called *The Children's Corner.* After the show ended in 1961, Rogers left Pittsburgh but returned in 1966 to begin work on his legendary children's program *Mister Rogers' Neighborhood.* Not only did the show provide quality education to children, it also offered an opportunity for many Pittsburghers, such as director George A. Romero and actor Michael Keaton, to get experience in the business. *Mister Rogers' Neighborhood* was also the launch pad for many veteran crew members in Pittsburgh.

When television station WIIC (now known as WPXI) was launched in 1957, Bill Cardille became the face of the station as he hosted nationally recognized shows, such as *Studio Wrestling* and *Chiller Theater.* Cardille's career leaped onto the big screen with his appearance in *Night of the Living Dead.* Between his *Chiller Theater* program and his appearance in *Night of the Living Dead,* Cardille became an American horror icon. On *Studio Wrestling,* Cardille also worked with some of the legends of professional wrestling, such as Bruno Sammartino and George "The Animal" Steele. The nationwide success of local programming from the various television stations such as WIIC during these years helped pave the way for the modern film industry in Pittsburgh.

Since Hollywood expanded outside of its boundaries, many cities worldwide contributed to major motion pictures. Whether it is an urban skyscraper or a rural farm, Pittsburgh has everything to offer filmmakers, unlike many of these other cities. With the region's unique topography and geography, Pittsburgh can stand in for most locations in the world. Even though Pittsburgh may not have beaches or famous landmarks found in other countries and cities, the establishment of 31st Street Studios (formerly Mogul Mind Studios) in 2009 and their green screen technology enables filmmakers to bring these unique sites to the city virtually.

The process of discovering a place to film involves location scouting. Like many other cities across the country, Pittsburgh has its own film office that assists these location scouts and productions in finding a suitable location in the region. Furthermore, Pittsburgh is an attractive location because it also has more crew workers than most other cities. Legislation (such as the Pennsylvania Film Tax Credit, for example) has even been introduced to entice location filmmaking in Pittsburgh. One of the most exciting aspects of filmmaking is when the actors and actresses show up on location for all to see. Locations vary all across the Pittsburgh region from inside the city to the surrounding rural areas. Movie productions do their best to avoid disruptions as they monetarily compensate home and business owners. These same productions also work in conjunction with the Pittsburgh Film Office in sending out letters to the community, alerting people of the disruptions that will occur and providing contact information for those with questions regarding the production and its schedule. Even though location filmmaking can bring disruptions, many Pittsburghers are excited at the chance of seeing major Hollywood stars in the community. The local citizenry even jumps at the chance to be in a movie. Those who are lucky enough to make it on set quickly discover that filmmaking consists of long days, a lot of standing around, and meeting new people. For some, the joy of meeting new people forges friendships. For others, it brings them face-to-face with a Hollywood star.

One

Establishing Film in Pittsburgh

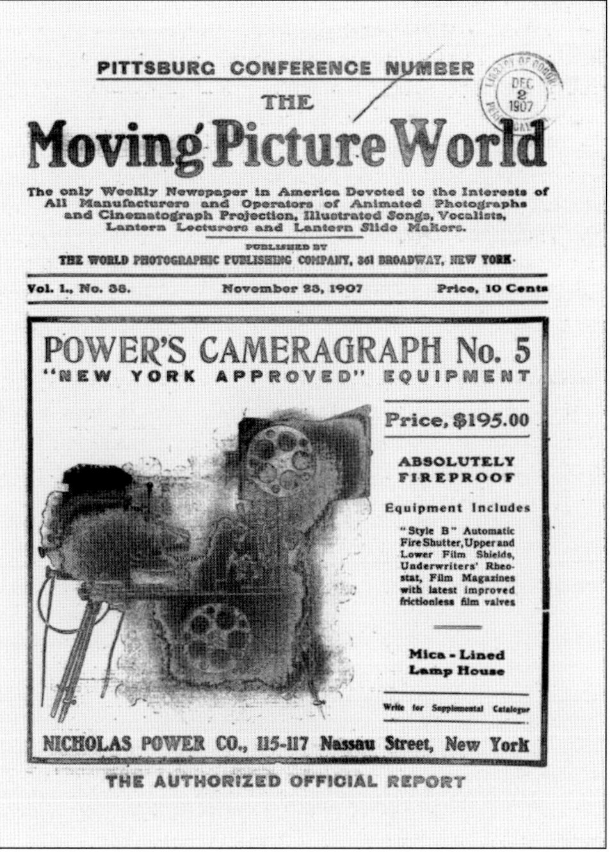

PITTSBURG CONFERENCE NUMBER

THE

Moving Picture World

The only Weekly Newspaper in America Devoted to the Interests of All Manufacturers and Operators of Animated Photographs and Cinematograph Projection, Illustrated Songs, Vocalists, Lantern Lecturers and Lantern Slide Makers.

PUBLISHED BY
THE WORLD PHOTOGRAPHIC PUBLISHING COMPANY, 361 BROADWAY, NEW YORK.

Vol. 1., No. 38. November 23, 1907 Price, 10 Cents

THE AUTHORIZED OFFICIAL REPORT

This issue of *The Moving Picture World* magazine from November 23, 1907, included an extensive article on a major conference in Pittsburgh among nationwide exhibitors. The conference took place on Saturday, November 16, and Sunday, November 17, 1907, at the Fort Pitt Hotel. Film manufacturers and renters from across the country met at this conference to discuss various ideas relating to the film business as well as submit their own suggestions and resolutions to problems the industry faced.

ARE YOU GETTING THE HEADLINERS ?

Why not hitch up with a live concern and get the best that is going. The season is now on. Don't trifle away your valuable time. Write quick for particulars

Wonderland Film Exchange

Suite 1308-9-10-11-12 Keenan Bldg.

PITTSBURGH, PA.

The Wonderland Film Exchange was in the T.J. Keenan Building, a structure that still exists to this day. In the beginning, many film exchanges didn't own their own buildings and were in large buildings with various other businesses that weren't necessarily film related. This Wonderland Film Exchange ad was found in the November 21, 1908, issue of *The Moving Picture World* magazine. In 1908, the Wonderland Film Exchange was only one of seven film exchanges in Pittsburgh authorized by the Motion Picture Patents Company to handle licensed films. The others included the American Film Exchange, the Columbia Film Exchange, the Duquesne Amusement Supply Company, the Pennsylvania Film Exchange, the Pittsburgh Calcium Light & Film Company, and Harry Davis.

We Are After 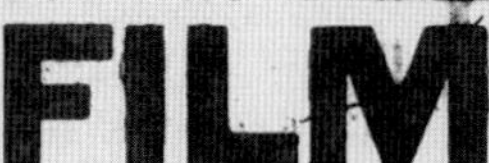

Customers Desiring Quality

A few words to those desiring the cream of all makes. To the many showing film after their competitors

FEATURE SUBJECTS

ALL BIOGRAPH SUBJECTS PURCHASED IN LARGE QUANTITIES
WIRE AND WE WILL SHIP IMMEDIATELY

The Pirate's Gold—Red Man and Child—After Many Years—The Guerrilla—Taming of the Shrew—Pilot's Daughter—The Clubman and the Tramp—Pirate's Honor—A Woman's Way

Twenty Independent Manufacturers Also Represented—Subjects Are All Winners

AMERICAN AGENTS:

GERMAN TALKING PICTURE ATTACHMENT CO.

ITS A MONEY GETTER

Special film with records to attach to moving picture machine and graphaphone.

Just received large assortment Talking Picture Film, Operas, Dramas, Vaudeville Sketches. All talk and sing. Get the exclusive right for your town.

NON-BREAKABLE CONDENSERS

Russian Optical Co.'s guaranteed lenses. We've got a large consignment. Money refunded if they don't do the work. While they last $1.00 each, any focus.

SONG SLIDE CARRIER, PRESSED STEEL, $1.00

AMERICAN FILM EXCHANGE - Wabash Building, Pittsburg, Pa.

This ad for the American Film Exchange from December 26, 1908, was taken from *The Moving Picture World* magazine. The Wabash Building, also known as the Wabash Pittsburgh Terminal, was demolished in 1953, leaving no trace of the company that once existed there. In fact, passengers were only received at the terminal until October 1931. The American Film Exchange likely resided in the old Wabash Pittsburgh Terminal due to the available space and instant access for travelers.

ECONOMY FILM SERVICE

410 LIBERTY AVENUE PITTSBURG

WE HAVE MORE FILM IN STOCK THAN ANY OTHER COMPETITOR

EVERY Reel is in first-class condition. The old stock has been disposed of. We have just received **Five Hundred Reels** from a foreign exchange, like new. We guarantee subjects to please any audience. We give all customers their proportionate share of new subjects. If you are paying big prices remember our service is **Quality and Low Prices.**

2 changes,	shipped	two at a time,	1000 feet each		.	$ 6.00
4 "	"	two	"	" "	.	10.00
6 "	"	three	"	" "	.	14.00
12 "	"	four	"	" "	.	25.00

POSTER AND SONG SLIDES WITHOUT ADDITIONAL CHARGE

The Economy Film Service was housed at 410 Liberty Avenue in Pittsburgh, a location that is in the vicinity of the film row along Ferry Street. In fact, the Economy Film Service would have been located near the Wabash Building downtown. Even though it wasn't on film row, it was still a prime location to be so close to the Wabash Pittsburgh Terminal. This ad was featured in the January 16, 1909, issue of *The Moving Picture World*.

Feature Films for Traveling Show

For Sale 40 reels feature films 2½, 3 and 4 cents per foot.

ECONOMY FILM COMPANY

314 Sheppard's Hotel

Sixth Street **Pittsburg, Pa.**

The Economy Film Company was located in the old Sheppard's Hotel along Sixth Street in Pittsburgh and was well positioned to do business in the city. This ad was taken from *The Moving Picture World* on January 16, 1909, the same time the Sheppard's Hotel was only a few blocks away from film row.

Beware! Mr. Manager

A very contagious disease exists (worn out sickly junk film service) means

Instant Death to your Theatre

LET US PRESCRIBE
OUR SELECTED FILM SERVICE

A tonic that is necessary for success. If you are worried, and need assistance, write for latest proposition; results will follow; we increase receipts.

PENNSYLVANIA FILM CO.

400-1-2-3-4 Lewis Building
PITTSBURGH, PA.

The Pennsylvania Film Company was located in the old Lewis Building at the corner of Sixth Avenue and Smithfield Street. This Pennsylvania Film Company ad was featured in *The Moving Picture World* on February 6, 1909.

EASTERN FILM EXCHANGE

Wabash Building
PITTSBURG, PA.

HIGH PRICE Exchanges have requested us repeatedly to increase our price on supplies and Film Service—you can bet **we have sat isfied more customers and have made good on low rentals. Why should we increase prices when our** profits justify us in purchasing large quantities of film. If you are dealing with **Mr. Stick-Him** you had better install our service immediately. Send list of subjects you have used. No repeaters guaranteed.

2 changes,	shipped	two at a time,	1000 feet	each	$ 5.00
4 "	"	two "	"	"	10.00
6 "	"	three "	"	"	14.00
12 "	"	four "	"	"	25 00

Song Slides and Beautifully Colored Posters FREE

SUPPLIES Tickets 9 cts, per 1000. Carbons 2 cts. each. Coudensing Lenses 50 cts. Moving Picture Lenses, $8.00. Stereopticon Lenses, $8.00. Film Cement, 10 cts. a bottle. Reels 50 cts. each.

NOTICE—We Guarantee to Fit a Lens for Any Curtain.

Like the American Film Exchange, the Eastern Film Exchange also resided in the Wabash Building. The first few floors of the building were devoted to the railway, while the upper floors housed miscellaneous businesses such as the film exchanges. This ad for the Eastern Film Exchange was found in *The Moving Picture World* of February 6, 1909.

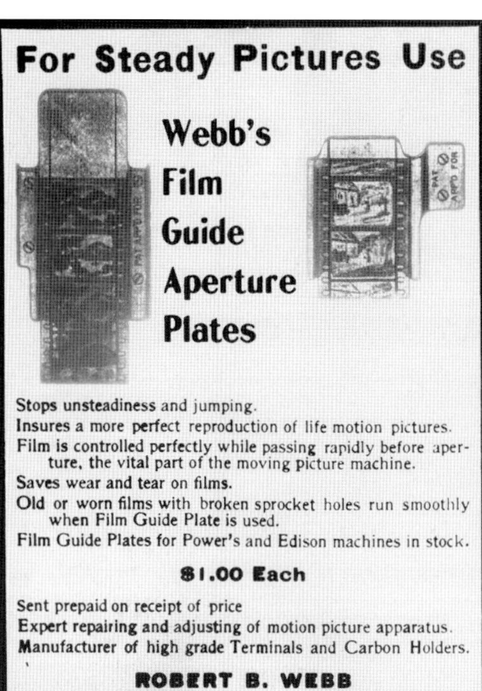

This Webb's Film Guide Aperture Plates ad was taken from *The Moving Picture World* magazine of September 7, 1909. This was one of several companies that provided film equipment for exhibitors. Aperture plates are pieces of metal with a rectangular cut in the center that is equivalent to the film's aspect ratio. Light is necessary to show films on a screen, but additional light can reflect on the film or distort it; aperture plates prevent that.

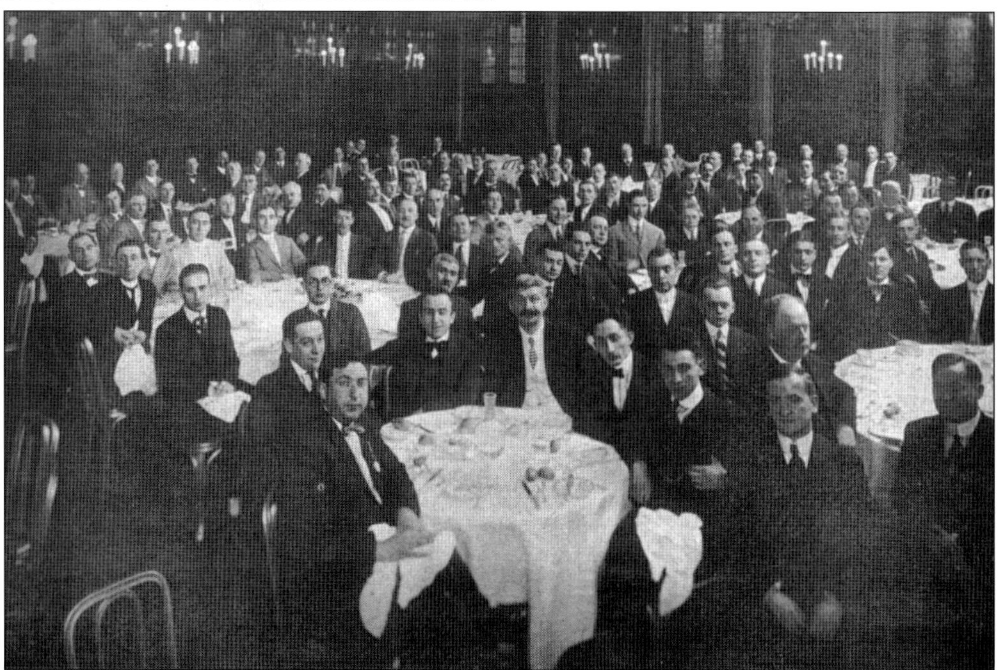

The Pittsburgh Screen Club consisted of all of the important figures involved in Pittsburgh's film community. Just as the important businessmen met on a nationwide level to discuss resolutions and solutions to problems facing the film industry, Pittsburgh did the same on a local level. This photograph from the September 1, 1915, edition of the *Pittsburgh Moving Picture Bulletin* shows the Pittsburgh Screen Club at a banquet held at the Fort Pitt Hotel on August 29, 1915.

OUR EXPOSITION

of everything that is useful in conducting a motion picture theatre can be seen daily at our ground-floor storeroom.

938-940 Penn Avenue

We will also have a big display at the coming Exhibitors' League State Convention, June 26, 27 and 28, in Moose Temple, Pittsburgh.

EXCLUSIVE DISTRIBUTORS

Powers, Simplex, Baird, Standard Machines

DEALERS IN ALL OTHER MAKES

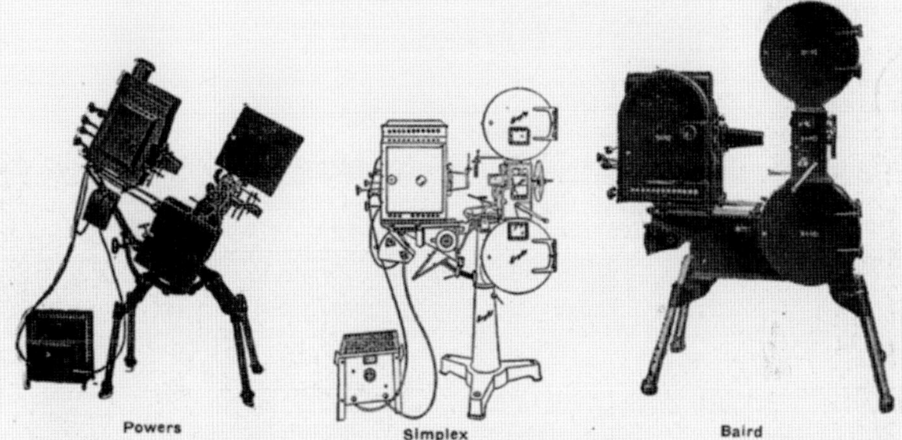

Why not Buy Your Supplies from the House That Carries Everything You Need?

Feature Film and Calcium Light Company

D. C. FRANCE, Manager

FIRST FLOOR, FILM EXCHANGE BLDG.,
938-940 Penn Avenue,

Phones Private Exchange 3511-3512 Grant PITTSBURGH, PA.

This Feature Film and Calcium Light Company ad was featured in the *Pittsburgh Moving Picture Bulletin* on June 14, 1916. The company, originally located along the Fourth Avenue section of film row, moved to 938–940 Penn Avenue during the first week of May 1916 along with most of the other exchanges from the old film row.

The A B C of the Film Business

Attention
Brains
Courtesy

At Your Disposal
and Gladly
Furnished by
Pittsburg Calcium Light & Film Co.

Pittsburg, Pa. **Des Moines, Ia.**
Cincinnati, O. **Lincoln, Neb.**
Rochester, N. Y.

The Pittsburgh Calcium Light & Film Company was founded by Richard A. Rowland, whose family owned a calcium light company. It was Rowland's interest in motion pictures and film that brought calcium light to the film industry. Rowland's mother loaned him $2,000 to begin the film aspect of the business. He charged nickelodeons $15 a week for film and eventually established this company across America. The Calcium Light & Film Company was initially located on First Avenue until the fall of 1907 when it moved to film row on Fourth Avenue. This ad was taken from *The Moving Picture World* magazine of February 6, 1909. Rowland sold the Pittsburgh Calcium Light & Film Company to the General Film Company in 1910 when he was around 30 years old.

Quick Work in the Box Office

A well-known moving picture man was asked recently: "What method do you employ to safeguard your box office receipts and take care of your patrons?" Pointing behind the counter in his box office, he answered: "That Automatic Machine answers both your questions, for thru its use my patrons receive their tickets quickly and my cashier makes change without fear of mistake, knowing that the correct number of tickets have been issued.

"We consider it absolutely necessary because it accounts for all receipts."

The Automatic Ticket Selling & Cash Register

"Protect the Employe---Remove the Temptation"

USED WHEREVER TICKETS ARE SOLD
THE AUTOMATIC TICKET SELLING AND CASH REGISTER CO. INCORPORATED

Please send me free of charge, literature illustrating your method of Daily Receipts, also Prices and Terms.

NAME ________
STREET ________
CITY ________

This intensely interesting booklet tells the story of the development of mechanical addition and accuracy written by one who has a deep understanding of the subject—it shows that the Automatic principle of pressing a button for the required number prevents congestion—and that the key to the register is the key to the situation.

AUTOMATIC TICKET SELLING & CASH REGISTER CO.

1476 BROADWAY, NEW YORK
5923 ALDER ST., PITTSBURGH
THIRD NAT'L BANK BLDG., ST. LOUIS
815 DIME BANK BLDG., DETROIT

Tickets and cash registers remain a part of the theater experience today and were already in great demand during the early 20th century, with all the new nickelodeons and theaters emerging. This ad for the Automatic Ticket Selling & Cash Register Company was taken from *The Moving Picture World* magazine of April 11, 1914.

THE MOVING PICTURE WORLD 713

Novel Use of Pictures.

Interurban Railway Company Installs Projecting Machine In "Party Car" With Pleasing Effect.

Moving pictures have found their way into a new channel, this time being used by street railway managers for the entertainment of passengers who charter private cars for long runs. The Pittsburgh, Harmony, Butler and New Castle Railway Company, with general offices in the Diamond National Bank Building, Pittsburgh, Pa., and whose lines extend from Pittsburgh to Butler thence to New Castle, Pa., is the first road to use the moving picture machine.

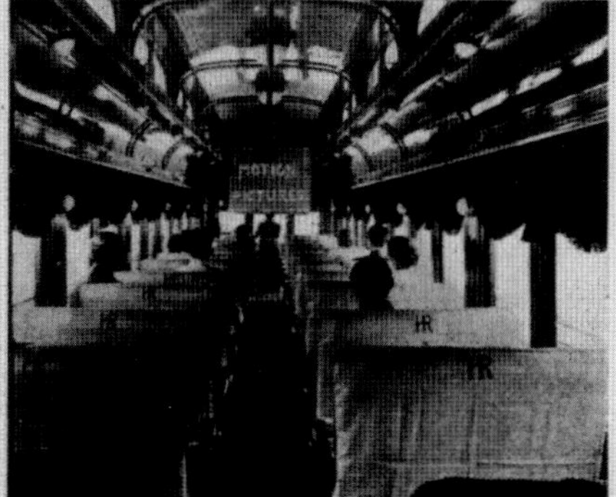

Interior View of Car, Showing Screen.

The "Party car," in which the first machine has been installed, is a rebuilt car, for this piece of equipment was badly damaged by being in a wreck not many months ago. When the car was rebuilt, General Superintendent Harry Etheridge conceived the idea that a "Party car" with a moving picture equipment would be a new traffic producer.

When the matter was given serious consideration, it resulted in the most modern motion picture machine on the market being bought and installed in the rebuilt car, it being attached to the inside of the roof on the rear platform.

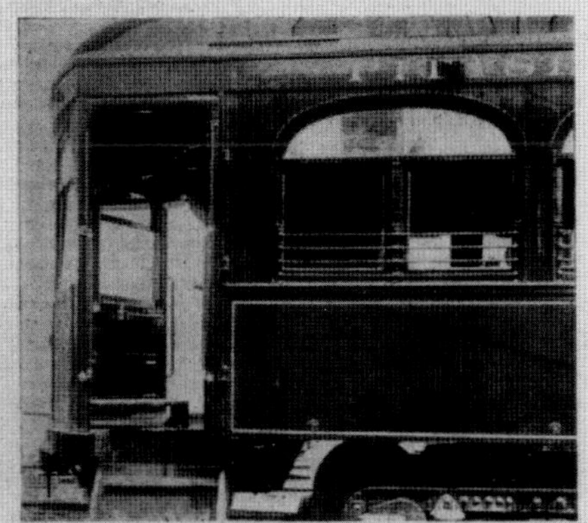

Showing Machine in Vestibule.

A small platform three feet square was built and high enough for the operator to stand upon to work the machine. When the trip is ended, the platform is lifted out of the way of passengers alighting from the car.

The screen is in the front of the car, and directly back of the motorman. This is lifted and lowered just as a blind is in the home. It also serves as a "blind" for the motorman, no light penetrating through the screen, thus giving the motorman a clear vision with the headlight of the car.

The electric lights in the car are turned out after the trip has been started, and all is ready to start the reel. Window curtains are drawn, and the car then resembles a cozy theater on wheels.

Two reels of pictures are shown and these reels are never repeated. Reels of the longest length are demanded by the company, for the longest trip the car makes is about two hours—this while being operated as a special between New Castle and Pittsburgh.

When the car is returned to the barn after the return trip at night, the reels are forwarded to Pittsburgh on the first car the following day. When the car is to go out again, an advance order is sent to a Pittsburgh film exchange, and new subjects are then sent to the company.

It frequently happens that the company is compelled to send out two special cars on order for private parties, frequently 100 or more passengers forming theater parties from New Castle and Butler to Pittsburgh. On the trip from New Castle to Pittsburgh, say 50 of the party use the "party picture car" on the "going trip" and then the pictures are "run." Then on the return trip, those who rode in the regular special car change places with those who rode in the "party car" and for their benefit the pictures are "run" on the return trip.

The "party car" is becoming a most popular feature with the company, and is now in demand practically five nights out of a week. It is handsomely furnished, clean white linen being placed over the back of the high seats every time the car is chartered. The appointments of the car are perfect. Lunch and card tables are at the command of the passengers on the "Party car," individual electric lamps being placed on each card table and at each seat for this purpose.

A GOOD JUDGE OF GOOD PICTURES.

George H. Hines, one of the oldest subscribers to the Moving Picture World and holder of the Motion Picture Patents Company's license No. 1, ought to qualify as a good judge of pictures. Mr. Hines has been operating picture theaters in Chicago for a long time and is now owner and manager of the Lyda Theater in that city. Here is what he has to say about a good picture:

"Chicago, May 10th, 1912.

"Editor Motion Picture World,

"New York City.

"My Dear Sir—In my past nine years as an exhibitor I have never taken the liberty of recommending a picture, as I have always been more than pleased with the Association pictures. But yesterday I had the pleasure of showing Selig's 'Coming of Columbus,' and I have 1,000 seats and played a record business with 'Columbus,' so much so that I have to-day booked it back again. I never have seen, or run, a picture that has pleased my patrons as 'Columbus' has. This will prove a revelation to picturedom and I think the great success of 'Columbus' should greatly encourage other manufacturers to bring out big feature subjects. One or two special features will be appreciated and welcomed by all high class motion picture theaters every week. Success to the Selig Poliscope Company. Keep the good work up, as motion motion pictures are only in their infancy to-day. They are the pleasing amusement that is liked by all the amusement-going people. Nuf ced."

GEORGE H. HINES.

NEW THEATER FOR WINDSOR, ONTARIO, CAN.

The Builders' and Contractors' Association, of Essex, Thompson Building, Windsor, Ontario, Canada, advises us that one of its chief contractors, Mr. F. C. Poli, is starting to build one of the finest five-cent moving picture theaters in Windsor. The house will have a seating capacity of about 450 and all latest improvements and fittings will be made in it. Mr. Poli has built about thirty of the best showhouses for others in the city of Detroit, and has come to the conclusion that he wants a moving picture theater for himself.

NEW OPEN AIRDOME ON BROADWAY, NEW YORK.

Messrs. Harris & Goldston are equipping a fine open air show on Broadway, near 99th street. They purchased a Powers No. 6 M. P. machine from J. H. Hallberg, "The Economizer Man." Mr. Hallberg reports the sale of an A. C. to D. C. Economizer 40 amp. size to W. C. Grau, Hopkinsville, Ky. A No. 6 Powers with full line of supplies to Earl & Carroll, Cornwall, N. Y. Many places are equipping their theaters with Hallberg A. C. Economizers, throwing out the cheaper devices on account of the better light produced by the Hallberg.

A page taken from *The Moving Picture World* magazine of May 25, 1912, depicts the advent of motion pictures being shown in railway passenger cars. The "Party Car" was a rebuilt passenger car owned by the Pittsburgh, Harmony, Butler and New Castle Railway Company. The projector was hung from the roof of the rear of the car, with the screen in the front.

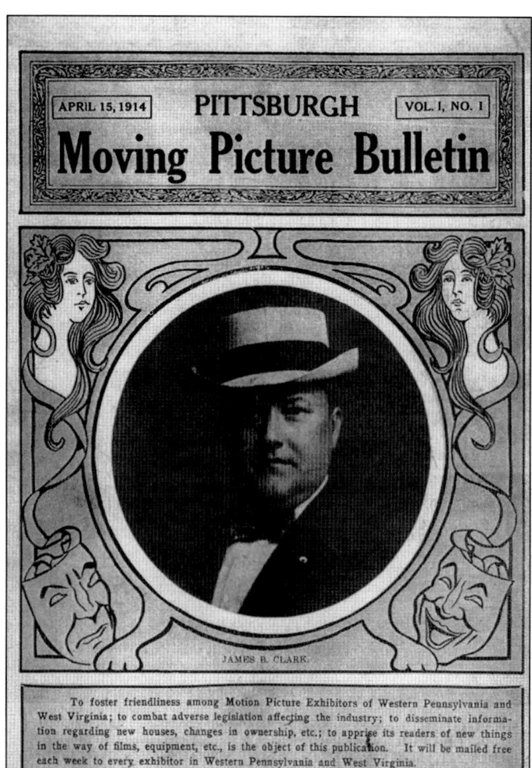

APRIL 15, 1914 PITTSBURGH VOL. I, NO. I

Moving Picture Bulletin

JAMES B. CLARK.

To foster friendliness among Motion Picture Exhibitors of Western Pennsylvania and West Virginia; to combat adverse legislation affecting the industry; to disseminate information regarding new houses, changes in ownership, etc.; to apprise its readers of new things in the way of films, equipment, etc., is the object of this publication. It will be mailed free each week to every exhibitor in Western Pennsylvania and West Virginia.

The *Pittsburgh Moving Picture Bulletin* served as a way for the Pittsburgh film community members to communicate among themselves. On April 15, 1914, the *Pittsburgh Moving Picture Bulletin* made its debut with a picture of James B. Clark on the cover. Clark was arguably the most important figure in the Pittsburgh film industry during the early part of the 20th century. He was the treasurer and director of the Pittsburgh Calcium Light & Film Company, the director of the Independent Film Company, the director of the Pittsburgh Photoplay Company, and the treasurer and director of the Feature Film and Calcium Light Company. Clark was involved with many other film businesses and local theaters.

FAMOUS PLAYERS FILM CO. NOW OCCUPIES NEW HOME

Paramount Pictures Building at Twelfth and Penn, Pitttsburgh, Finest Film Exchange of Country—Convenient, Commodious, Complete in Every Detail.

Occupying the largest and most complete film exchange in the United States, the Famous Players Film Service, Inc., distributors of the Paramount Pictures in Western Pennsylvania, Ohio, West Virginia and Ky., now has abundant room for expansion, and while the service rendered by this company in the past has been faultless, the new quarters insure the same grade of efficiency for the future. The new quarters at the corner of Penn avenue and Twelfth street, a new five-story building, with a floor space of 12,000 square feet, is divided into departments in such a manner that the highest grade of efficiency in every department of the business is attained.

The removal from the old locations in Ferry street and the Wabash building was effected last Saturday and by Monday morning the business of the exchange was transacted and the service was continued uninterruptedly as if no change in location had taken place. In spite of the tremendous task of moving, every film was shipped on schedule time and not a single exhibitor was disappointed, thanks to the capable management of the officials of the company and the hard work of the large corps of employes.

A page from the April 14, 1915, *Pittsburgh Moving Picture Bulletin* provides evidence of the migration of film row and the Paramount Film Exchange to Penn Avenue. Most of the other film businesses along the intersection of Fourth Avenue and Ferry Street moved just two weeks later. The first two Paramount Film Exchanges were located on Ferry Street and in the Wabash Building. The third exchange was at the corner of Twelfth Street and Penn Avenue, and the final, most popular location was along the Boulevard of the Allies.

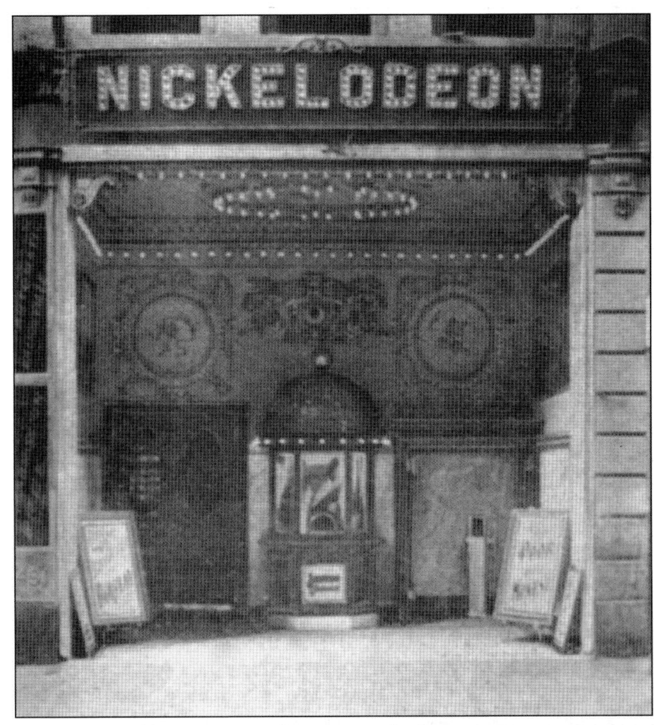

Harry Davis was, and possibly still is, highly regarded as the father of the moving picture theater. With his brother-in-law John P. Harris, Davis opened the very first nickelodeon in the United States along Smithfield Street in Pittsburgh on June 19, 1905. Photographs of the theater are extremely rare because it was demolished just five years after it opened. These images of the first nickelodeon were taken from the November 30, 1907, edition of *The Moving Picture World* magazine. The photograph of the interior below is exceptionally rare. The theater could seat a total of 96 guests to watch the estimated 15-minute motion picture display.

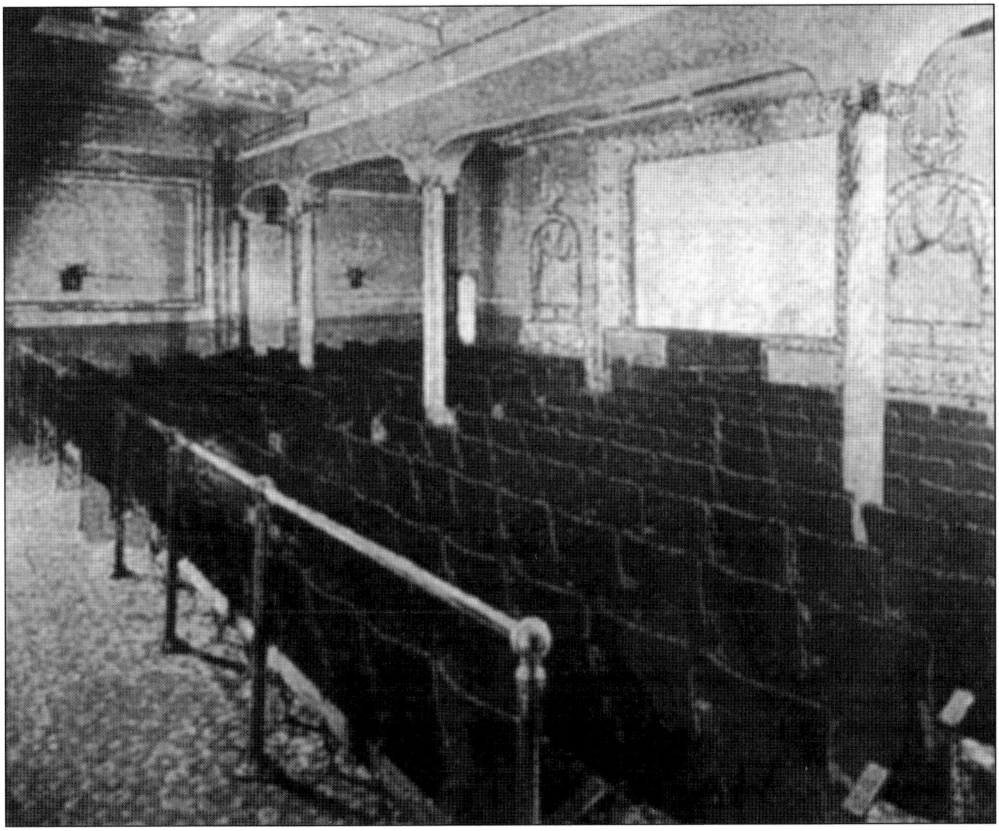

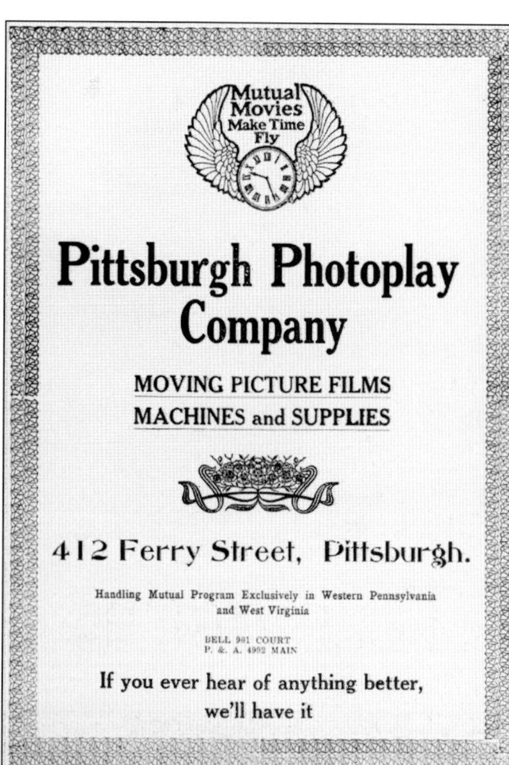

Many records indicate that Pittsburgh Photoplay Company began in January 1911 with the primary purpose of manufacturing, buying, selling, leasing, and dealing in films, appliances, and accessories for motion picture exhibitors—known today as theaters. This Pittsburgh Photoplay Company ad was featured in the May 20, 1914, edition of the *Pittsburgh Moving Picture Bulletin*.

This incarnation of film row in downtown Pittsburgh was at the intersection of Fourth Avenue and Ferry Street. The *Pittsburgh Moving Picture Bulletin* might be the only publication to have ever featured photographs of film row. This image of the Fourth Avenue section of film row was taken from the May 13, 1914, edition of the *Pittsburgh Moving Picture Bulletin*. Unfortunately, the print quality of the bulletin was very poor and resembled newspaper quality.

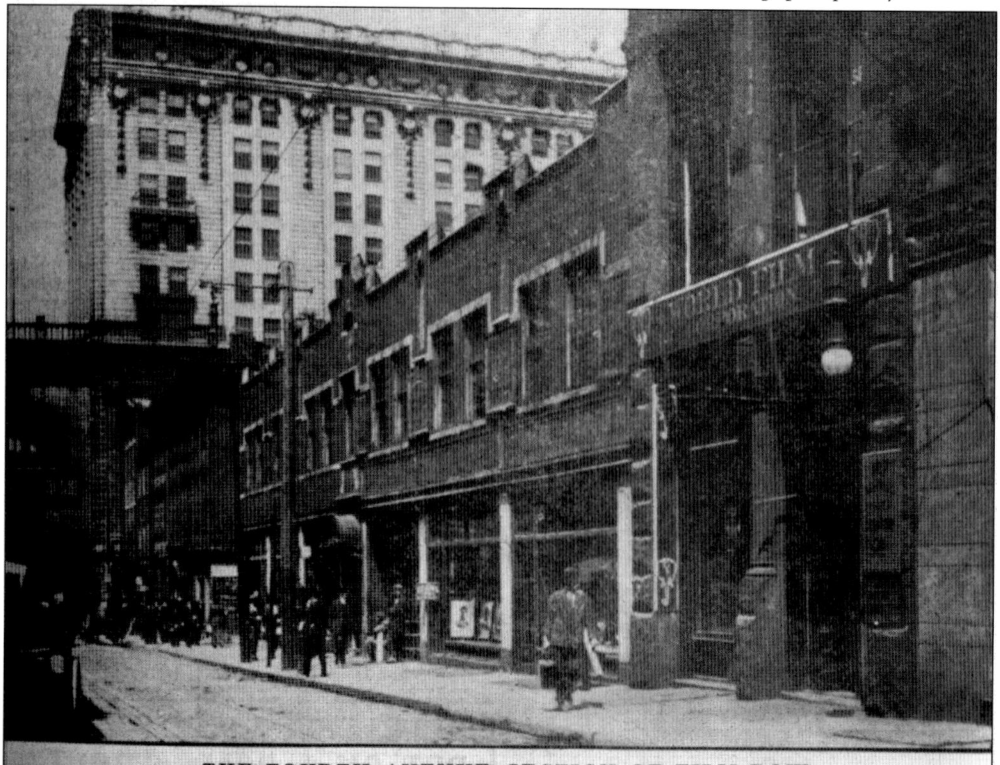

THE FOURTH AVENUE SECTION OF FILM ROW

Two

PIONEERING PITTSBURGH TELEVISION

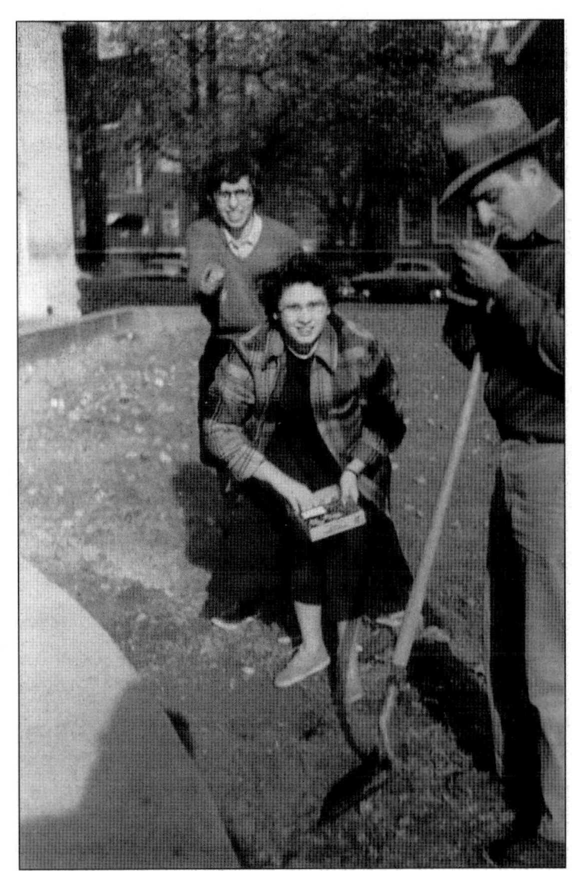

This outdoor photograph of Josie Carey and Fred Rogers in December 1956 was taken during their years making *The Children's Corner* at WQED. The duo made a wonderful team. One example of their teamwork involved the music for the children's program. Carey wrote the lyrics while Rogers wrote the music, which had to accommodate Carey's vocal range.

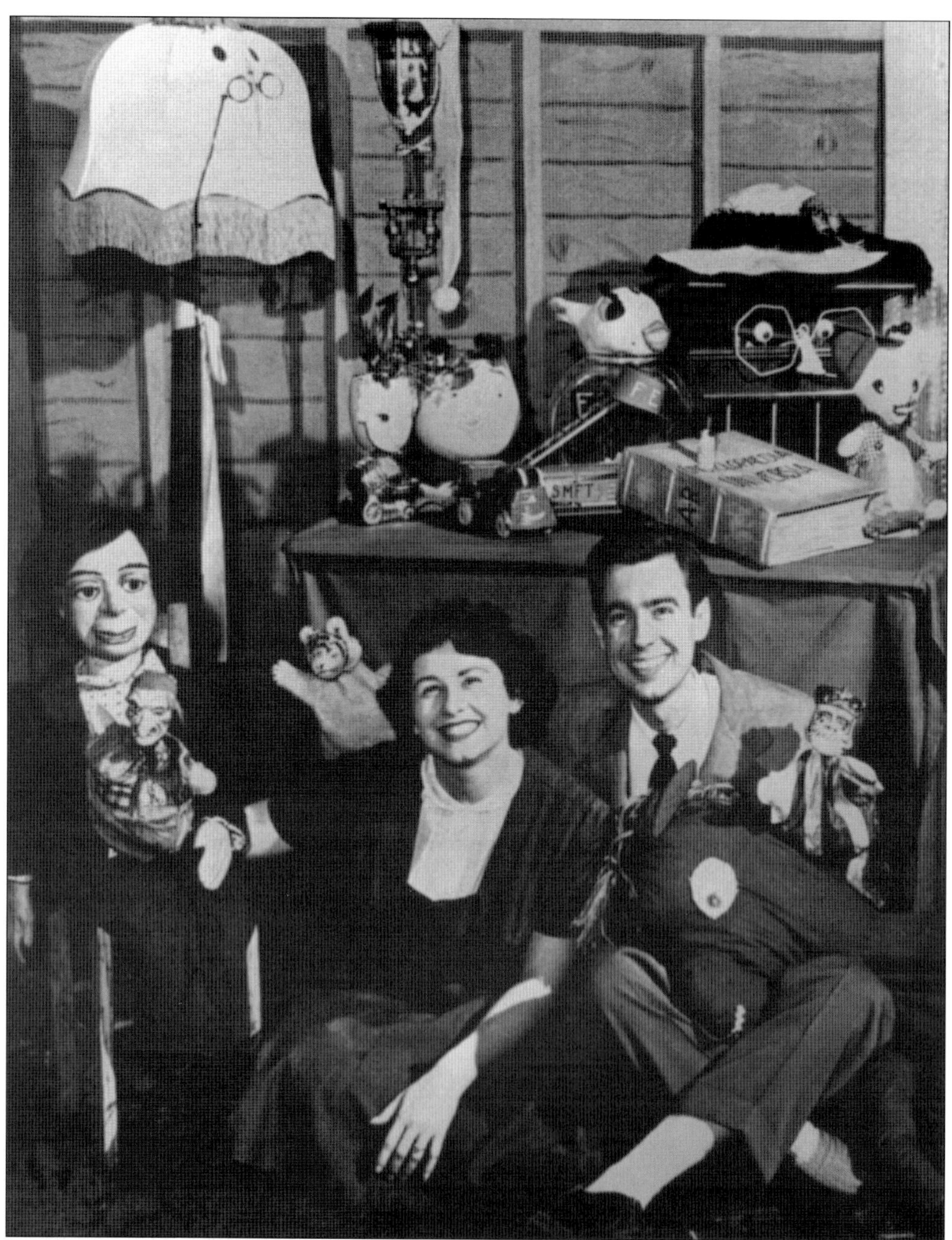

Carey and Rogers pose with some of the puppets featured on *The Children's Corner.* Although Carey was the star of the show, Rogers provided individual personalities to the puppets he controlled from behind the scenes. Children cared about the puppets as if they were real. (Courtesy of © The Fred Rogers Company, used with permission.)

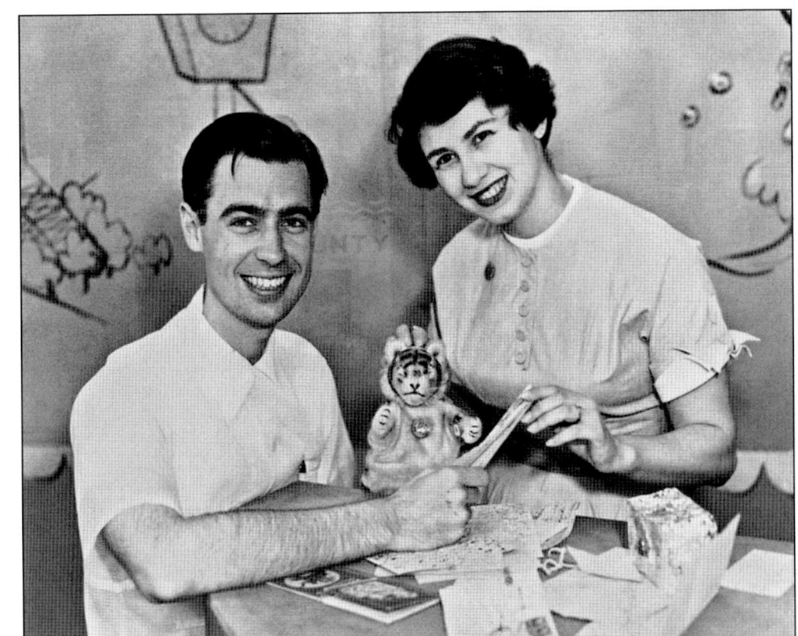

Carey and Rogers are pictured on the set of *The Children's Corner.* They both devoted their time on television to children and didn't make it a secret that they hoped to make a positive impact on their lives. (Courtesy of © The Fred Rogers Company, used with permission.)

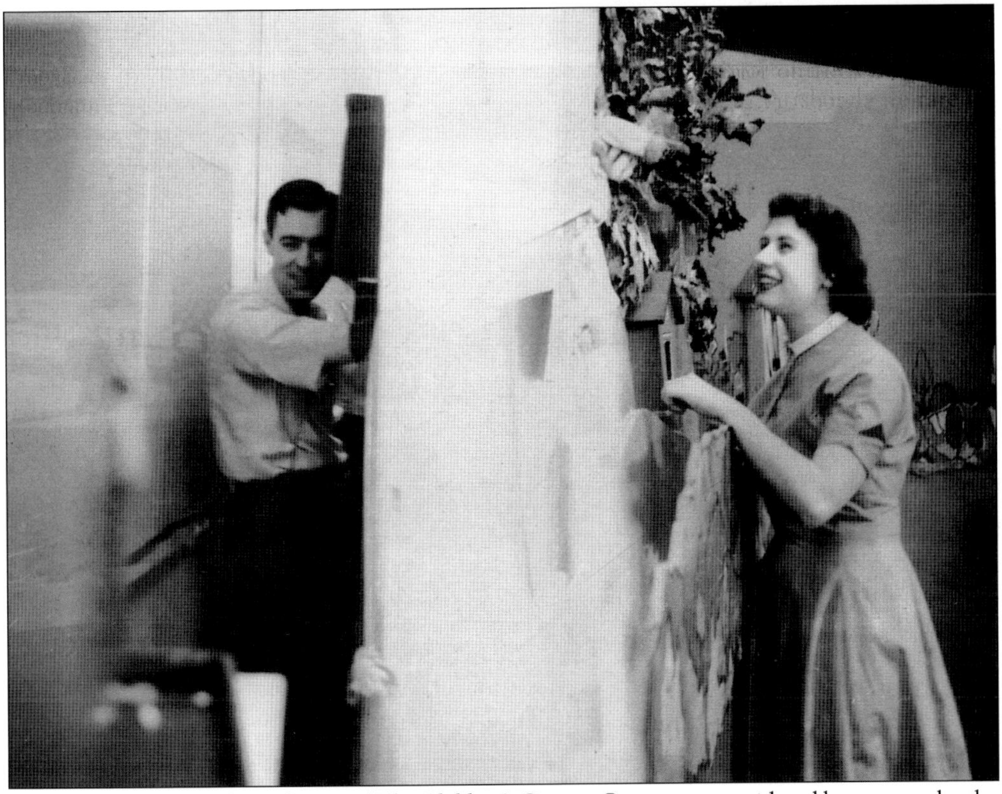

Carey and Rogers work on the set of *The Children's Corner.* Carey was considered by many to be the first star of WQED, as she primarily appeared in front of the camera as the host of *The Children's Corner,* while Rogers mostly used his talents behind the scenes. (Courtesy of Sam Silberman, © The Fred Rogers Company, used with permission.)

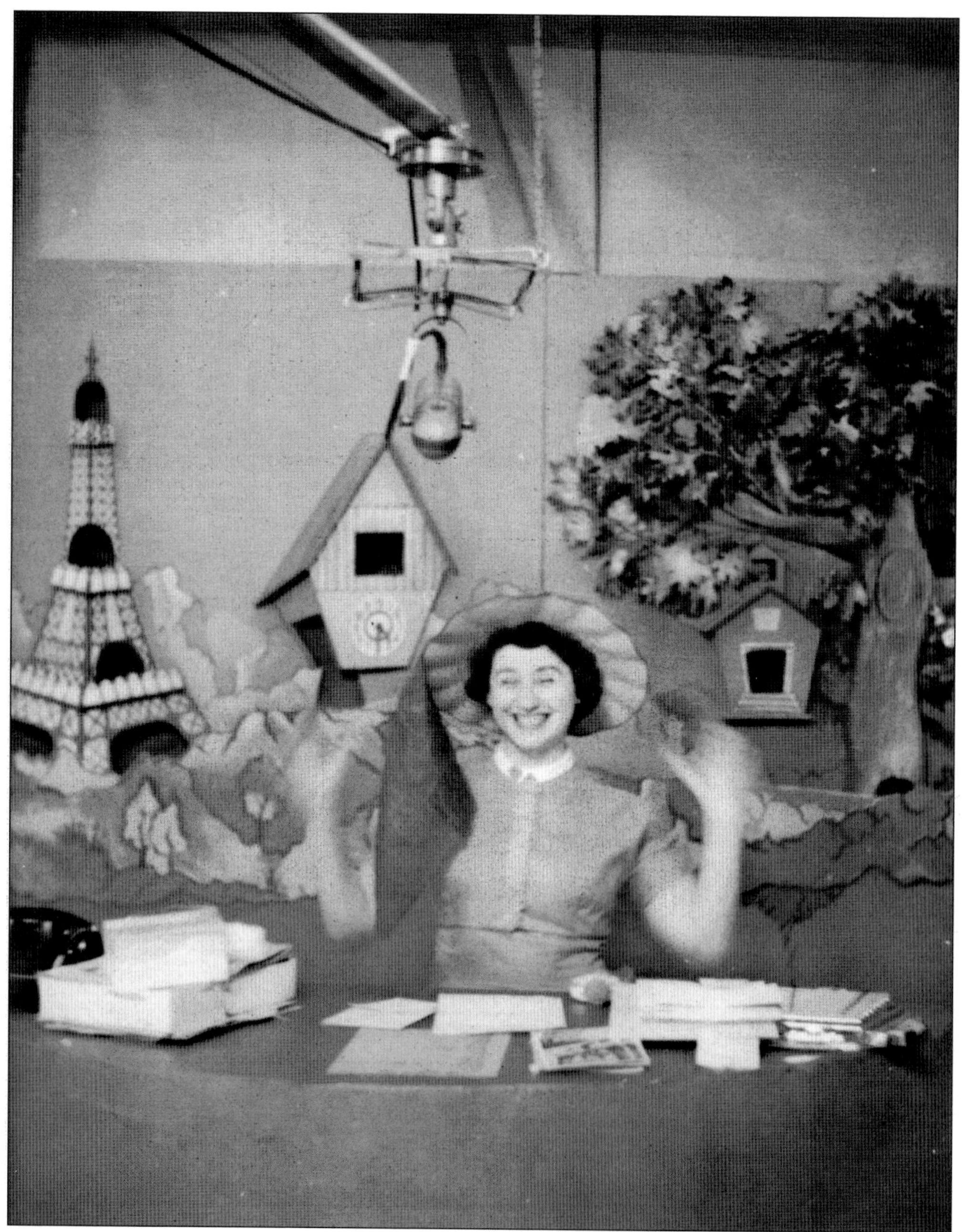

This image shows Carey having fun on the set of *The Children's Corner.* Although working on the show had its fun times, Carey devoted hours of work, even when the cameras were off, in order to make the show a success. (Courtesy of Sam Silberman, © The Fred Rogers Company, used with permission.)

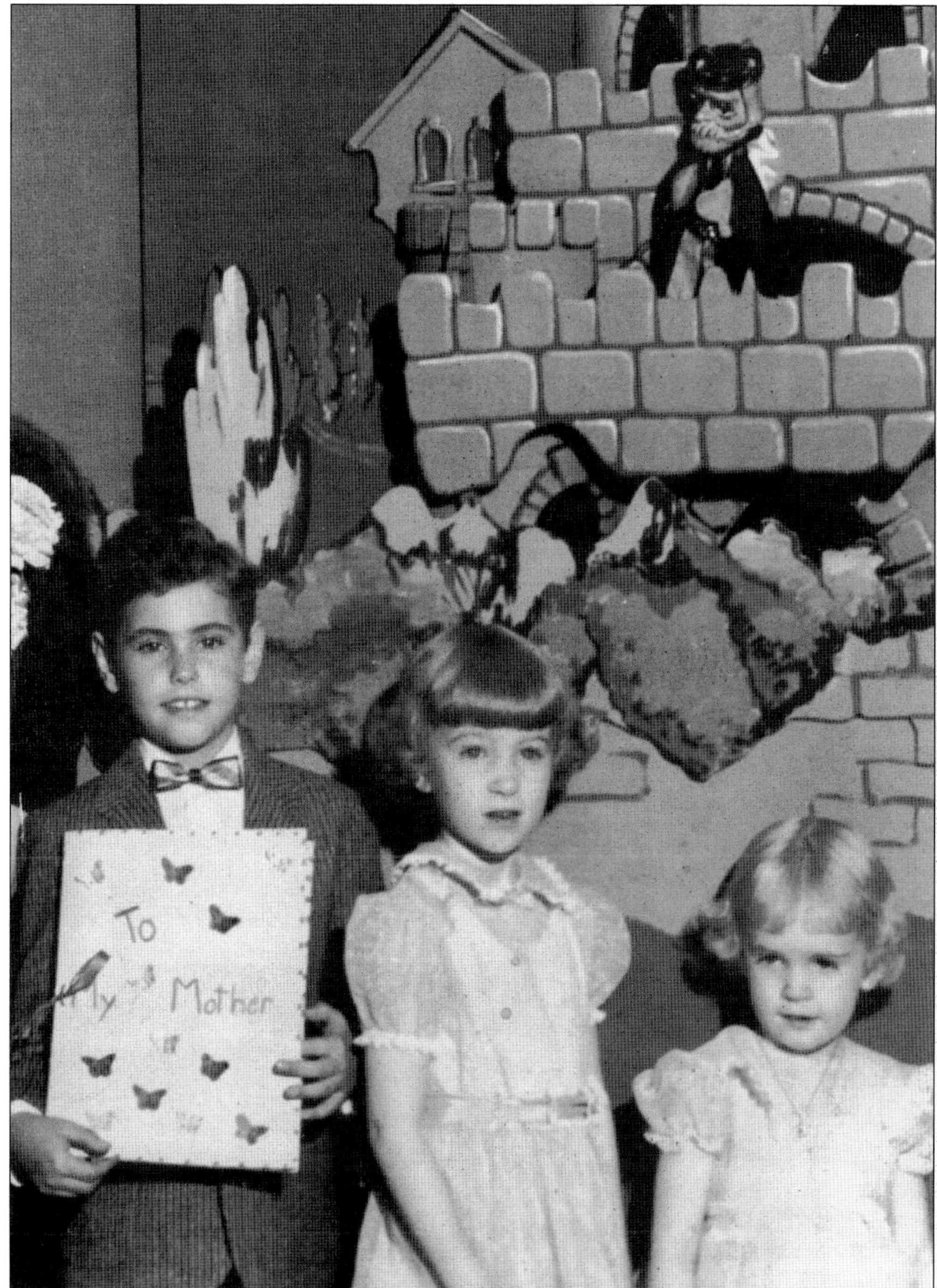

Kids visit *The Children's Corner* set at WQED. Children had a key role in the success of the show, as their drawings and birthdays were celebrated on camera. However, children weren't the only special guests to appear on the show. Johnny Carson, Shirley Jones, and Charles Schultz also made appearances on the popular program.

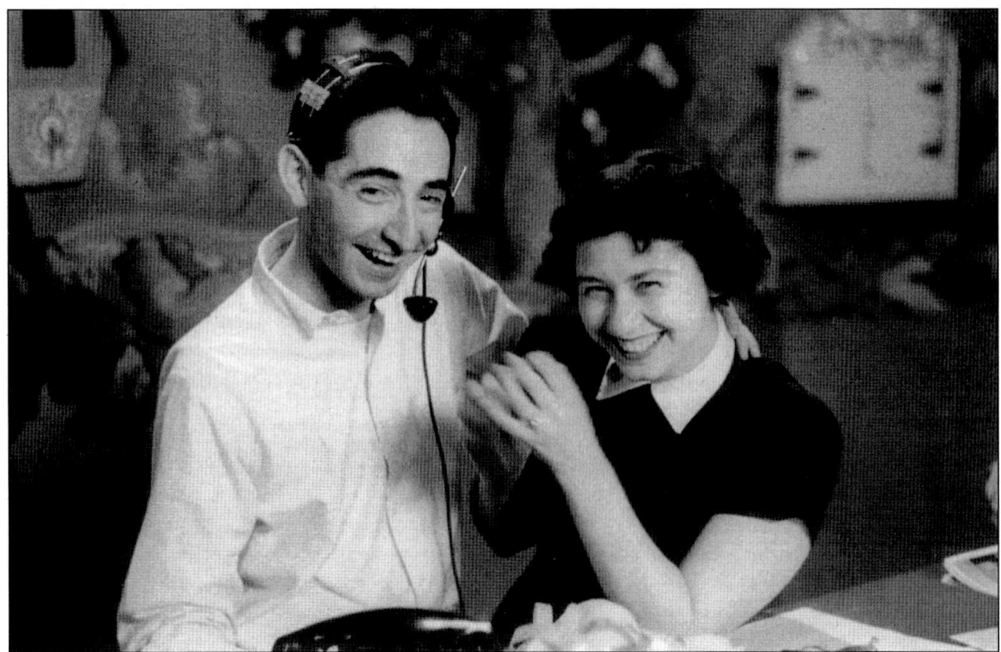

Sam Silberman and Josie Carey pose on the set of *The Children's Corner* in January 1958. Silberman was a director and producer for WQED. His body of work behind the camera included *The Children's Corner* and *Mister Rogers' Neighborhood*, among many other WQED programs.

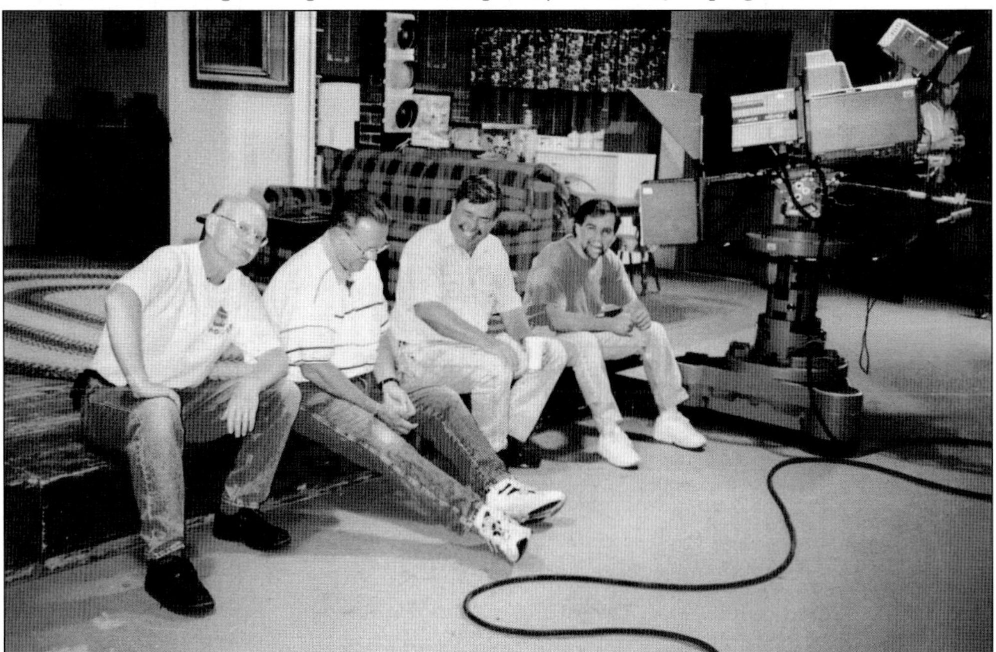

Even when the cameras weren't rolling, the *Mister Rogers' Neighborhood* set at WQED has been described by many as a nice, pleasant atmosphere, with Fred Rogers behaving the same way off camera as he did on camera for the world to see. From left to right are crew members Joe Abeln, camera operator Art Vogel, bass player Carl McVicker, and assistant floor manager Jimmy Seech. (Courtesy of Sam Silberman, © The Fred Rogers Company, used with permission.)

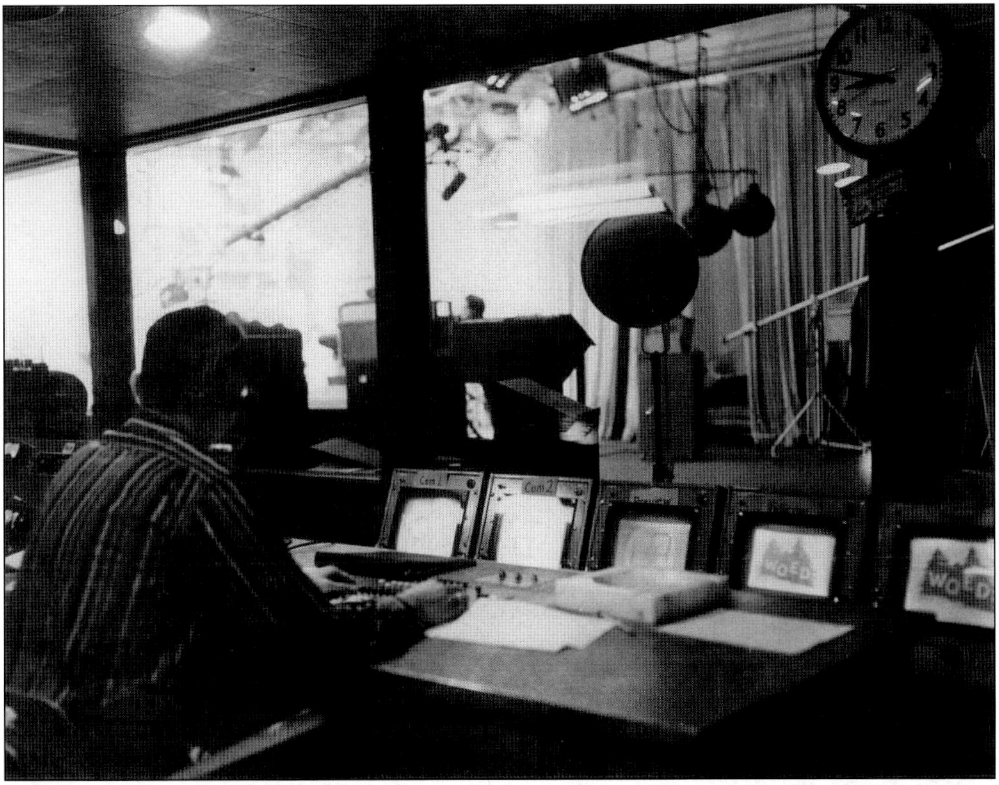

In these photographs, WQED employees work the equipment behind the scenes. At the time, the equipment used at the station was state of the art to produce quality broadcasts and programs. WQED provided valuable learning experience, helping workers to master their craft. The exceptional skills they learned at WQED even allowed some of them to progress in the film and television industry if they so desired.

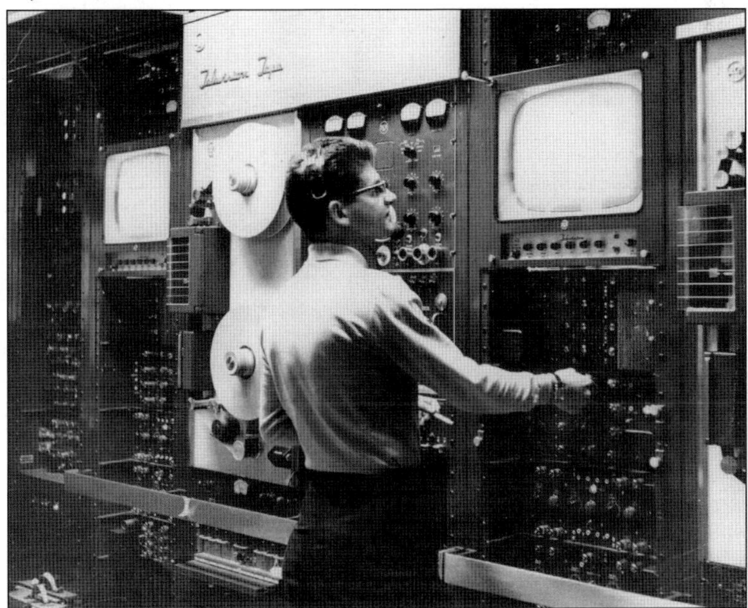

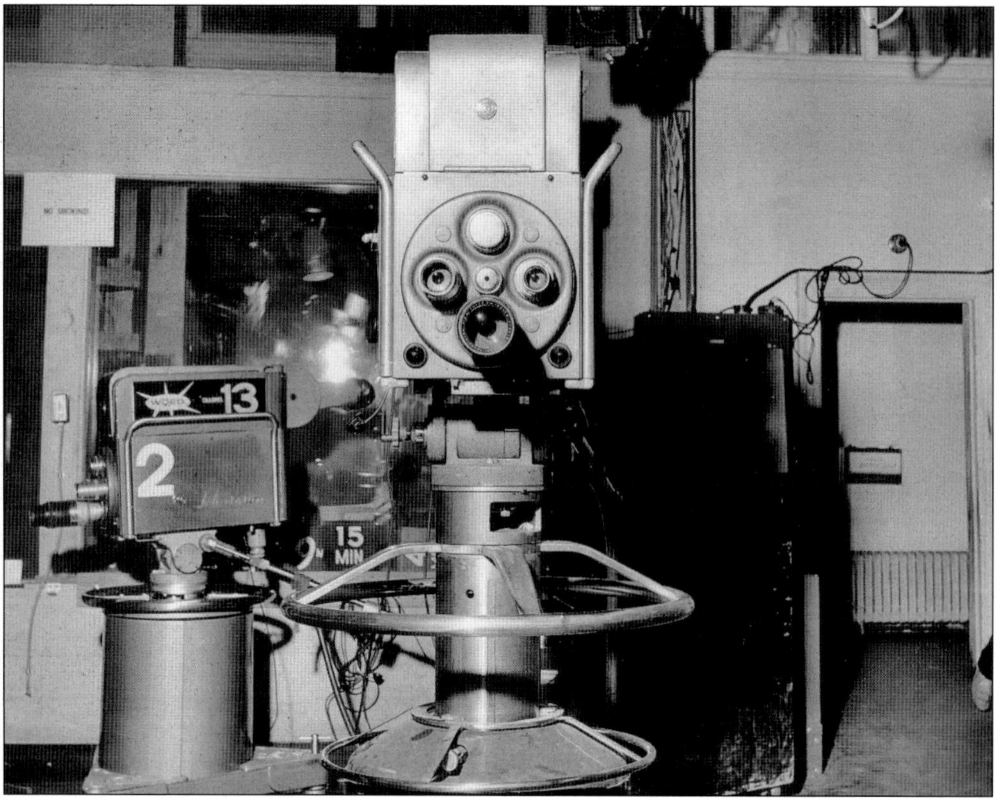

Shown here are some of the cameras that were used during the early days at WQED. Cameras such as these were used for some of the most proud moments in the station's history. However, these weren't the only cameras to grace the set of WQED. Film productions for *Bob Roberts*, *Roommates*, and *Only You* also brought in their cameras to make these movies during the 1990s. Sting, Tim Robbins, Susan Sarandon, Bill Clinton, Danny Glover, Marisa Tomei, and Robert Downey Jr. have all visited or performed at WQED, among many others.

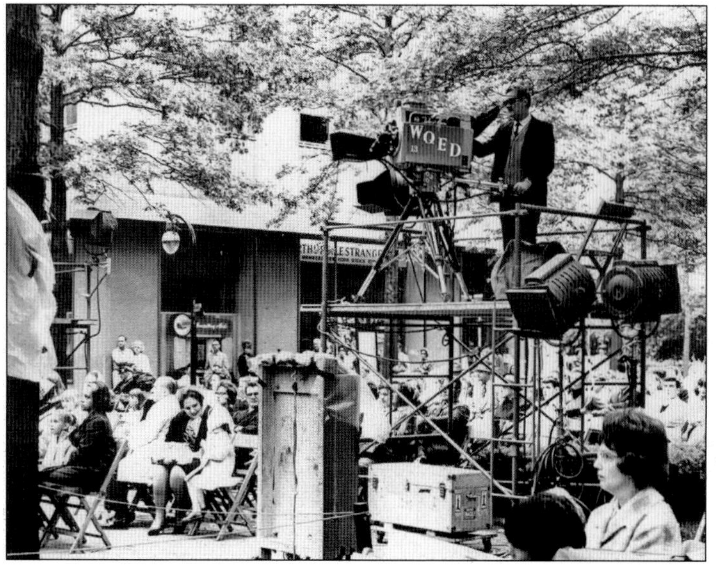

WQED has established an exceptional rapport with the community since its inception. This photograph shows WQED cameraman Dick Reschoff on top of a scaffolding platform, filming the Three Rivers Arts Festival at Gateway Center. A focus on community programming in Pittsburgh still exists at WQED.

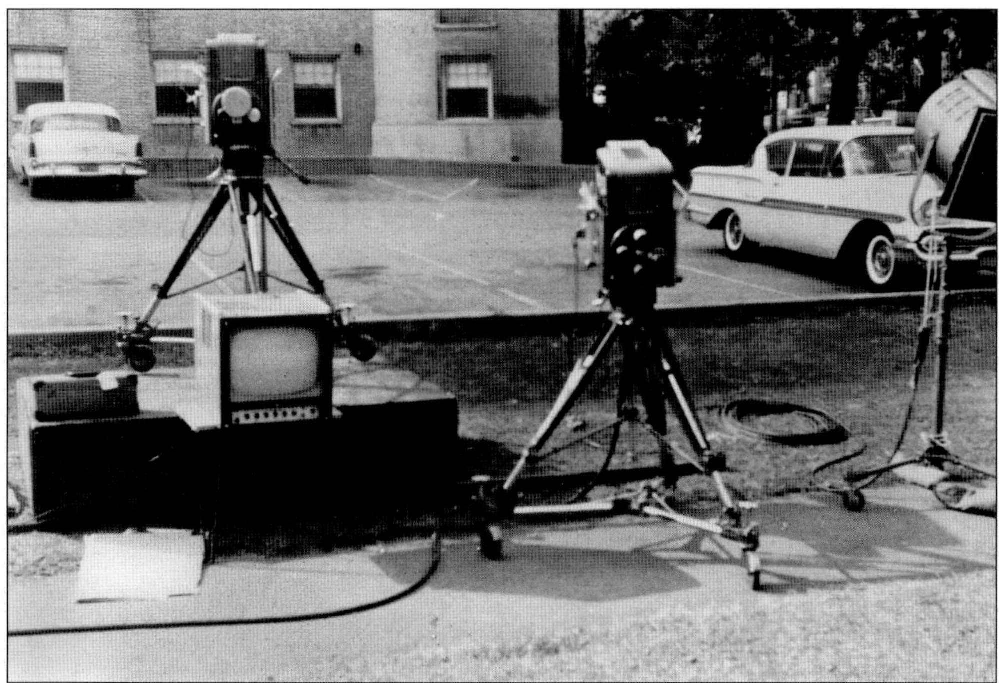

WQED equipment is pictured here outside in a parking lot. The photograph may have been taken with the intention to show the equipment that was being used at the time; it is unclear if this equipment was about to be loaded onto a production vehicle and used for filming.

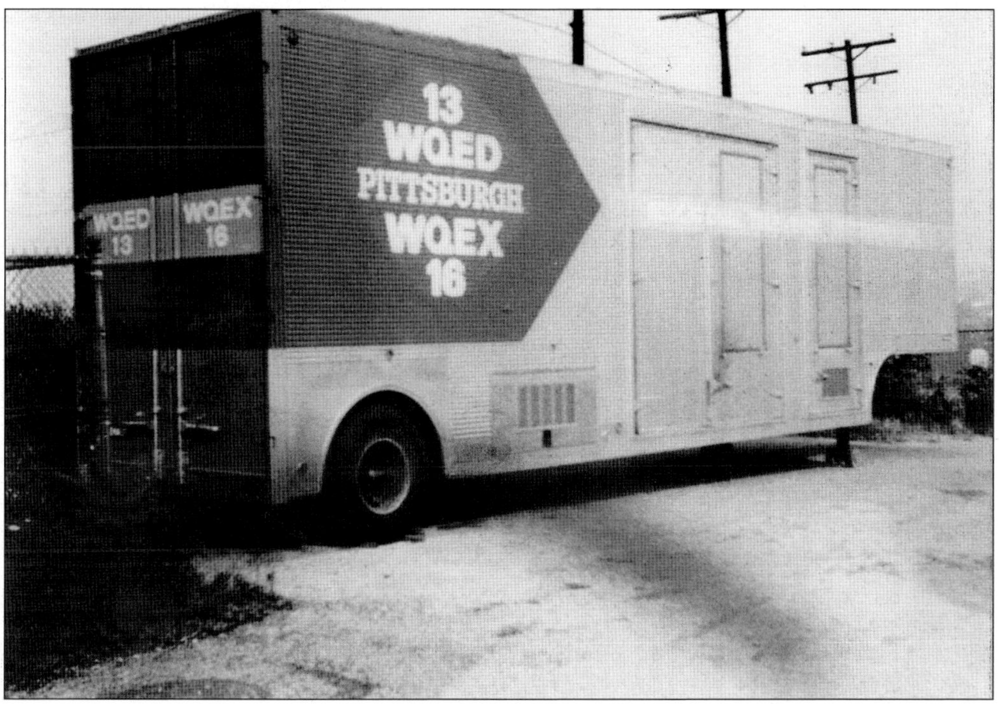

This July 1967 photograph showcases a WQED trailer that was being used at the time. Like any television station, WQED had to be prepared for the substantial job of transporting equipment.

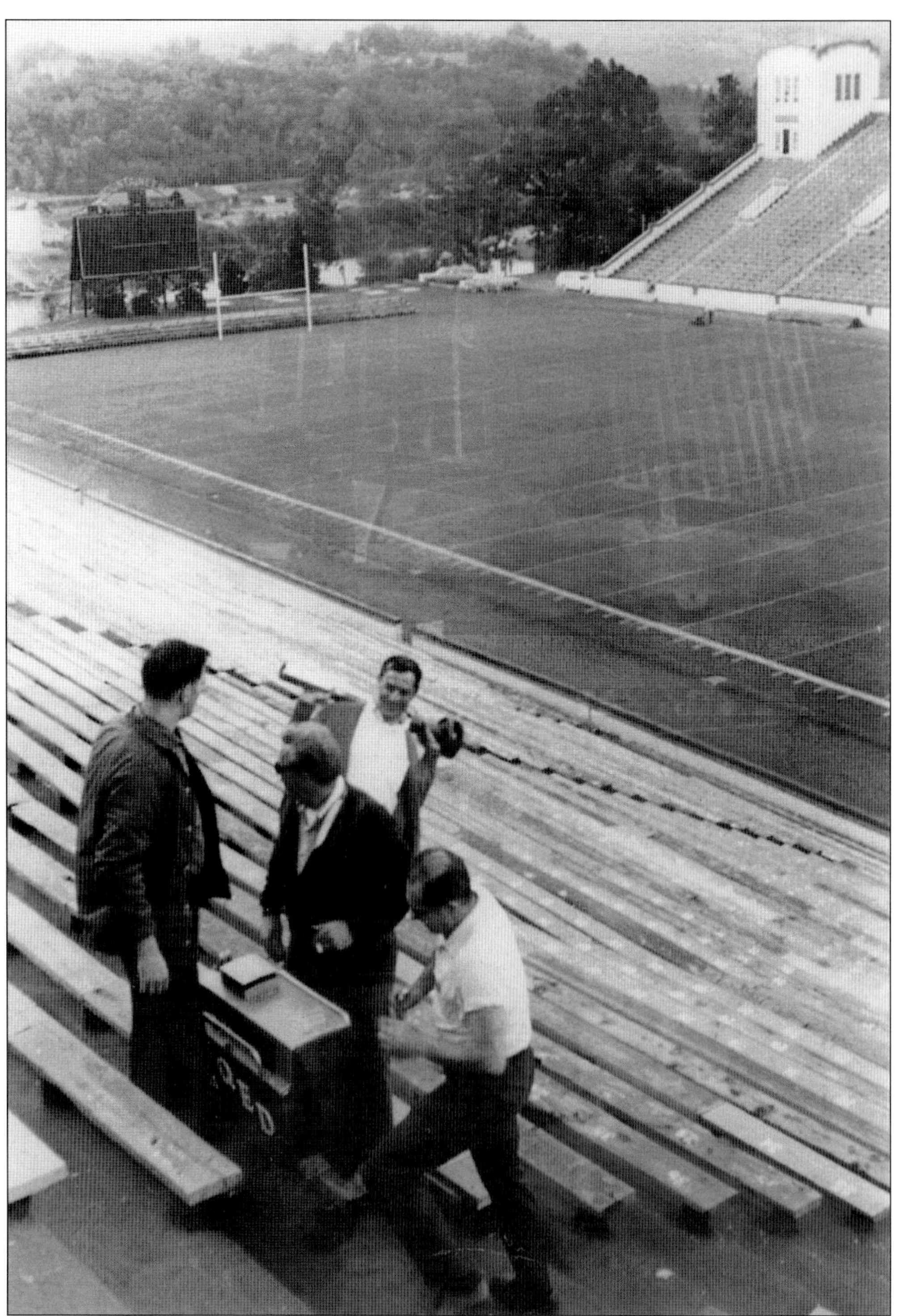

WQED crew members are working at a local Pittsburgh stadium. Over the years, WQED has been found all over the Pittsburgh region, filming the various surrounding communities and the people in them. This longstanding tradition holds true today in a variety of programming.

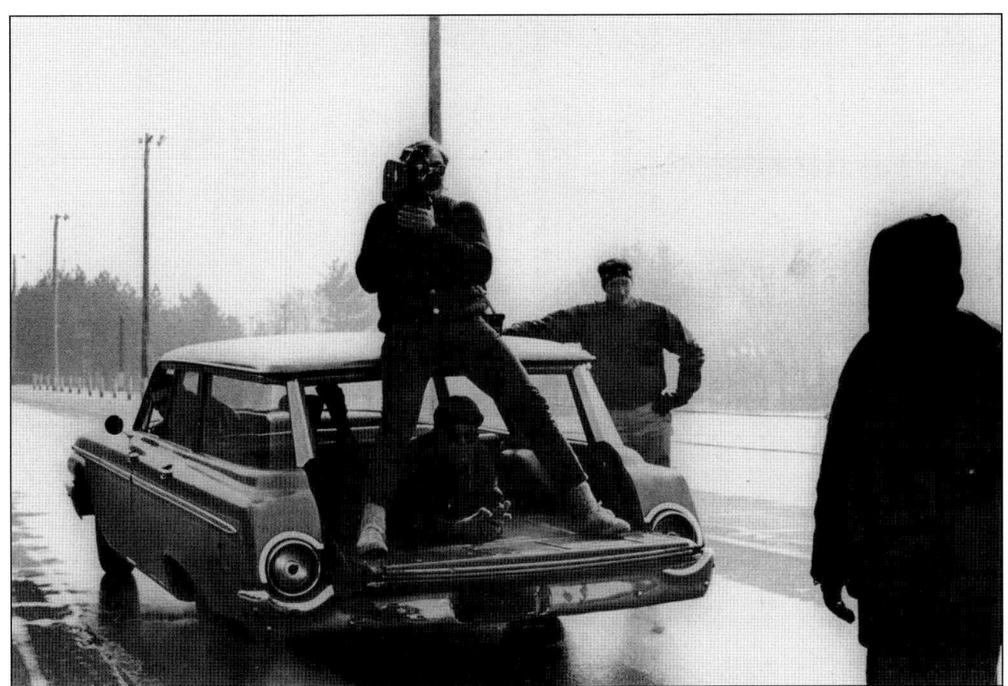

The WQED crew films *Ofoeti* in South Park Township, Pennsylvania, in 1966. The man on the floor of the station wagon is director Bill Francisco, the cameraman is Joe Pytka, the production assistant standing along the side of the station wagon is Jerry Gallagher, and the actor they are filming in silhouette is John Tragard.

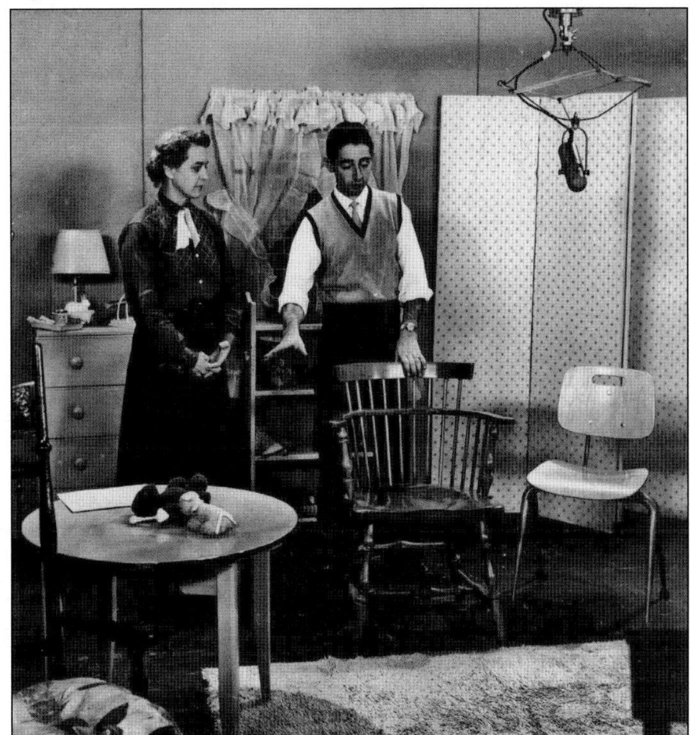

Sam Silberman gives instructions to the host of a WQED program that shows new mothers what to do when a baby comes home from the hospital. The station did not limit educational programming to children, providing informative shows to viewers of all ages.

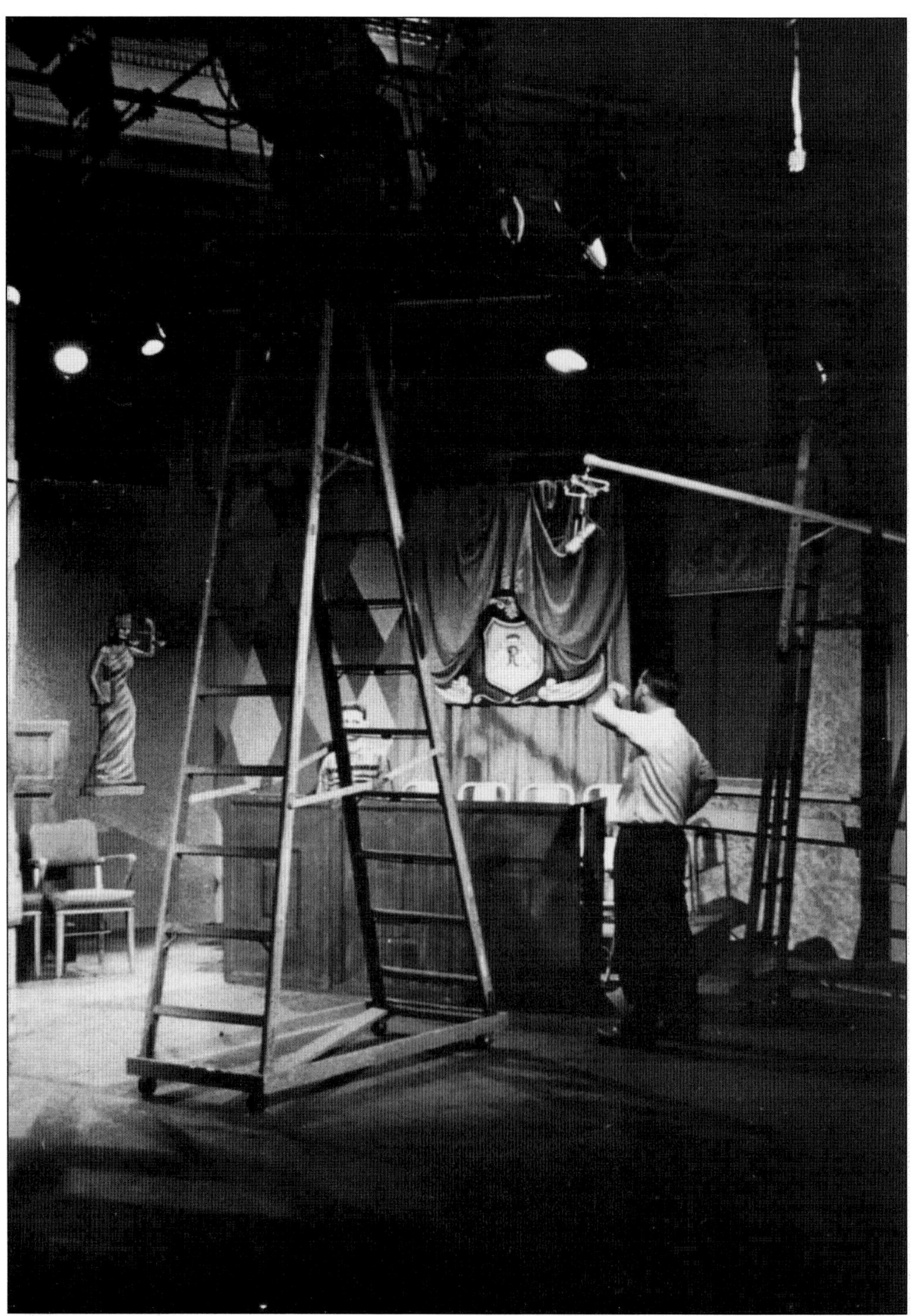

Bill Evans directs the lighting on the WQED program *Legally Speaking*, produced in cooperation with the local bar association. Although this show never earned the popularity of others such as *The Children's Corner* and *Mister Rogers' Neighborhood*, *Legally Speaking* was broadcast on WQED for several years from the late 1950s to the mid-1960s.

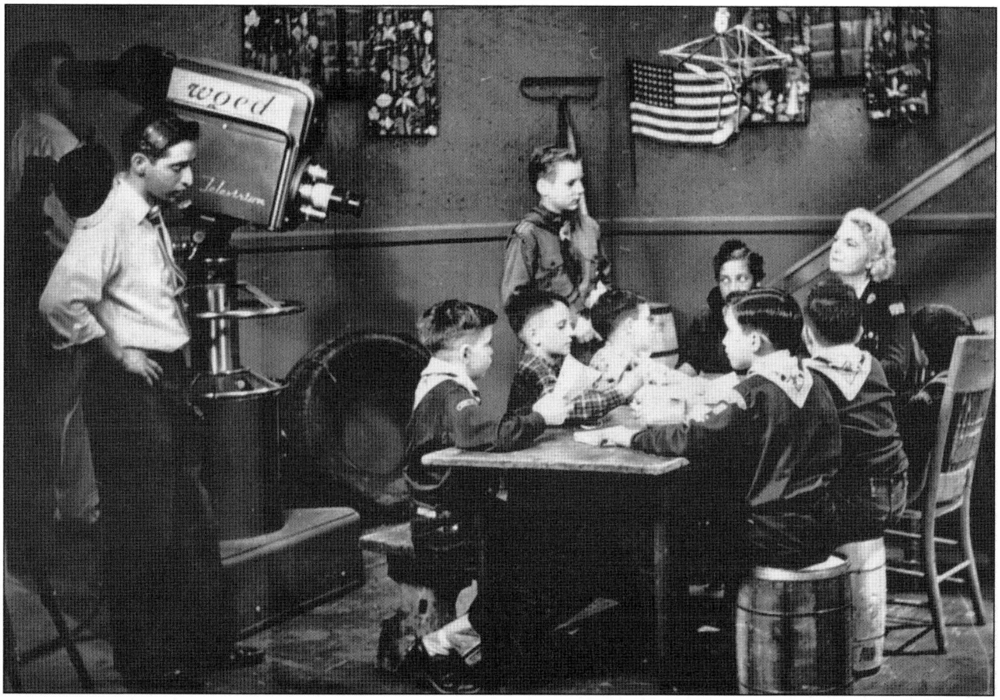

Sam Silberman and the WQED crew film the Boy Scouts. WQED primarily filmed a wide variety of educational programming for people of all ages. Silberman became the program director and eventually president of WQED before retiring.

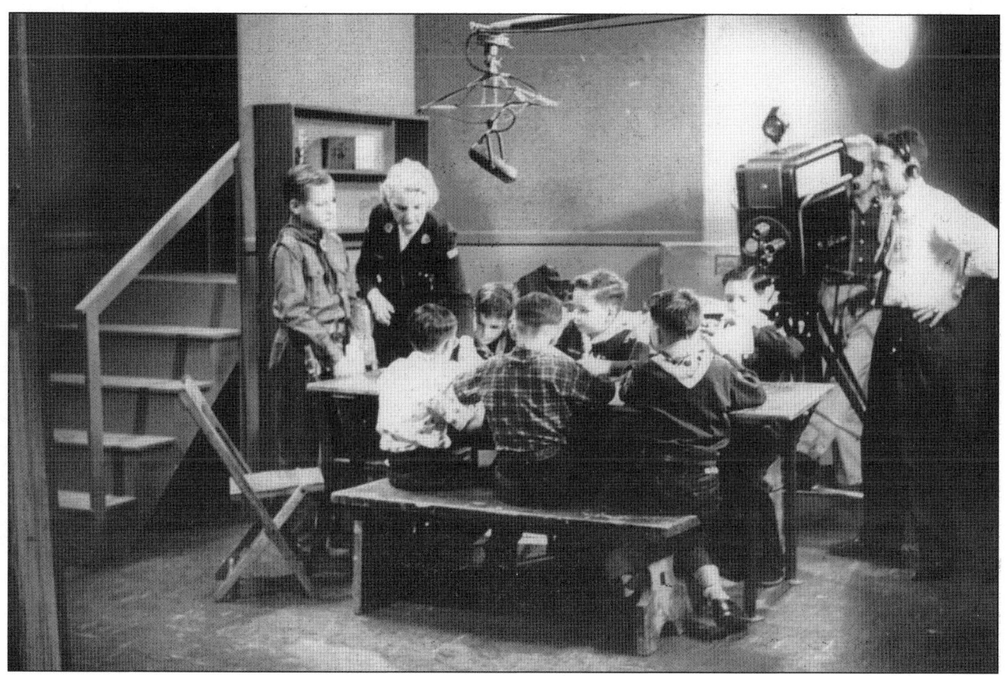

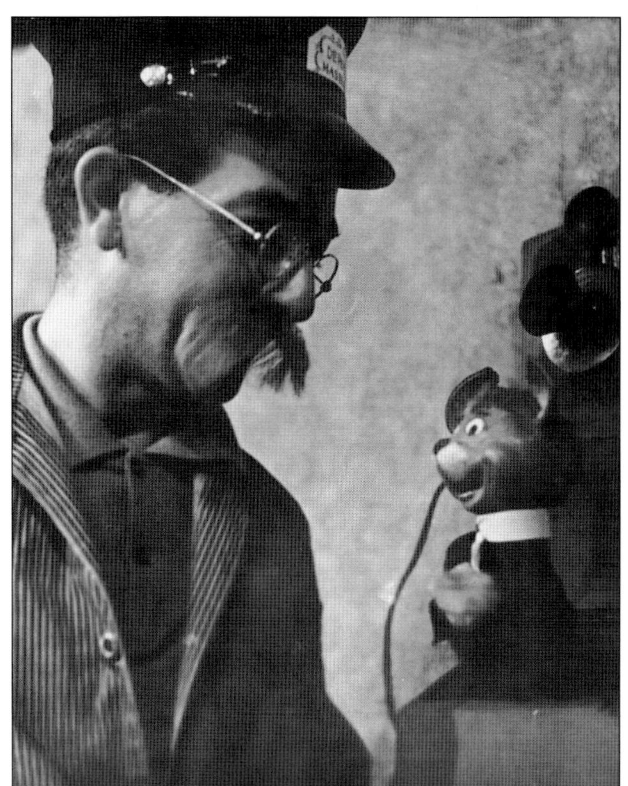

Dimple Depot was a short-lived WQED children's program that was meant to be somewhat of a successor to *The Children's Corner*. However, *Dimple Depot* didn't become anywhere near as popular as its predecessor. This picture shows Ernie Coombs looking at a puppet on the set of *Dimple Depot*. Before *Mister Rogers' Neighborhood* aired on WQED, Rogers worked on a show for the Canadian Broadcasting Corporation (CBC) called *MisteRogers*. Coombs worked on *MisteRogers* with Rogers, but Coombs's popularity stems from a later show on CBC called *Mr. Dressup*.

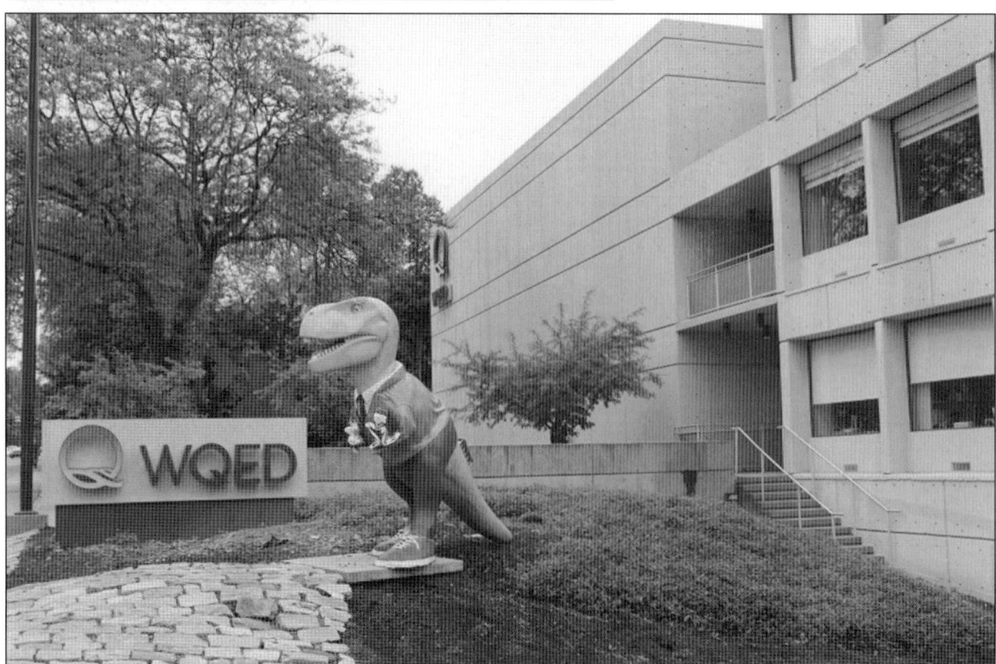

A recent photograph shows the current location of WQED in Pittsburgh. WQED is still committed to producing educational programming as well as shows that pertain to the Pittsburgh community. (Courtesy of Kailyn Trainer-Walters.)

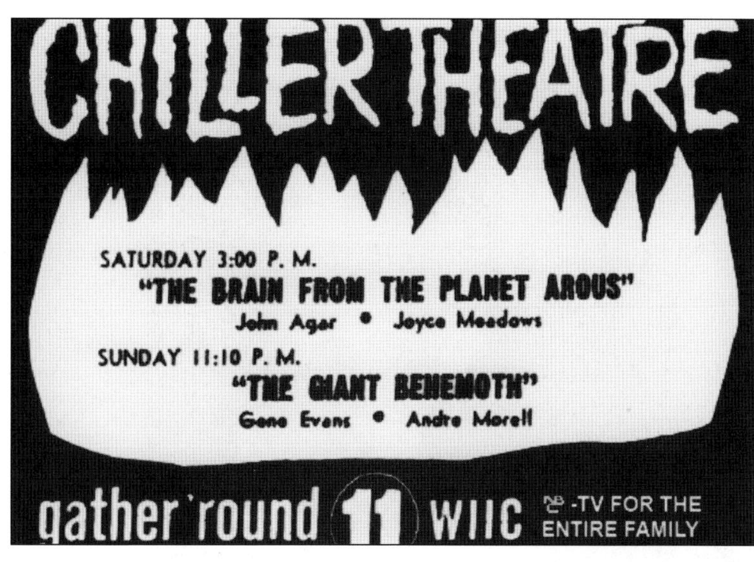

This is WIIC Channel 11's first *Chiller Theater* ad taken from a local Pittsburgh newspaper in September 1963. The show exploded in popularity, with Bill Cardille receiving fan mail from all across the country. (Courtesy of WPXI-TV.)

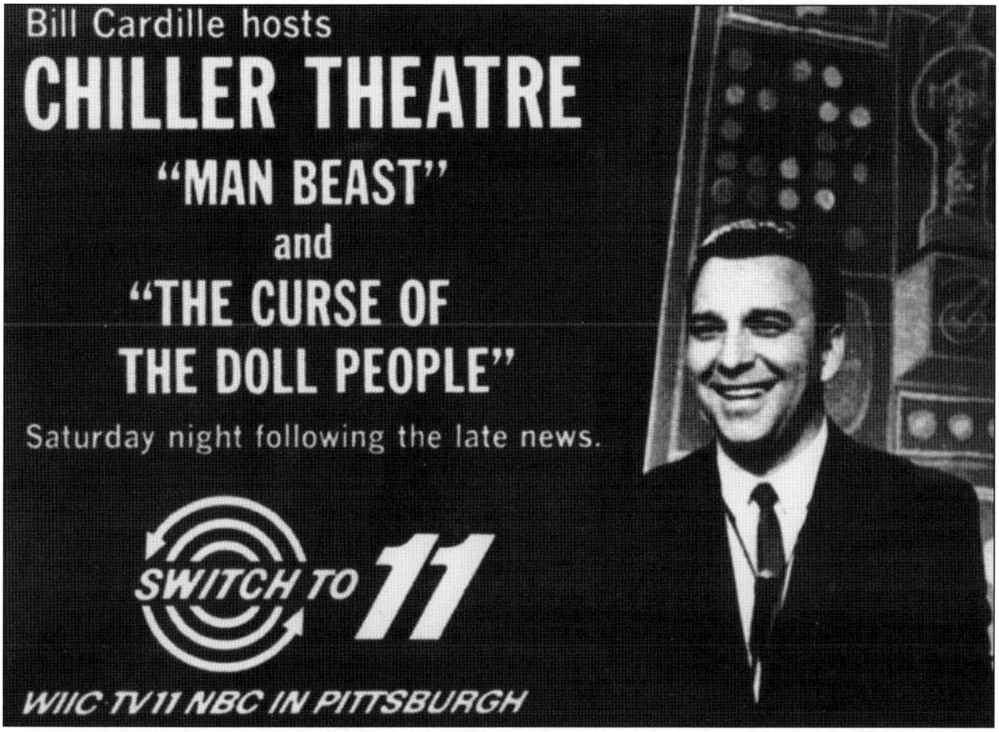

Bill Cardille hosts
CHILLER THEATRE
"MAN BEAST"
and
"THE CURSE OF THE DOLL PEOPLE"
Saturday night following the late news.
SWITCH TO 11
WIIC TV11 NBC IN PITTSBURGH

Another Channel 11 *Chiller Theater* ad from a local paper in August 1968 shows the legendary broadcaster Bill Cardille. The year 1968 was particularly special for Cardille, the horror genre, and Pittsburgh. Not only was *Chiller Theater* a huge success nationwide with Cardille being recognized as a horror icon, but he also made the move over to feature film when he was asked to be in George A. Romero's *Night of the Living Dead*, a film made in the Pittsburgh area. *Night of the Living Dead* became one of the most popular horror movies of all time, furthering the popularity of Cardille. (Courtesy of WPXI-TV.)

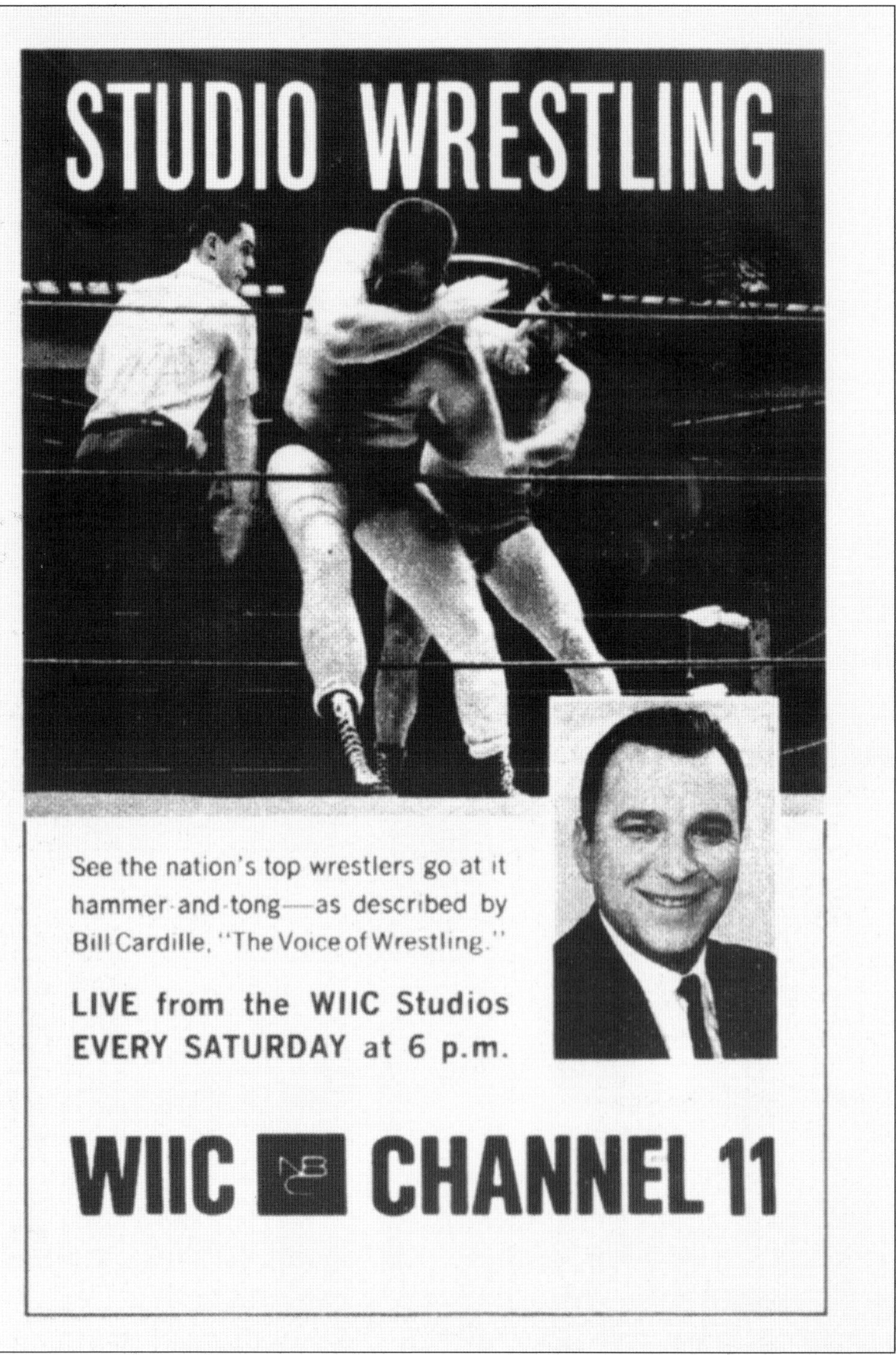

This is a Channel 11 ad for Bill Cardille's other television show, *Studio Wrestling*, which was somewhat of a predecessor to Vince McMahon's WWF/WWE wrestling show and featured many legendary wrestlers that were eventually featured on McMahon's show, such as Bruno Sammartino, Greg "The Hammer" Valentine, and George "The Animal" Steele. (Courtesy of WPXI-TV.)

Three

Location Filmmaking in Pittsburgh

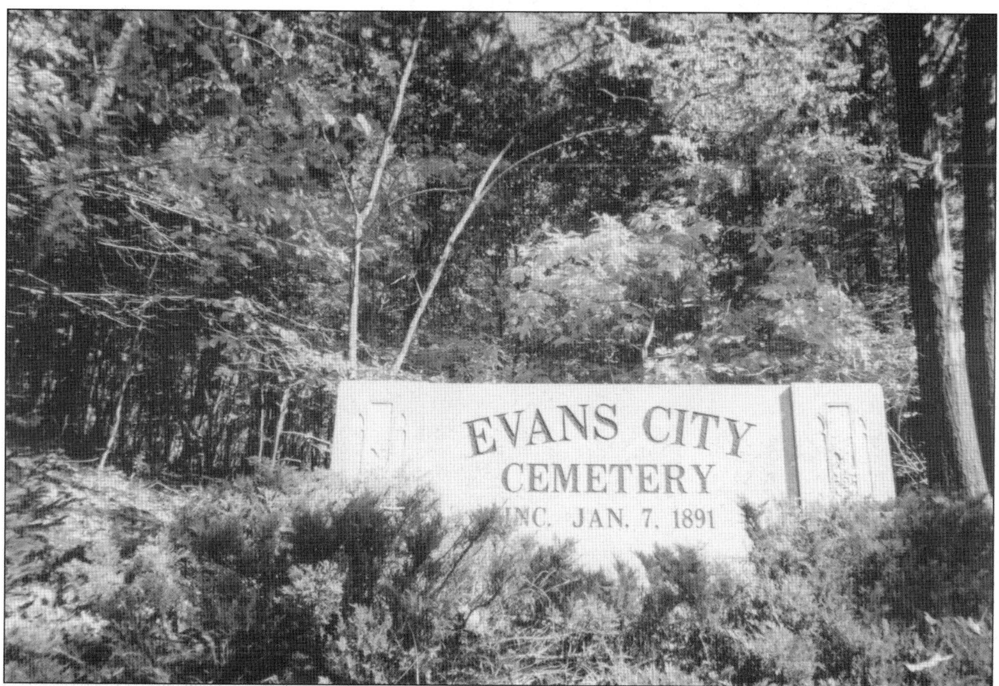

The entrance to the Evans City Cemetery has been somewhat modernized since it was used for *Night of the Living Dead* in 1967. One of the most noticeable differences between 1967 and the present is the cemetery sign.

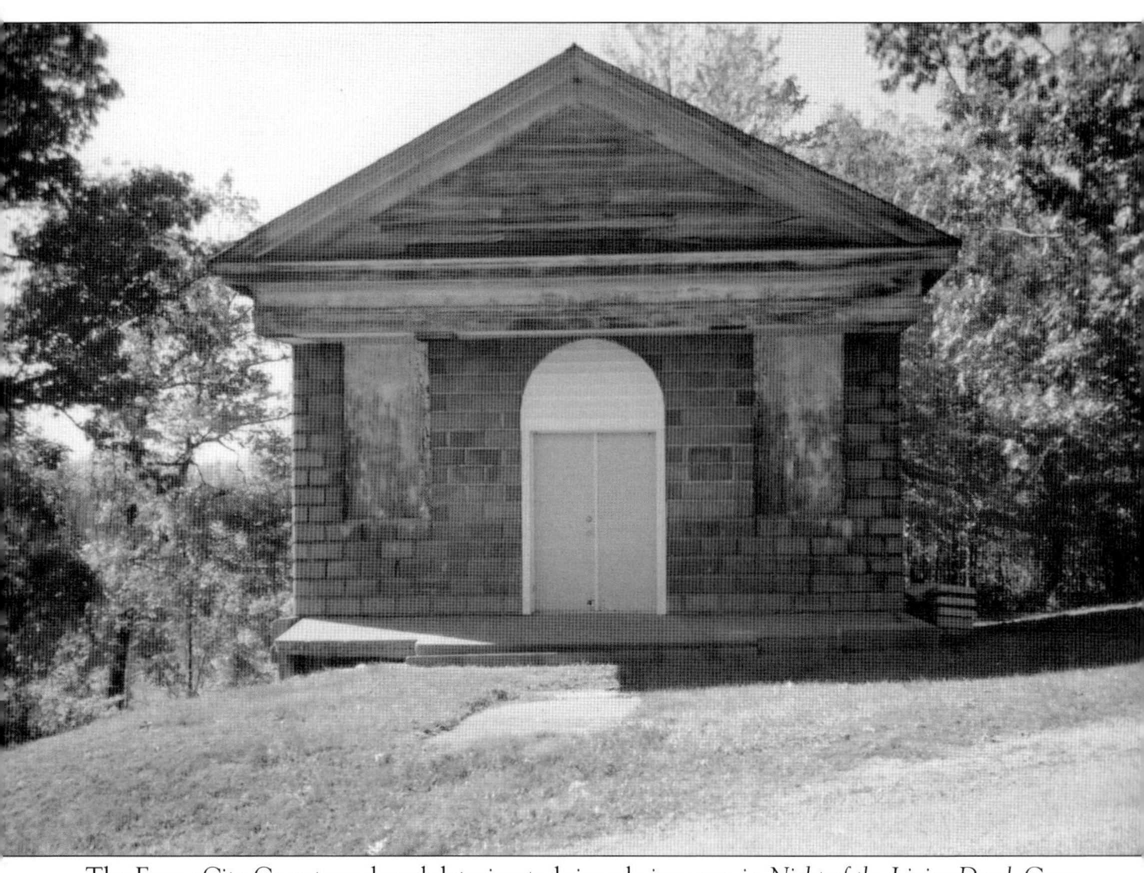

The Evans City Cemetery chapel deteriorated since being seen in *Night of the Living Dead*. Gary Streiner, who worked on *Night of the Living Dead*, recently raised the money to restore this cinematic landmark, a restoration that is currently underway. This picture of the chapel was taken right before its restoration. (Courtesy of Kailyn Trainer-Walters.)

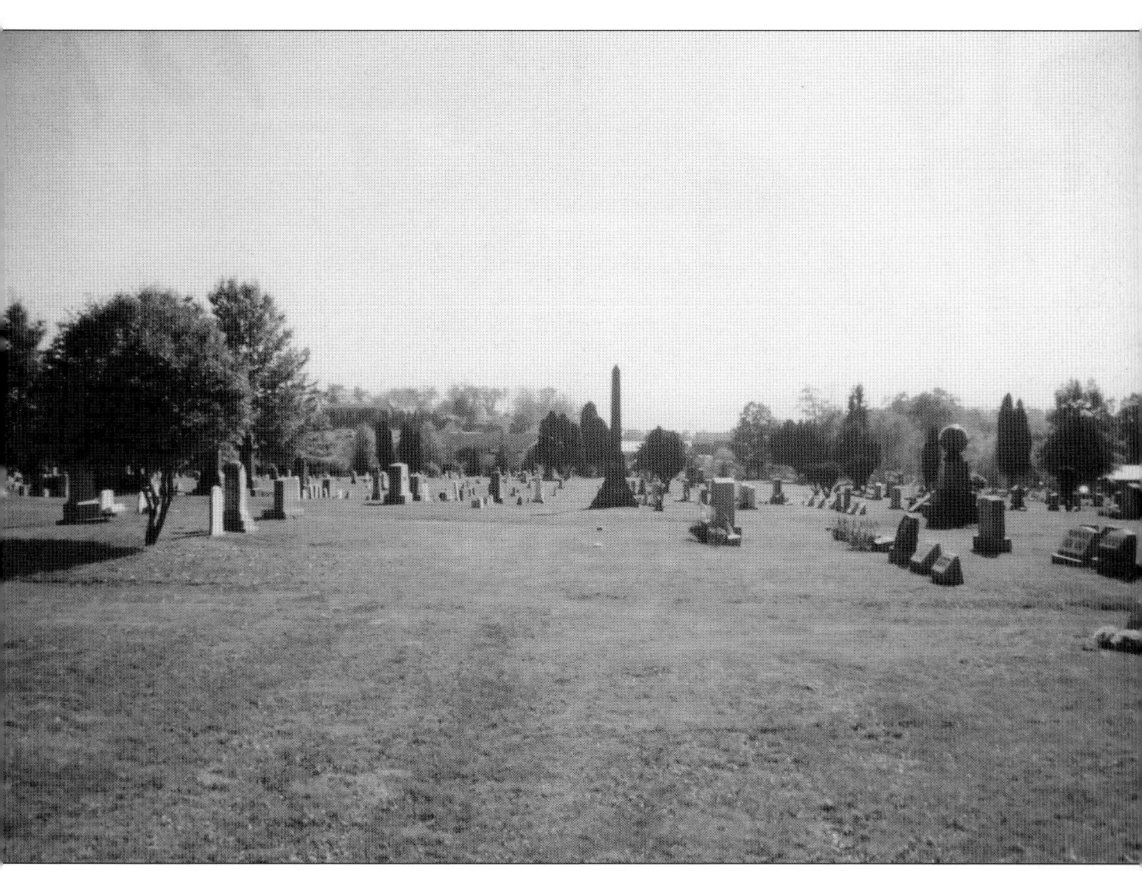

A modern-day view of the Evans City Cemetery depicts similarities and differences since *Night of the Living Dead* was filmed in 1967. Many of the unique gravestones stand out in this photograph as they do in the movie; however, many of the trees that once populated the cemetery are now gone.

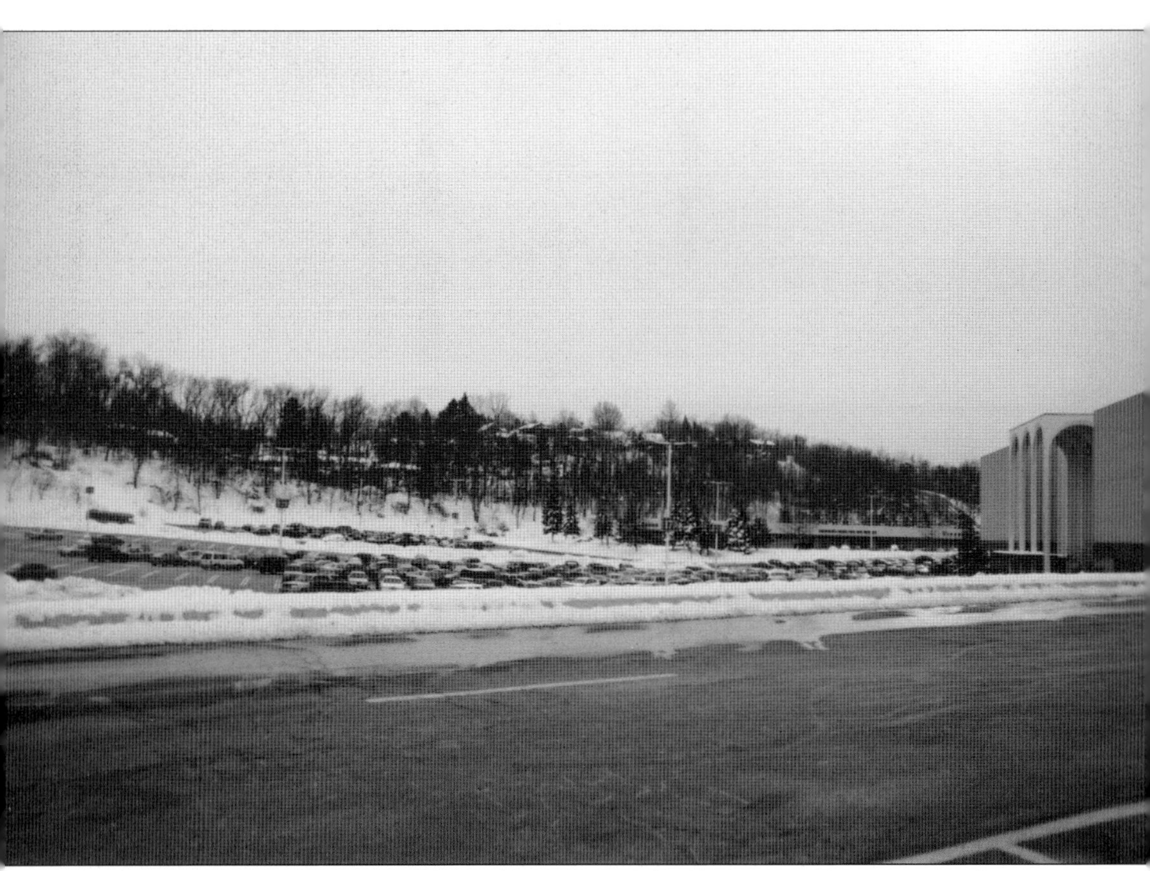

The parking lot of the Monroeville Mall was one of the filming sites for George A. Romero's *Dawn of the Dead* in late 1977 and early 1978. *Zack and Miri Make a Porno* was also filmed at the mall in 2008.

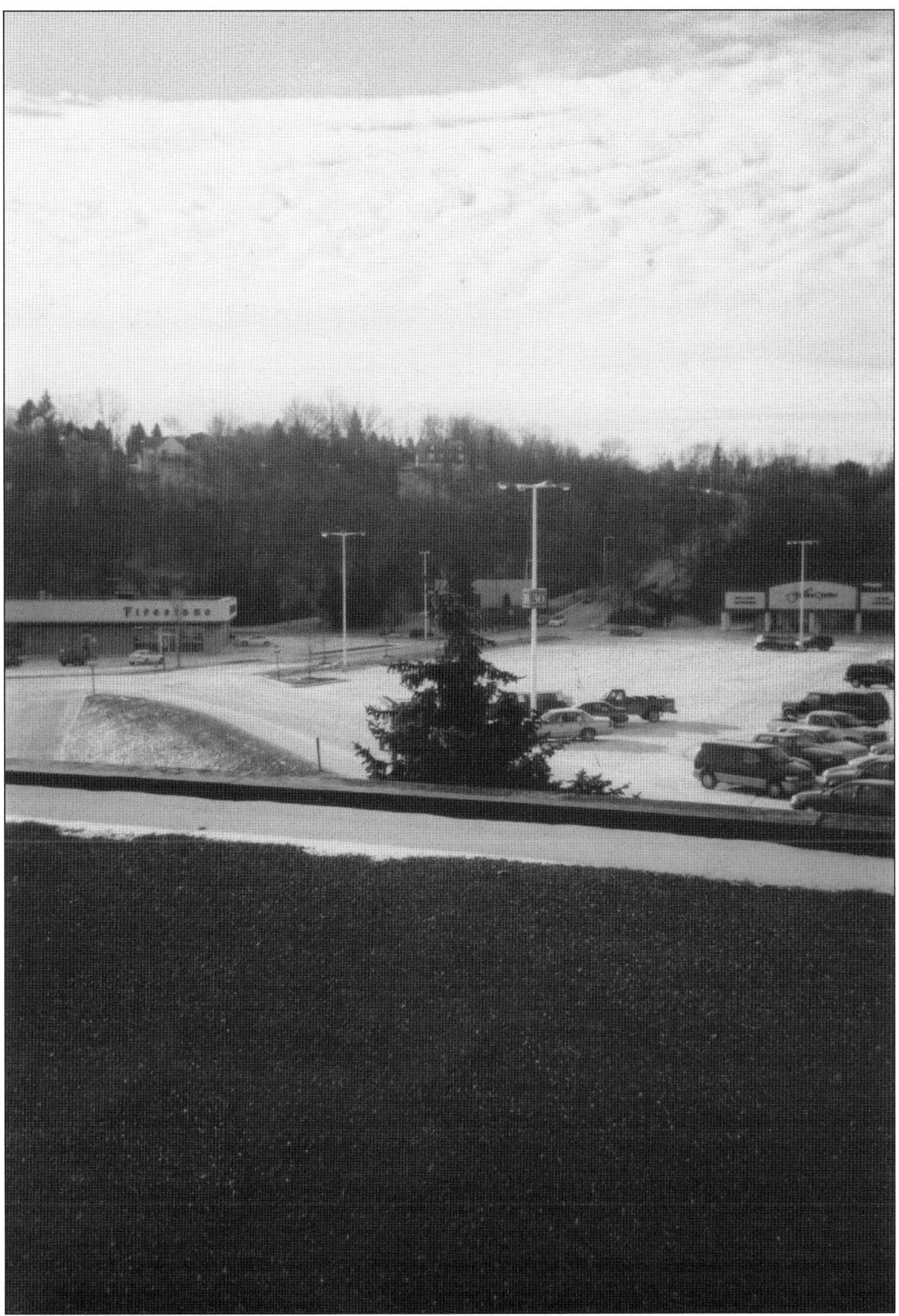

This road and portion of the Monroeville Mall parking lot can be seen in several shots throughout *Dawn of the Dead.* One of the key scenes this exterior location was seen in was during the biker raid toward the end of the film.

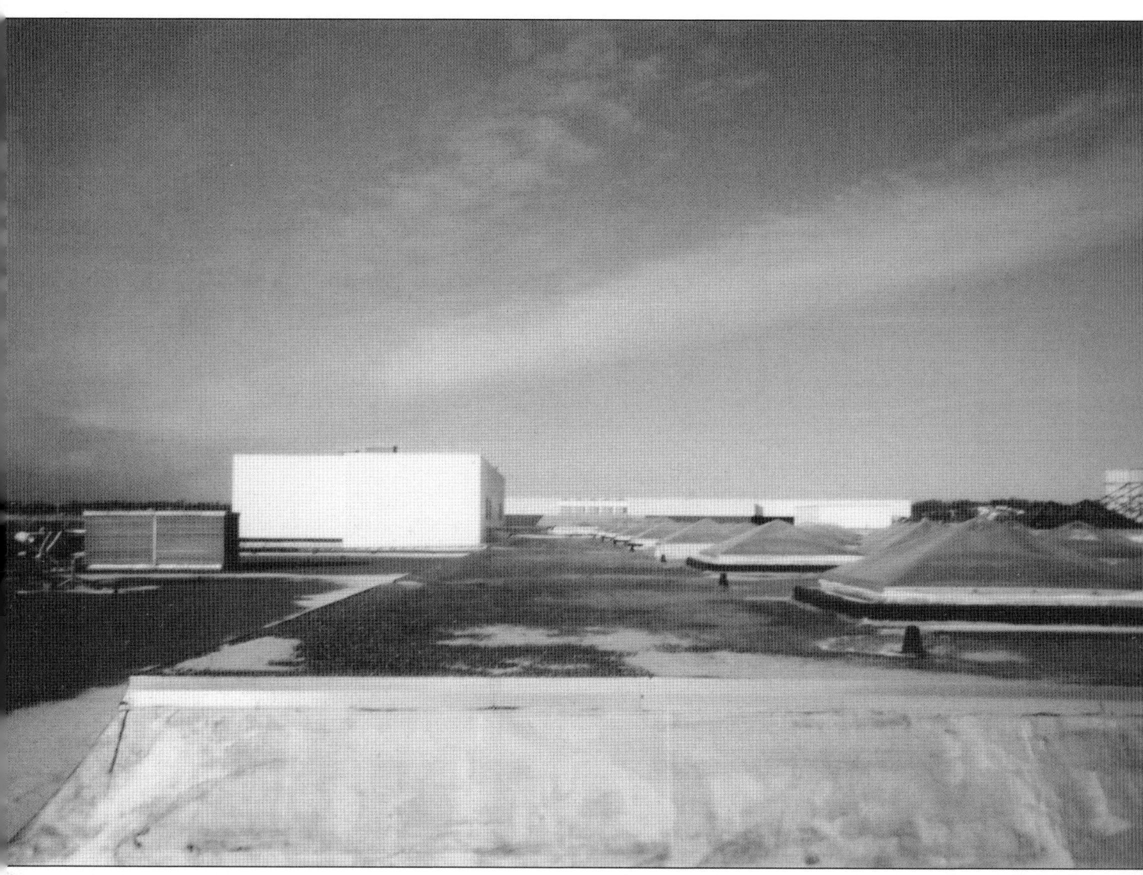

A photograph taken several years ago shows the roof of the Monroeville Mall. The pyramid-like objects along the roof are actually windows that provide sky lighting for the mall. In *Dawn of the Dead*, the characters look through these windows.

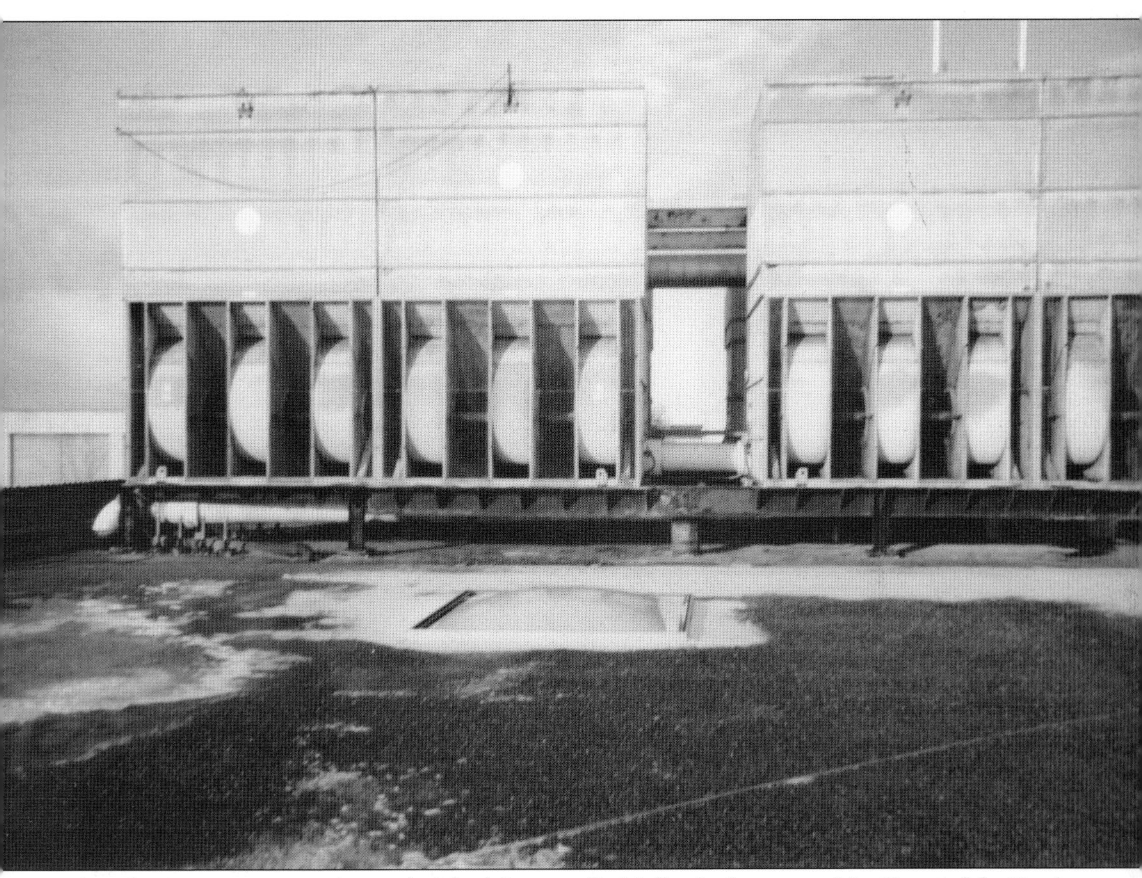
Another image presents the roof of the Monroeville Mall, which was used for *Dawn of the Dead*. For the most part, the roof has remained the same since the filming for the zombie movie over 30 years ago.

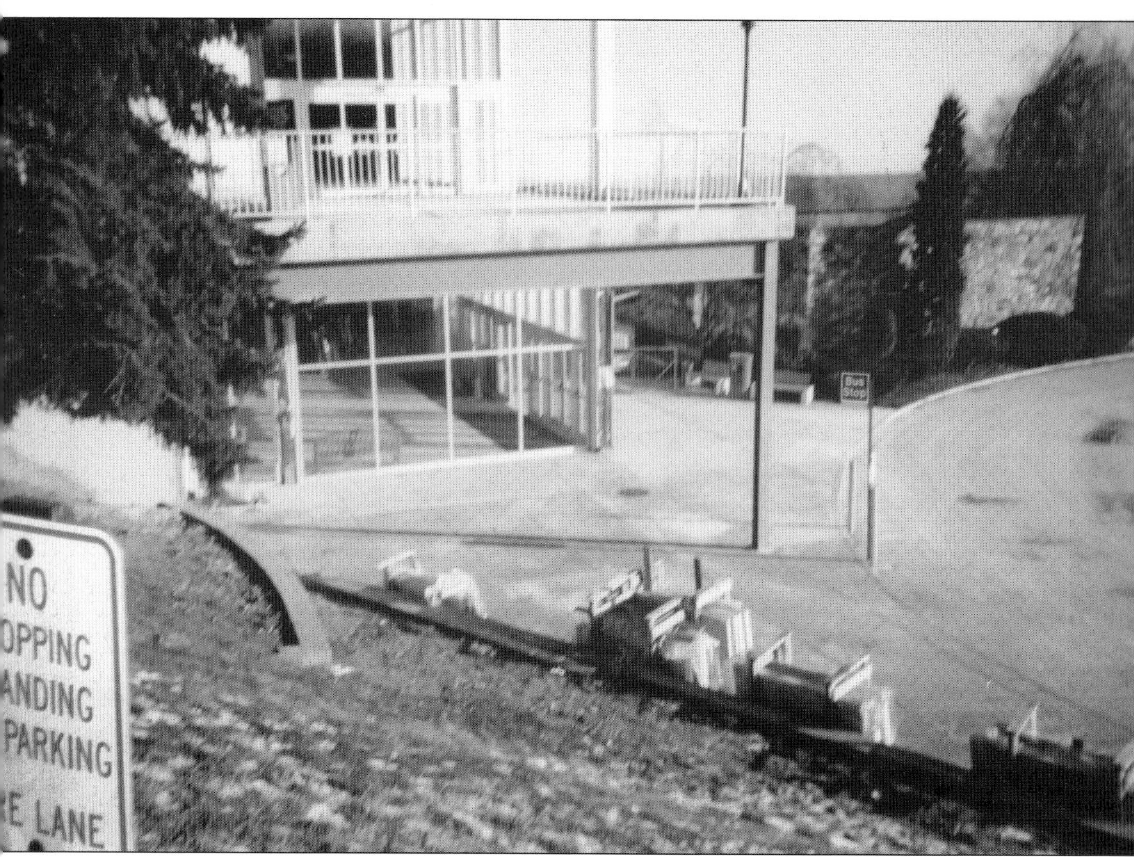

This entranceway for the Monroeville Mall was used for *Dawn of the Dead*. It can be seen in several shots throughout the film. One of those scenes featured the main characters driving a car down an interior passageway. In a similar shot, a biker gang also drives down the same corridor.

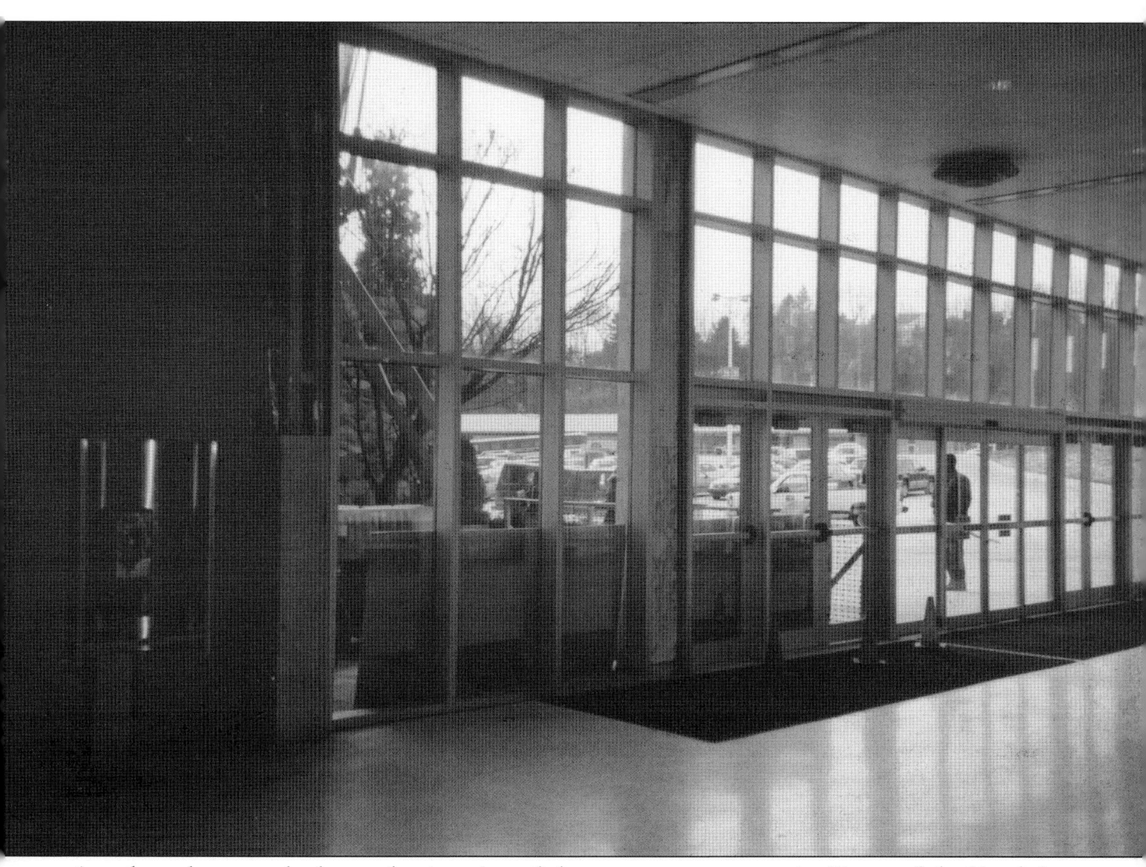

Another photograph shows the interior of the entranceway seen in *Dawn of the Dead*. In the film, the doors shown here were blocked with large trucks, preventing the zombies from breaking through.

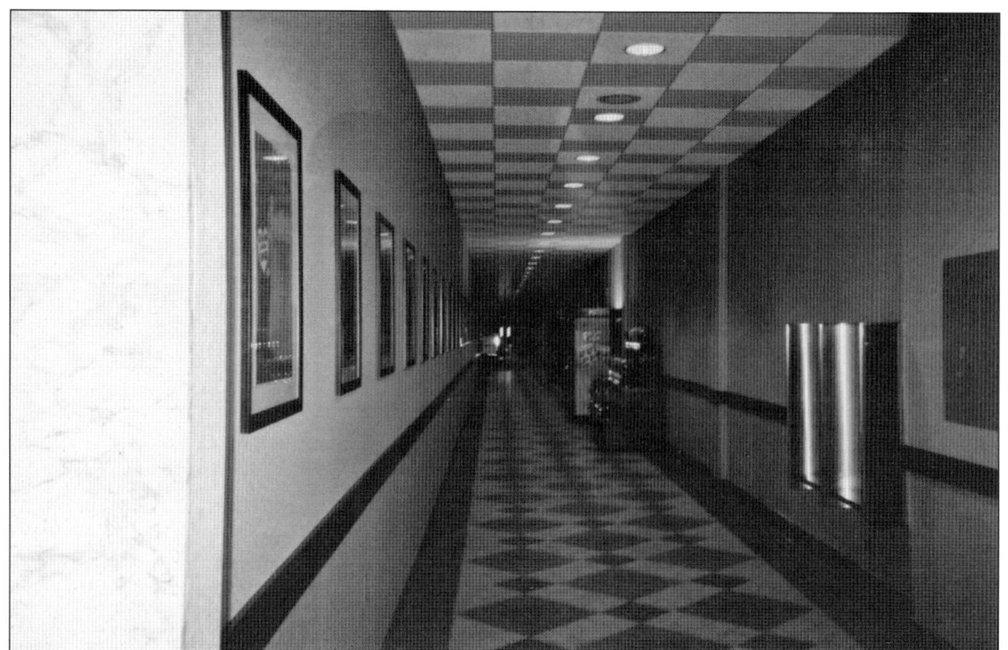

This hallway inside the Monroeville Mall was used for the filming of *Dawn of the Dead* and can be seen several times in the movie. George A. Romero's production filmed inside the mall right before Christmas 1977 and right after New Year's Day 1978 because they could not film inside the mall with all the Christmas decorations. All of the filming in the mall took place after hours.

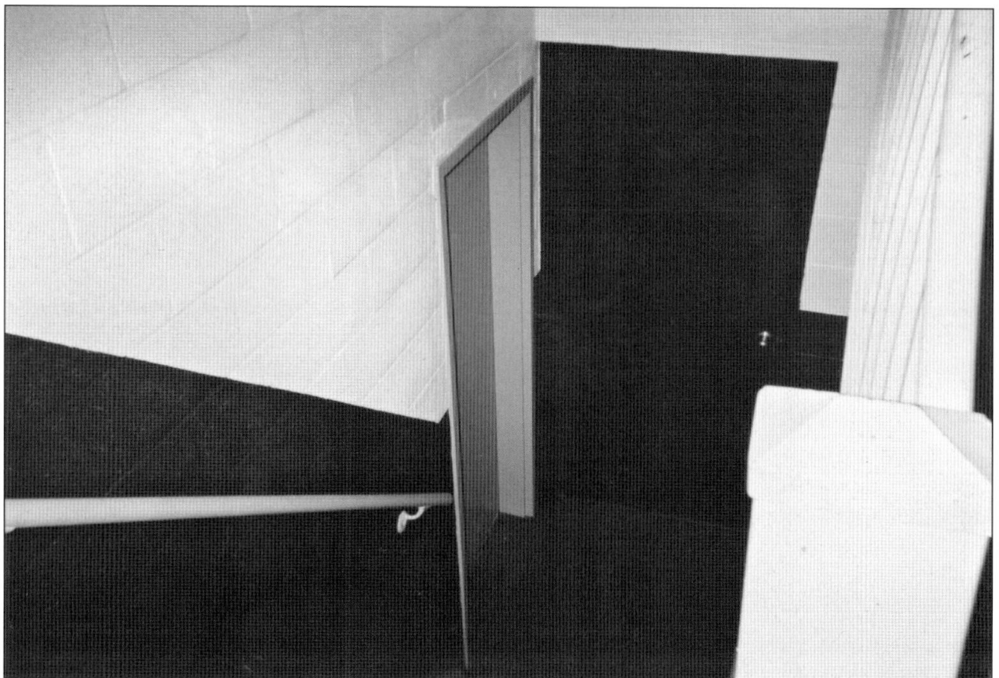

This private stairwell in the Monroeville Mall was used for the filming of *Dawn of the Dead.* In the movie, this stairwell led to the hideout where the main character lived in the mall. The filmmakers were given exclusive permission to film in the private areas of the mall.

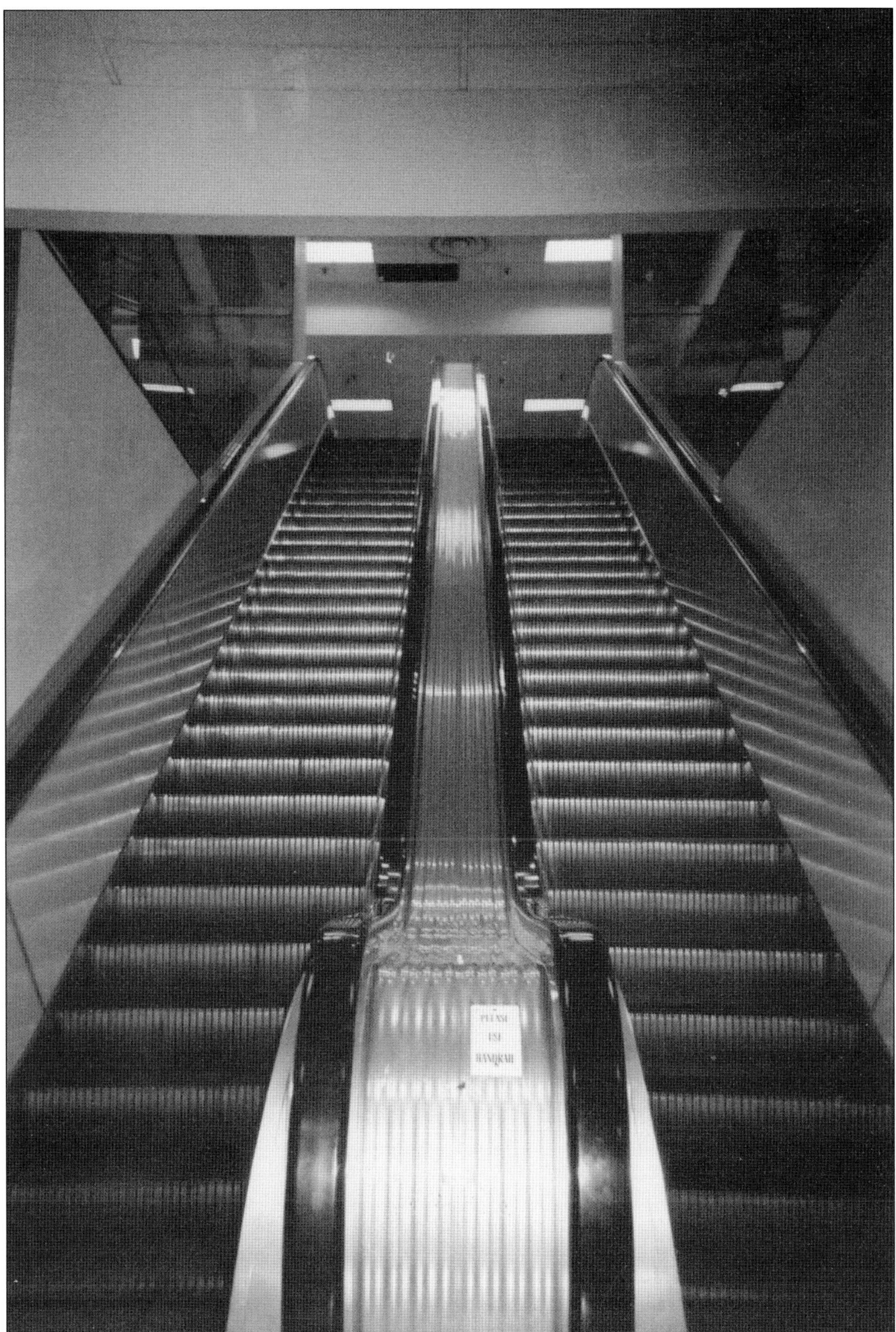

This c. 2004 picture of an escalator inside the Monroeville Mall was featured in *Dawn of the Dead*. The escalator is located in the JCPenney store.

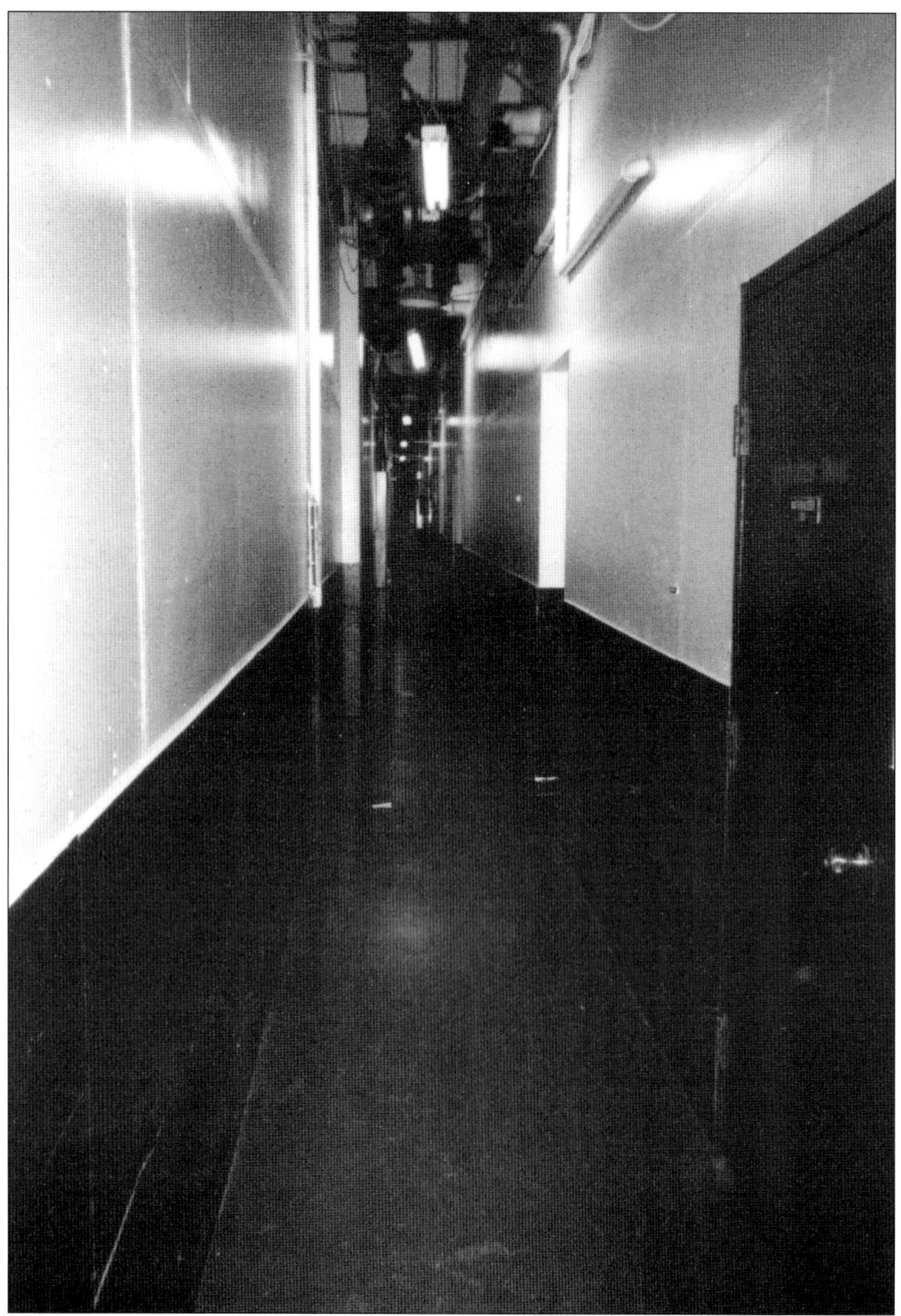

This private hallway inside the Monroeville Mall is briefly seen in *Dawn of the Dead*. The main characters travelled down this hallway as part of the labyrinth of passageways that led to their hideout in the mall.

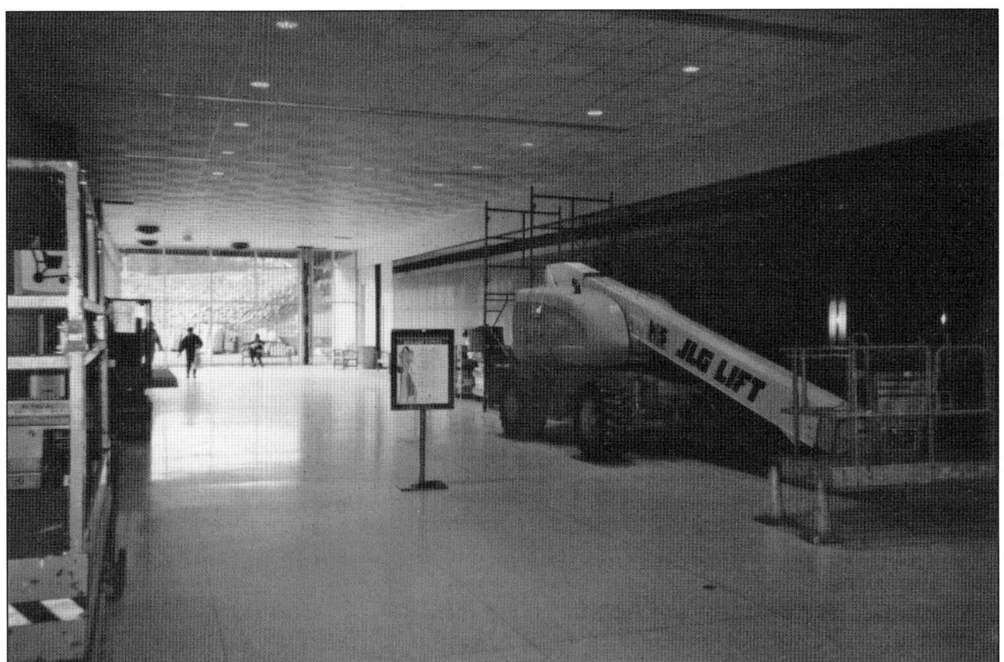

This picture shows an entranceway in the Monroeville Mall that was featured in *Dawn of the Dead*. In the film, some of the main characters drive a car through here. Real bikers were also brought onto the set to drive motorcycles here. The production was given permission to drive cars and motorcycles in the mall.

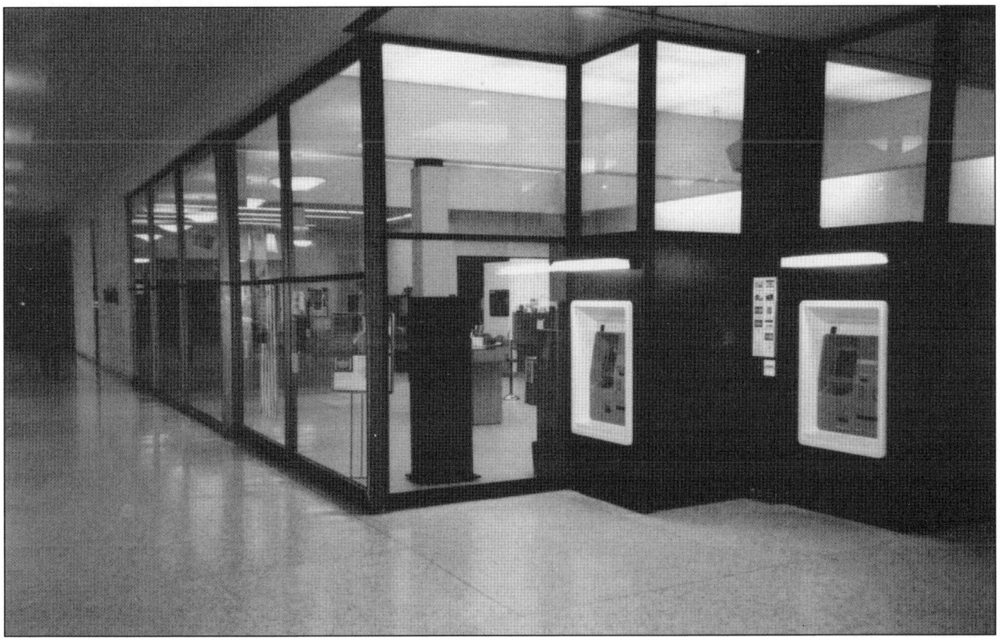

The bank on the upper level of the Monroeville Mall is pictured around 2004. This bank was featured in *Dawn of the Dead* but no longer exists in the mall, along with many other aspects of the mall that have disappeared since the filming took place over 30 years ago. One of the most notable differences is the disappearance of the ice rink, which has been replaced with the food court.

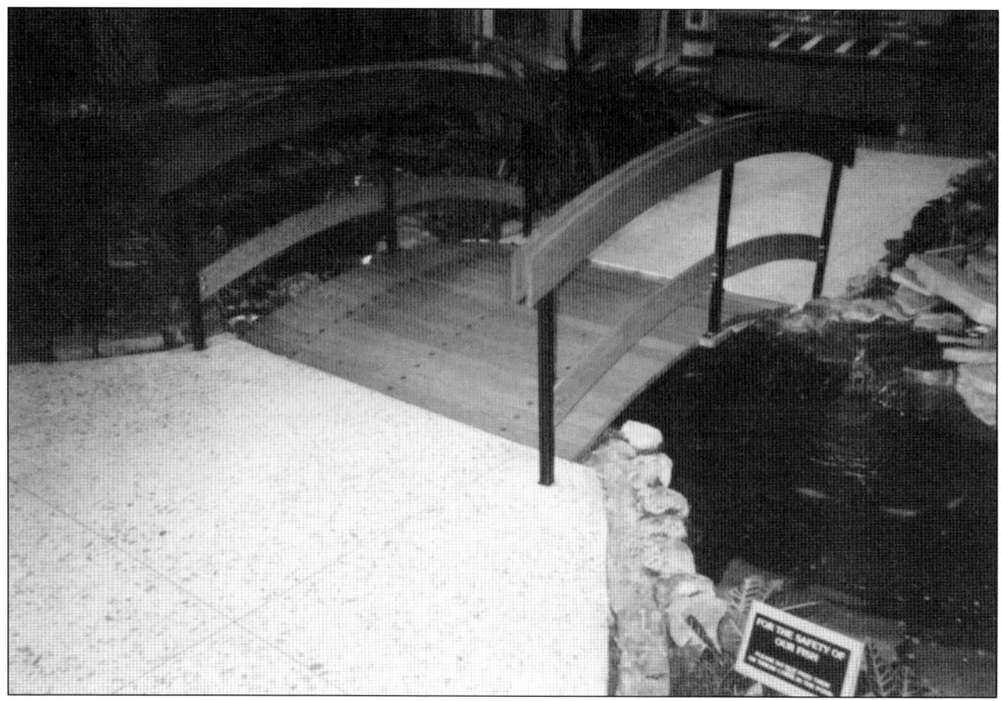

This small wooden bridge inside the Monroeville Mall is seen in *Dawn of the Dead*. It is one of the few remaining physical features of the mall since the filming took place.

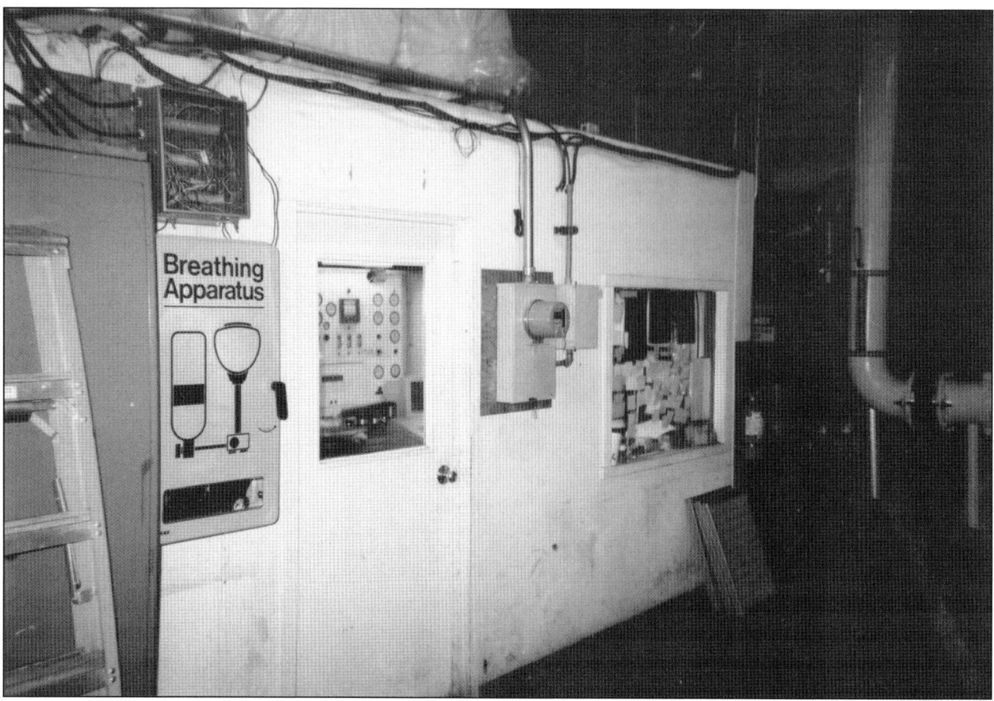

The exterior of the Monroeville Mall control room can be briefly seen in *Dawn of the Dead*.

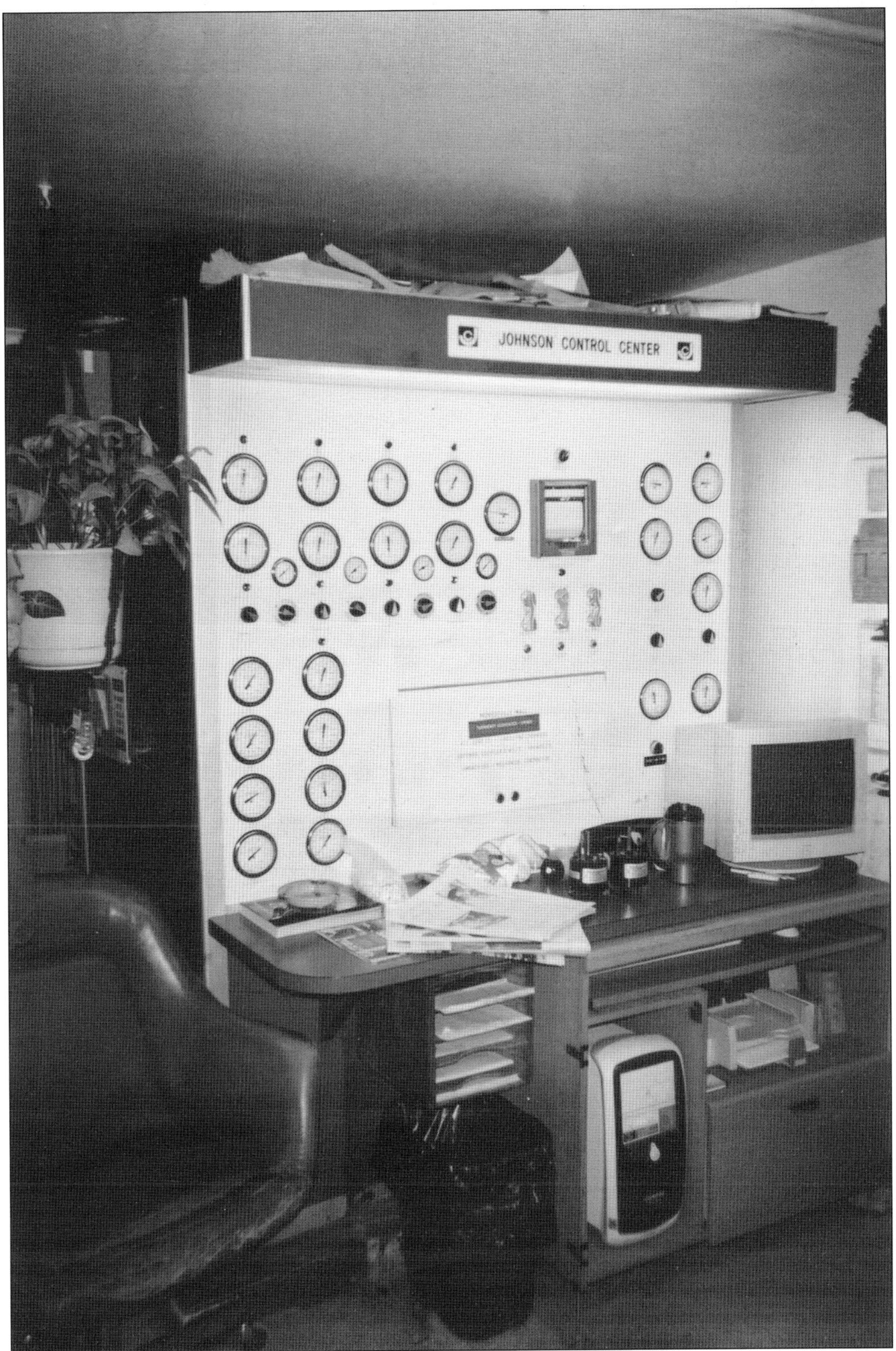

The interior of the Monroeville Mall control room was featured in a scene for *Dawn of the Dead*.

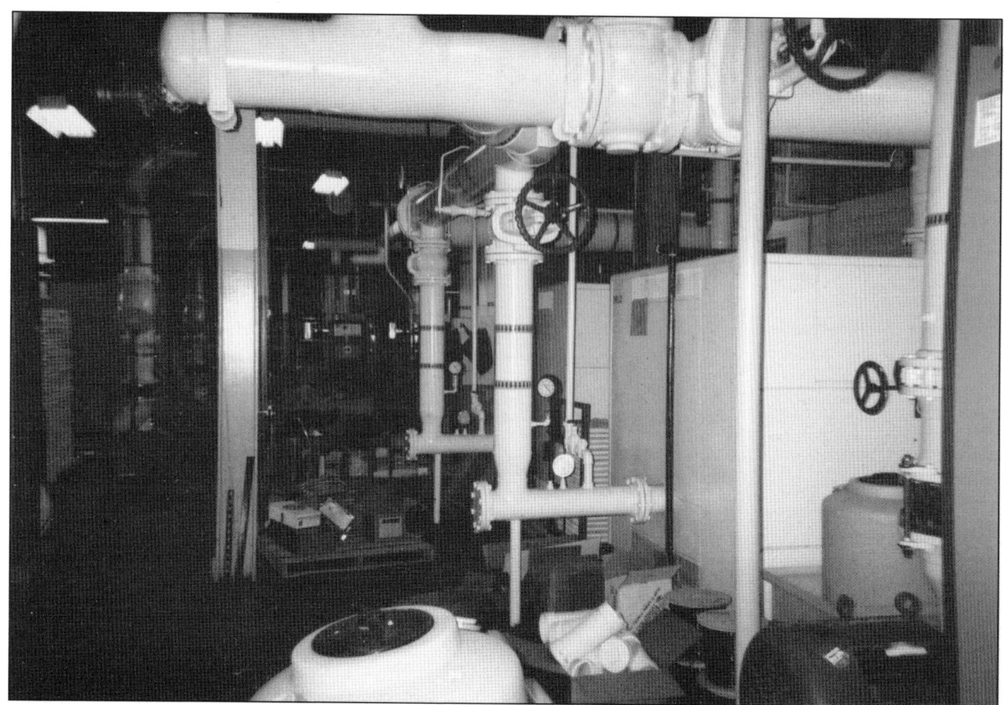

A recent shot of the boiler room inside the Monroeville Mall reveals that the scene has not changed much since being used in *Dawn of the Dead*.

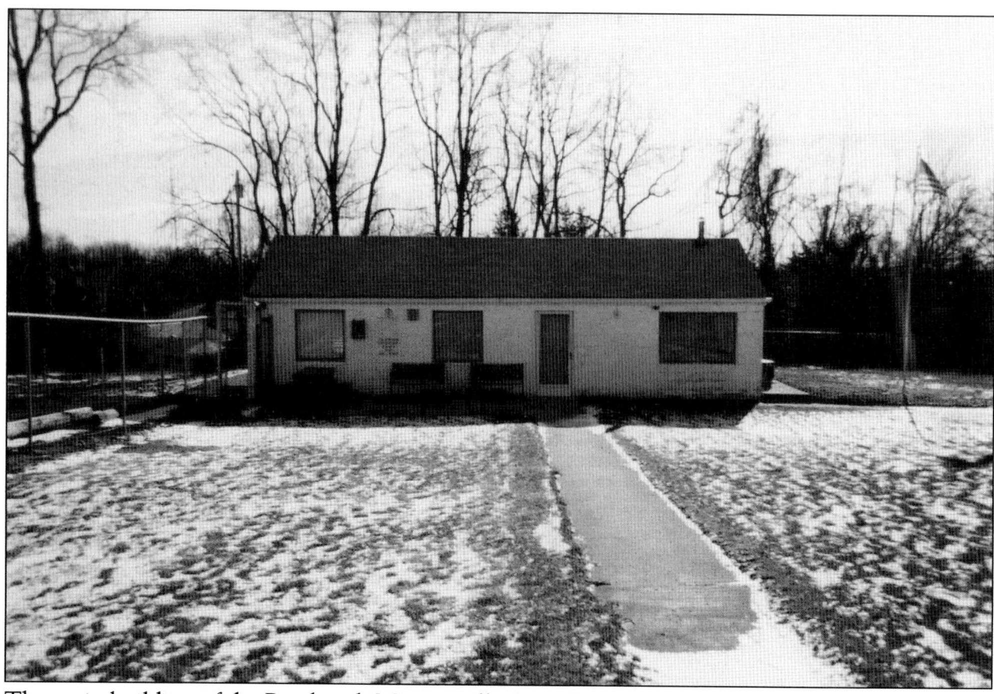

The main building of the Pittsburgh Monroeville Airport was used for George A. Romero's *Dawn of the Dead*. From the outside, the building remains quite similar to its appearance in the film over 30 years ago.

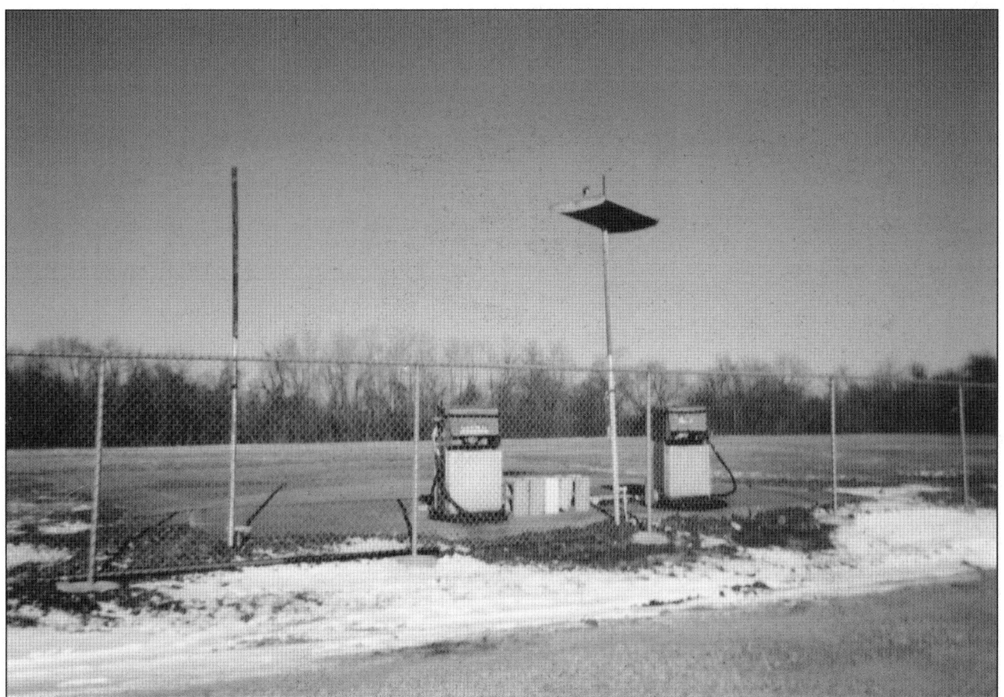

Another picture from the Pittsburgh Monroeville Airport shows the aviation fuel pumps that were featured in *Dawn of the Dead*. These pumps may have been changed or upgraded since the filming took place over 30 years ago.

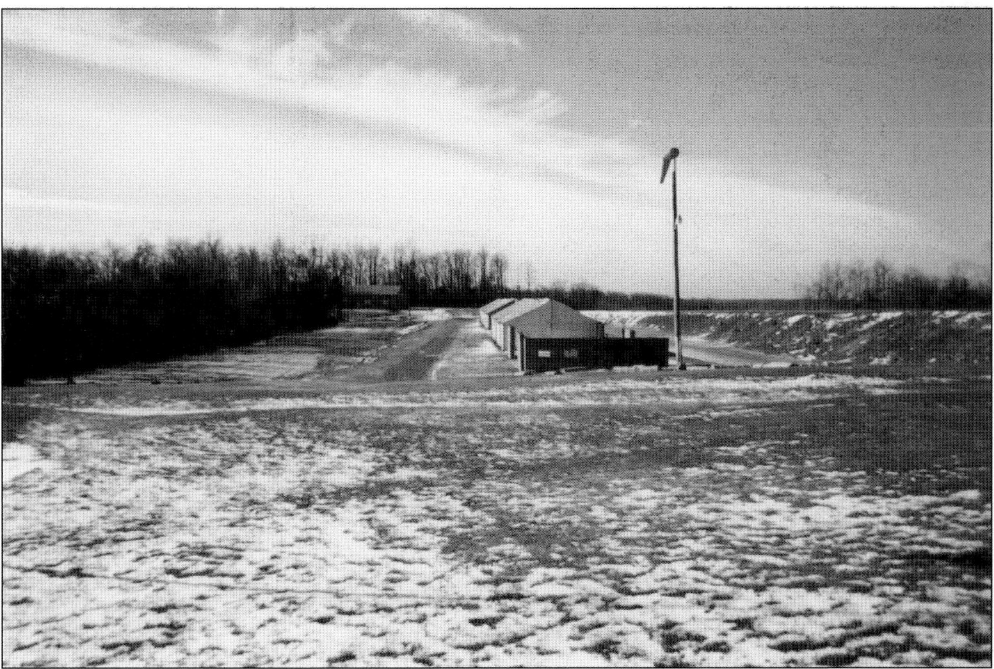

A wide shot of the Pittsburgh Monroeville Airport depicts a similar view to that seen in *Dawn of the Dead*. Although the geography pretty much remained the same, the buildings have noticeably changed since being filmed in the late 1970s.

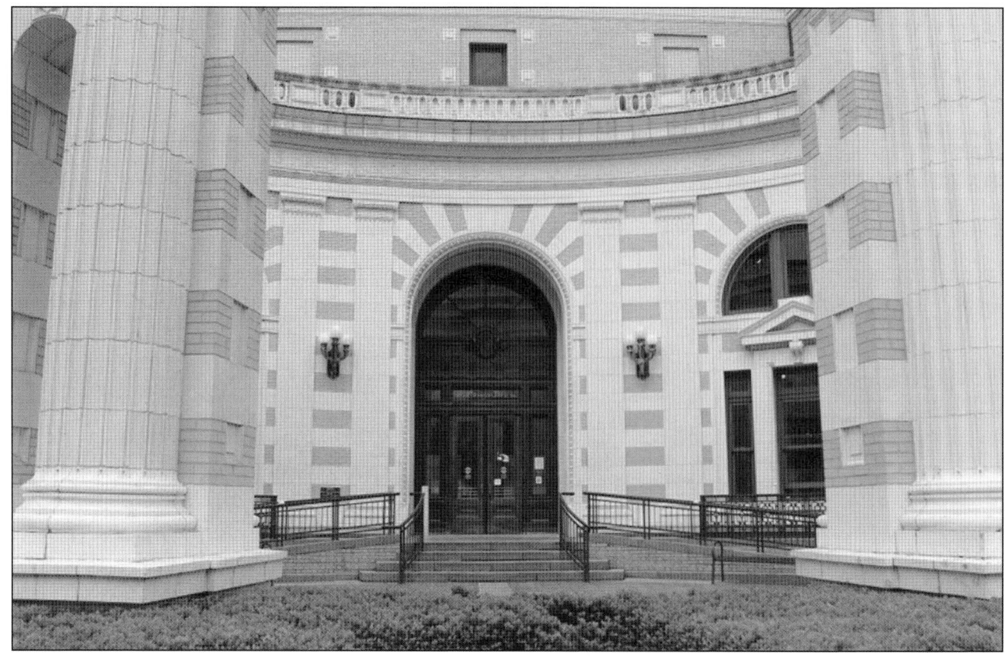

Carnegie Mellon University has seen a lot of movie magic over the years. One of the buildings prominently featured on camera is Margaret Morrison Carnegie Hall. The building gained most of its recognition from George A. Romero's *Creepshow* in 1982. It was also used in the television movie *Against Her Will: An Incident in Baltimore* starring Walter Matthau. (Courtesy of Kailyn Trainer-Walters.)

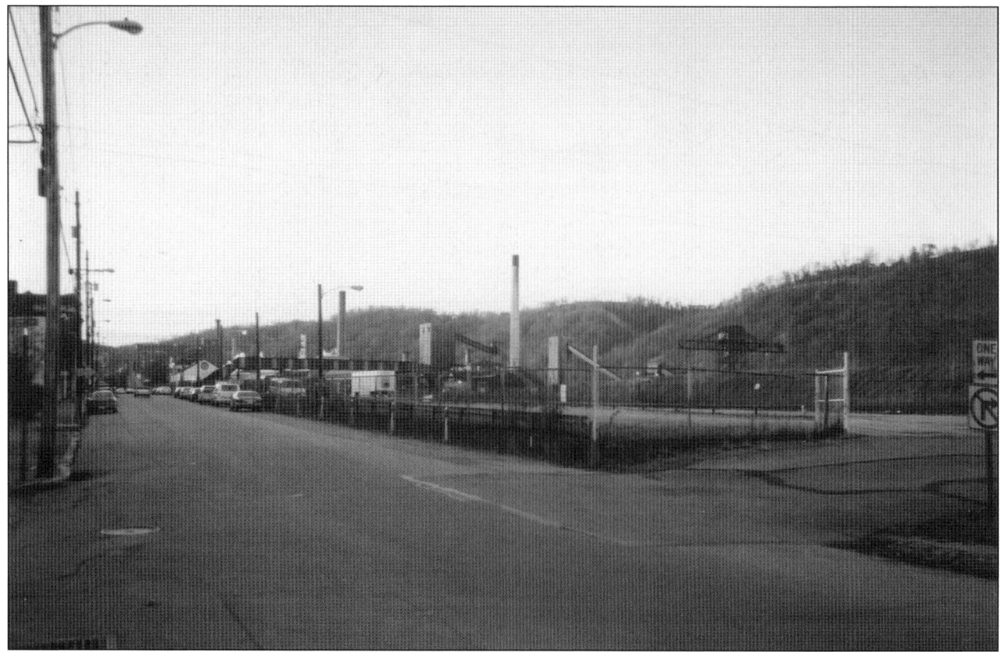

This modern photograph along Donner Avenue in Monessen, Pennsylvania, shows all that remains of the old Wheeling-Pittsburgh Steel Mill along the Monongahela River. The mill was used in 1986 for the film *Robocop*.

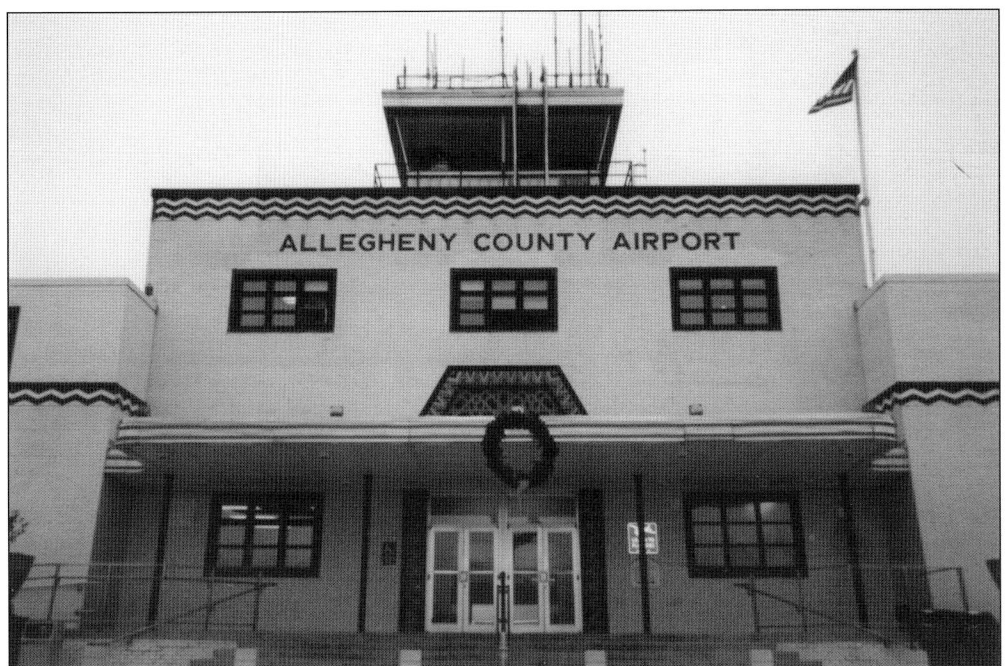

The Allegheny County Airport was used for the movies *Gung Ho* in 1986 and *The Mothman Prophecies* in 2001. Although this photograph shows the front exterior of the terminal, *The Mothman Prophecies* was filmed in the rear.

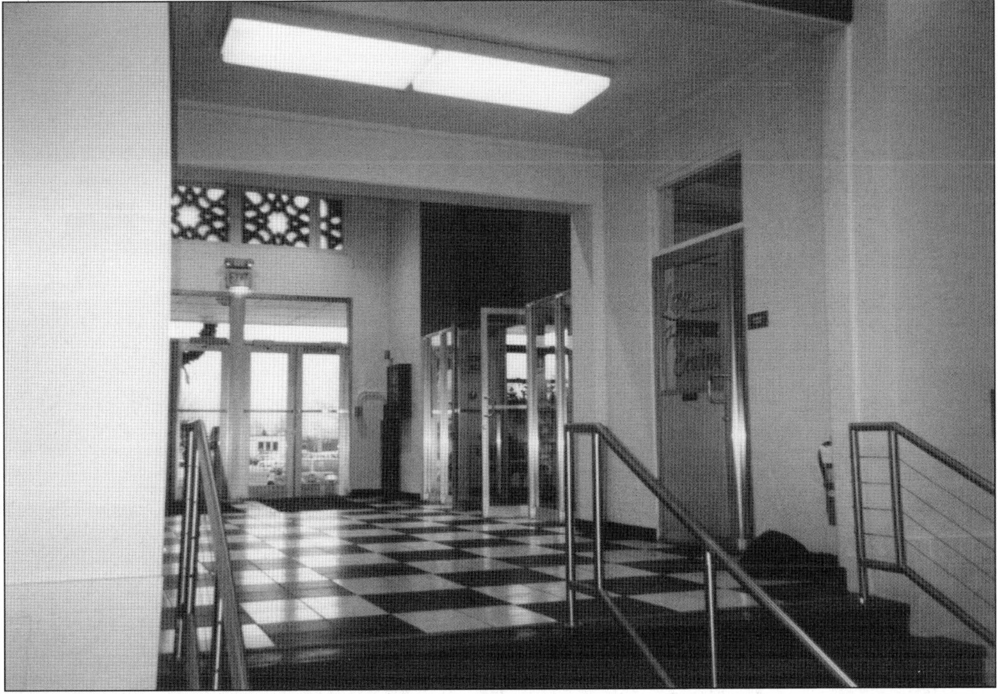

The interior of the Allegheny County Airport terminal was used for the film *Gung Ho*. The production crew had to construct a few props on the set, such as stands and booths. Markings for their placement remain on the floor to this day.

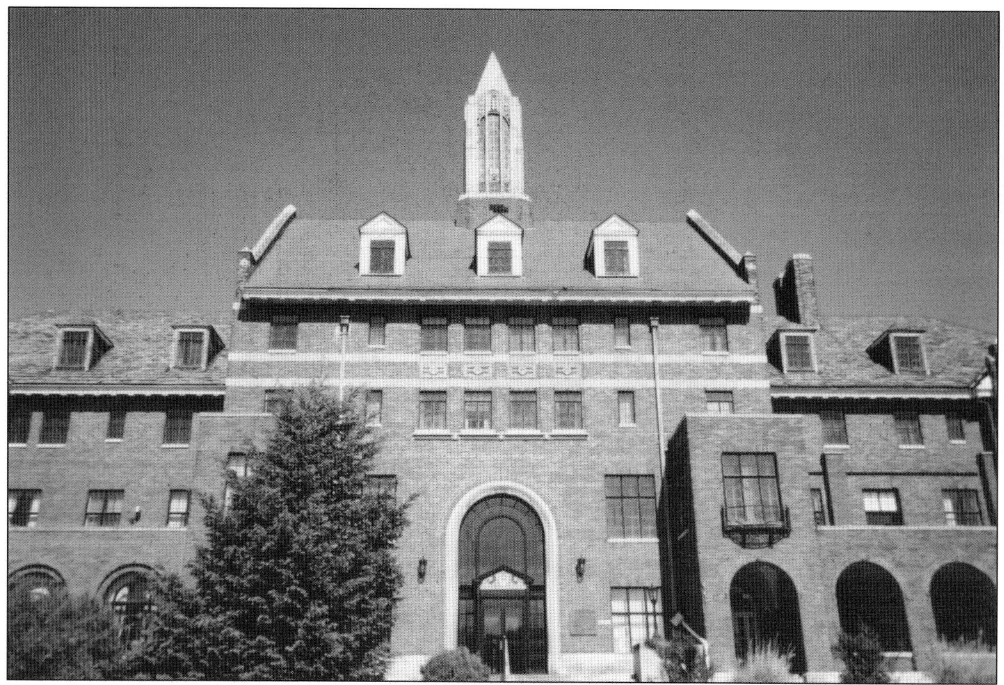

This is a frontal shot of the Western Center administration building in Canonsburg, Pennsylvania. The building was used in *The Silence of the Lambs* and was demolished in recent years.

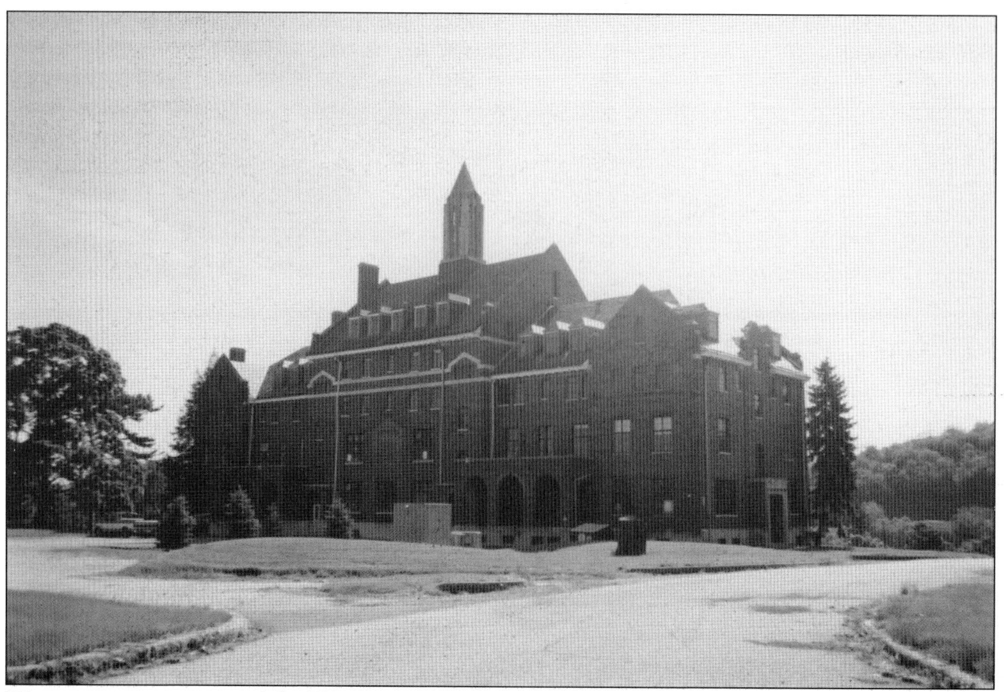

This rear exterior view of the Western Center is similar to what can be seen in *The Silence of the Lambs*. A prop sign rested on the small, grassy hill in front of the building in this shot. The sign read "Baltimore State Forensic Hospital."

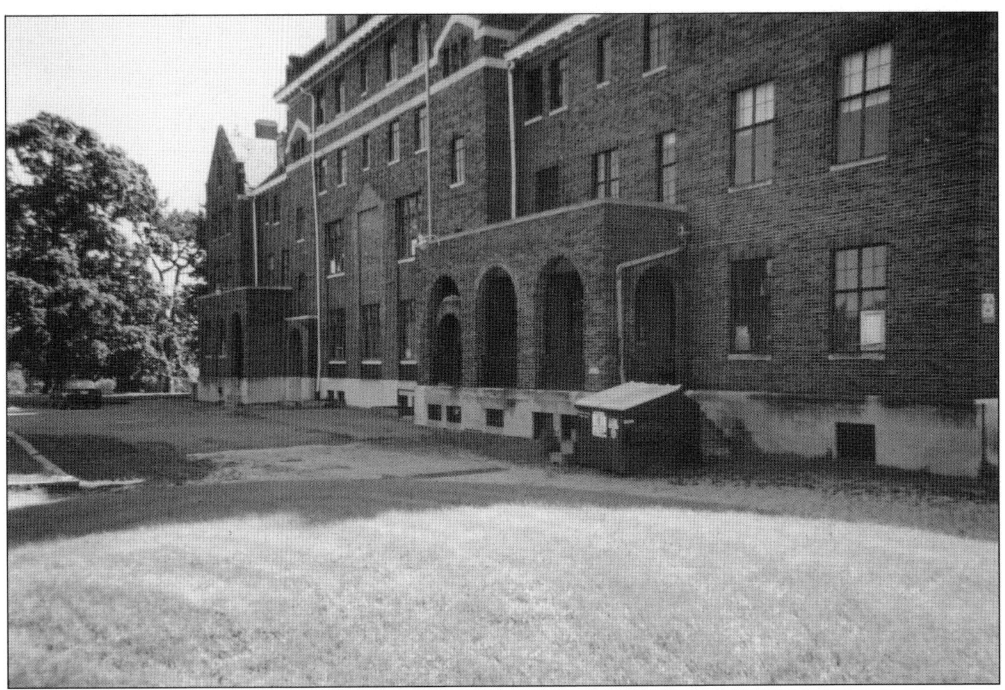

The rear exterior view of the administration building featured a few shots of Jodie Foster as Clarice Starling walking into and out of the building in *The Silence of the Lambs*. One of the more noticeable differences of the rear view of the administration building is the perpendicular section of the building that has been demolished.

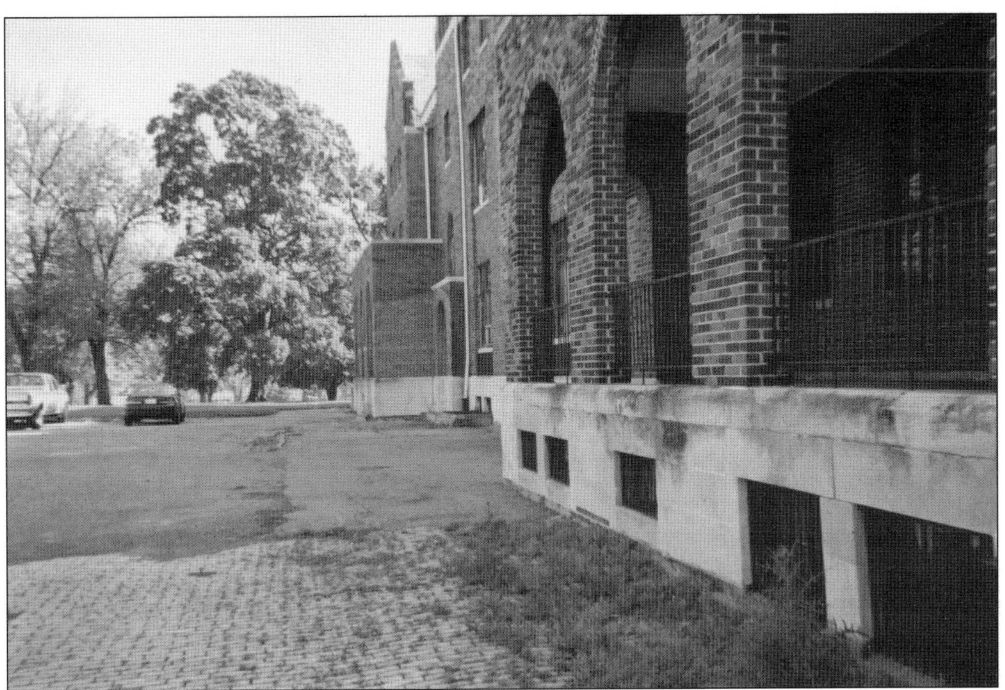

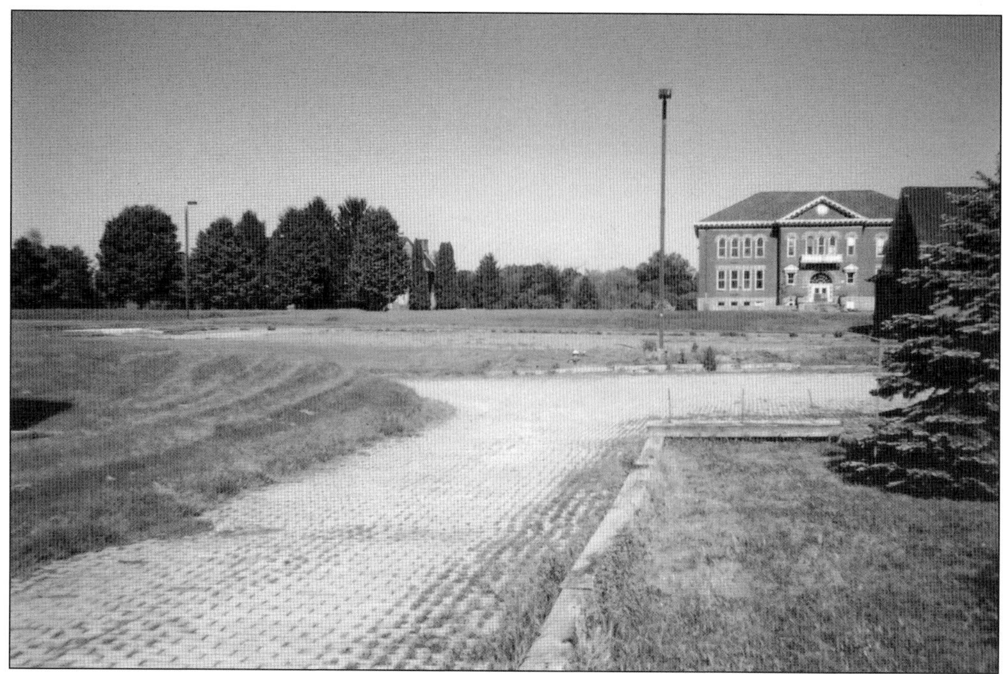

This photograph was taken from behind the Western Center administration building. In *The Silence of the Lambs*, Clarice Starling's car was parked in this shot. This view also shows the path Starling walked to her car in the movie.

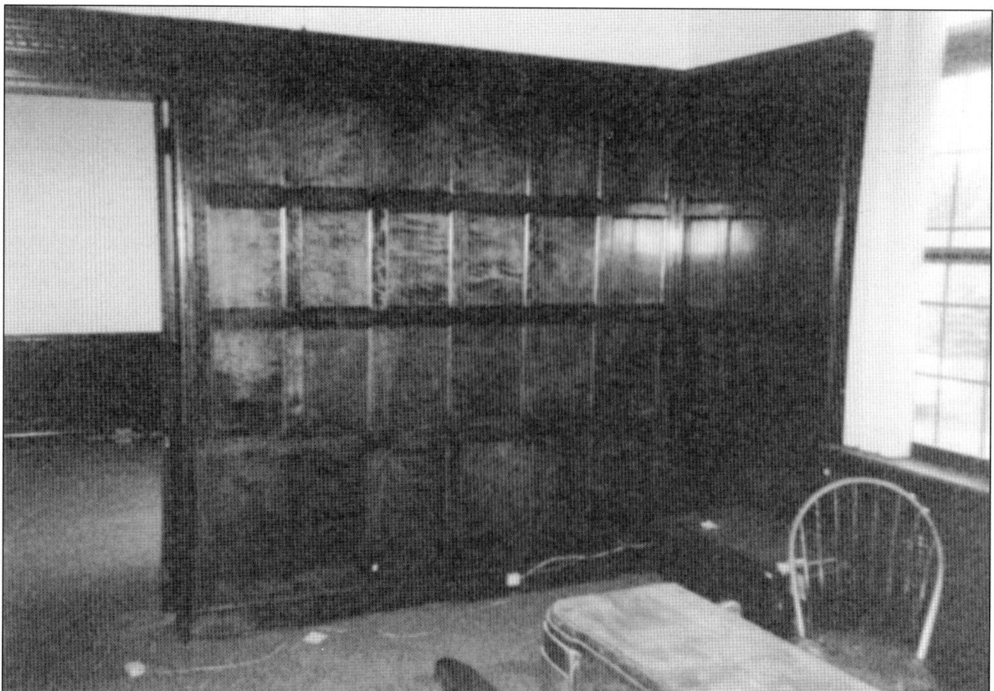

In *The Silence of the Lambs*, actor Anthony Heald's character Dr. Chilton had his desk in this corner inside the Western Center administration building. This room is featured in the scene where Dr. Chilton and Clarice Starling meet for the first time.

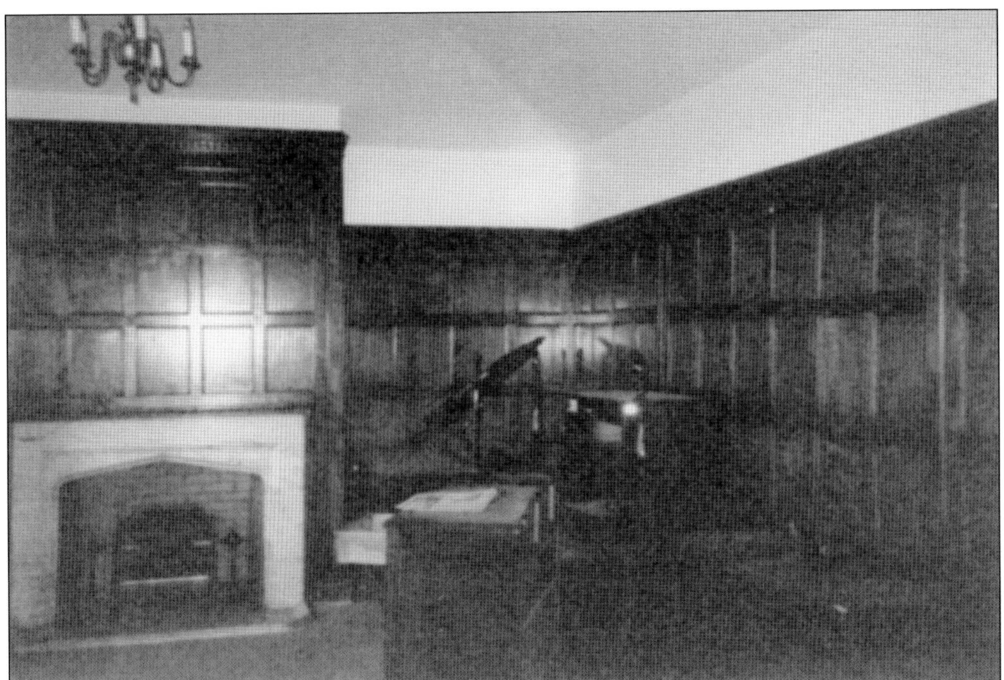

Clarice Starling stood in the vicinity of this shot as she talked to Anthony Heald in *The Silence of the Lambs*. This corner is directly opposite the corner in which Dr. Chilton's desk was positioned in the Western Center administration building.

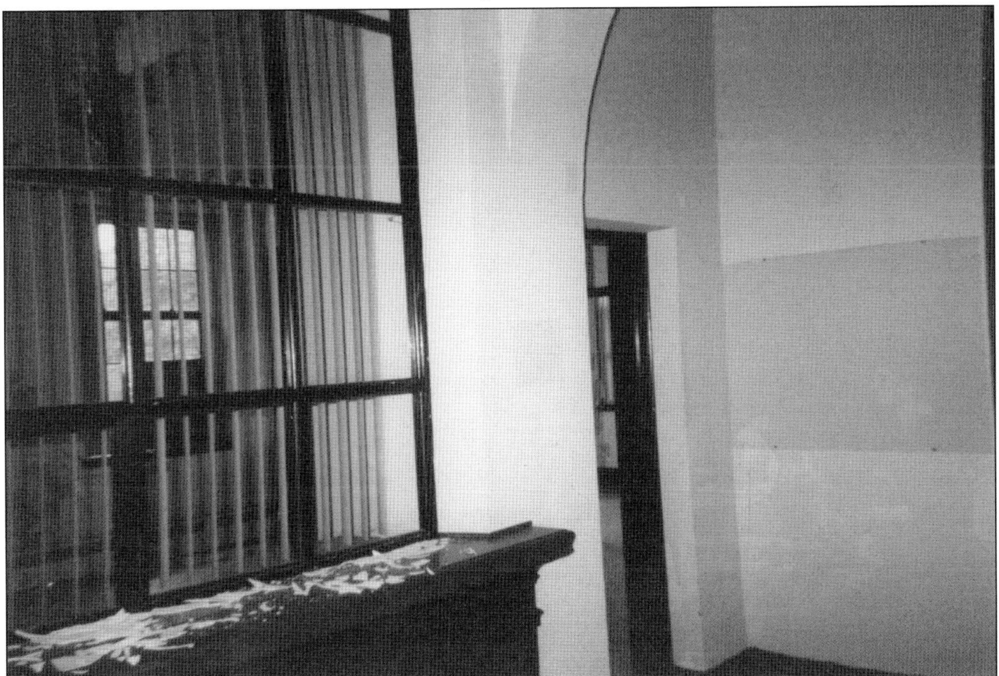

The hallway and room seen here was traveled by Dr. Chilton and Clarice Starling in *The Silence of the Lambs*. This location is part of the iconic scene when Dr. Chilton escorts Starling to the dungeon to see Hannibal Lecter for the first time.

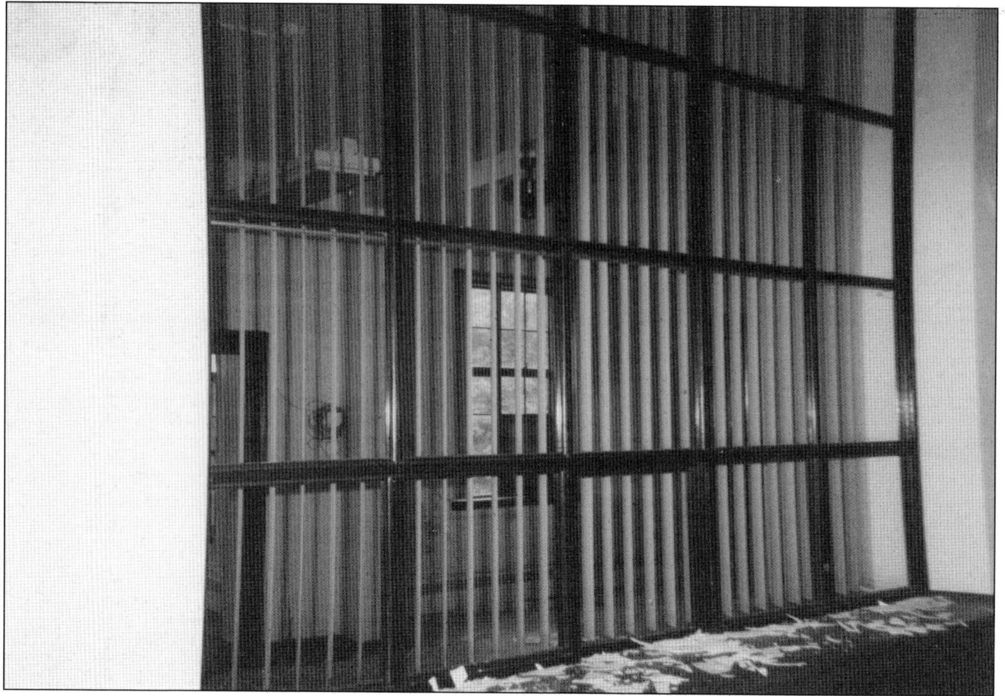

This is another view of the hallway traveled by Dr. Chilton and Clarice Starling in *The Silence of the Lambs*. This photograph, taken around 2003, shows a great deal of deterioration to the inside of the building since the movie was filmed there nearly 14 years earlier.

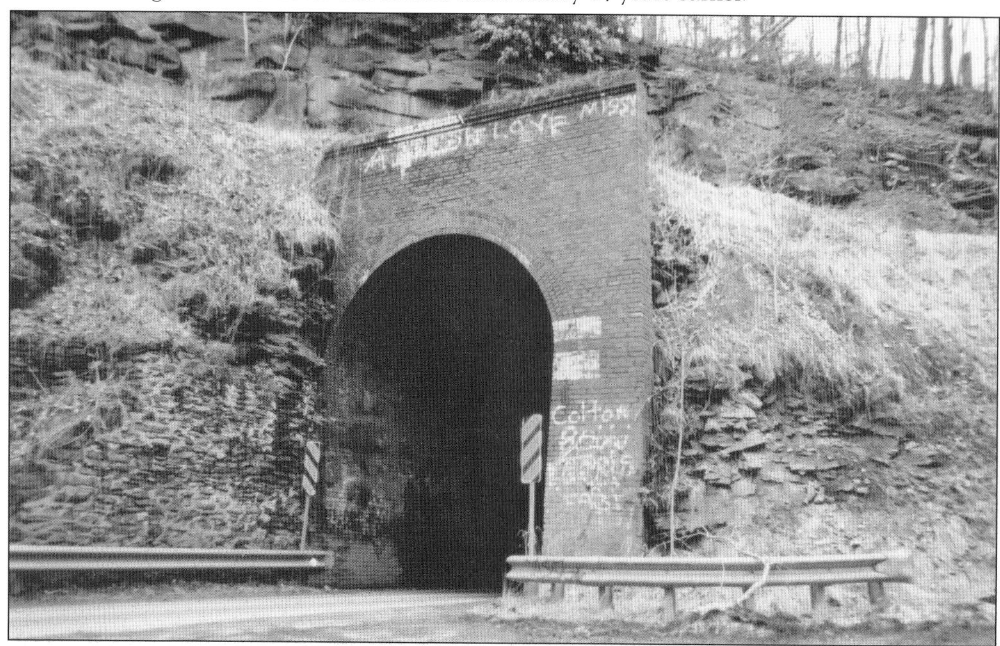

This tunnel is located outside Layton, Pennsylvania and was briefly seen in *The Silence of the Lambs* when Clarice Starling, Jack Crawford (played by Scott Glenn), and agent Terry (played by Chuck Aber) are in a car together as they head to a funeral home. This tunnel is also seen in the movie *Riddle*.

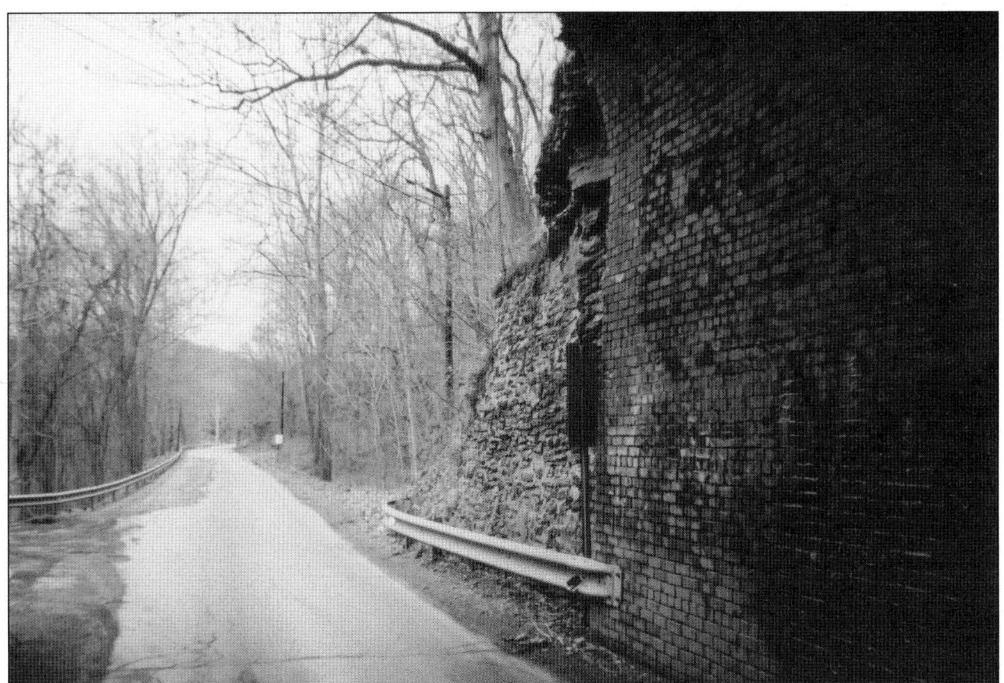

The view from inside the tunnel shows the road that was traveled by Clarice Starling, Jack Crawford, and agent Terry in *The Silence of the Lambs*. Actress Elisabeth Harnois also traveled this road in *Riddle* as main character Holly Teller. In *Riddle*, Teller drives to the fictional town of Riddle, where her car eventually breaks down.

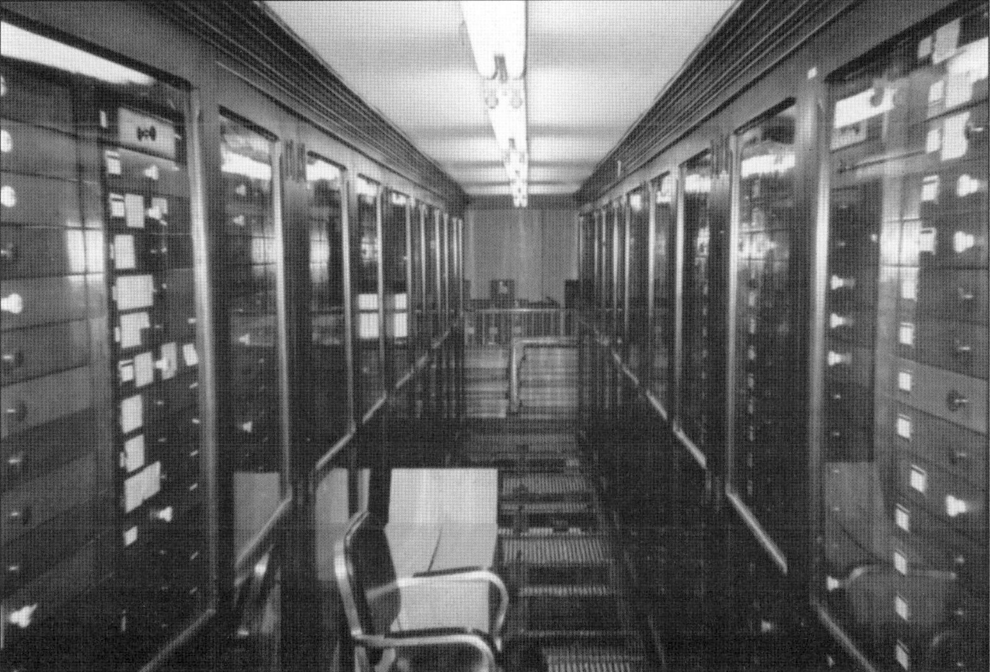

This hallway in the Carnegie Museum of Natural History is a behind-the-scenes area in the invertebrate zoology section. Jodie Foster walked down this hallway in *The Silence of the Lambs*.

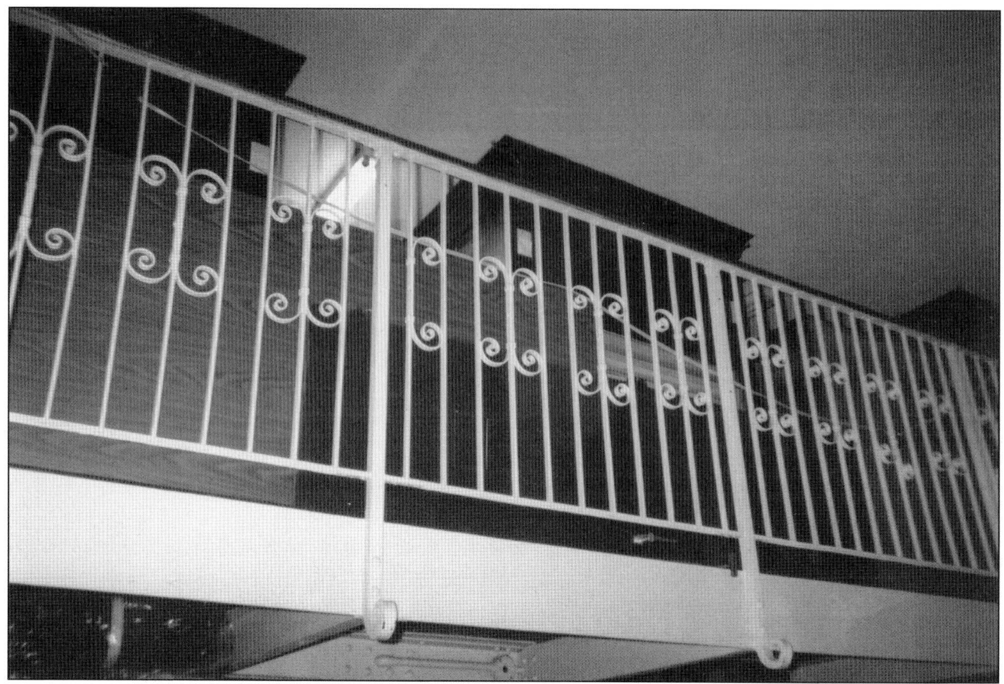

This is the balcony railing at the end of the hallway located behind the scenes in the invertebrate zoology section at the Carnegie Museum of Natural History. Clarice Starling stood looking over this railing in *The Silence of the Lambs.*

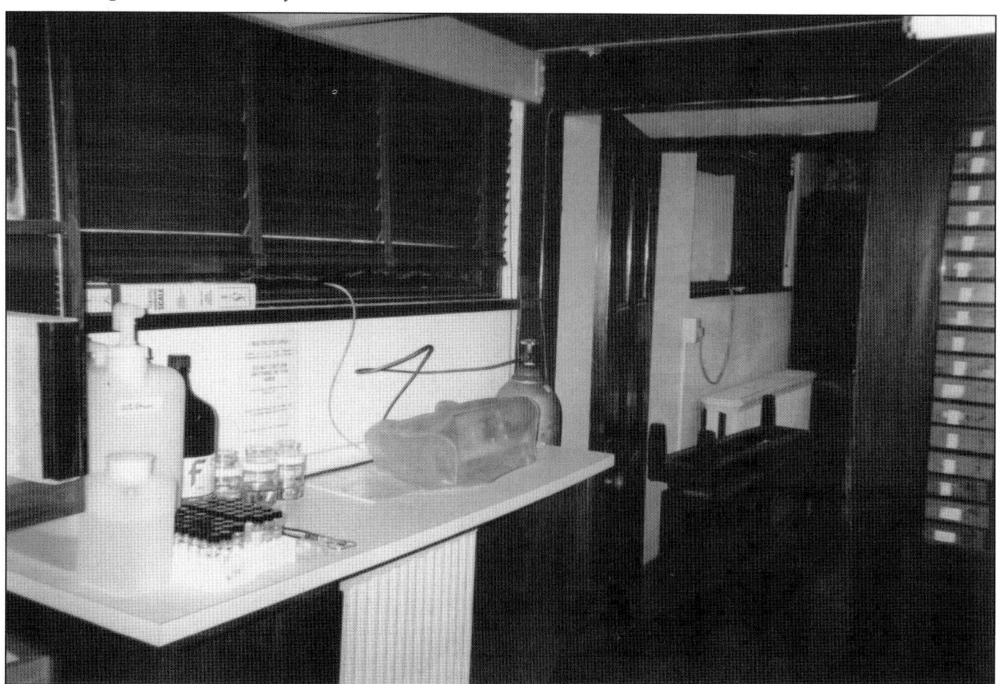

This doorway is located in the invertebrate zoology section at the Carnegie Museum of Natural History. Clarice Starling can be seen walking through the doorway with two men in *The Silence of the Lambs.*

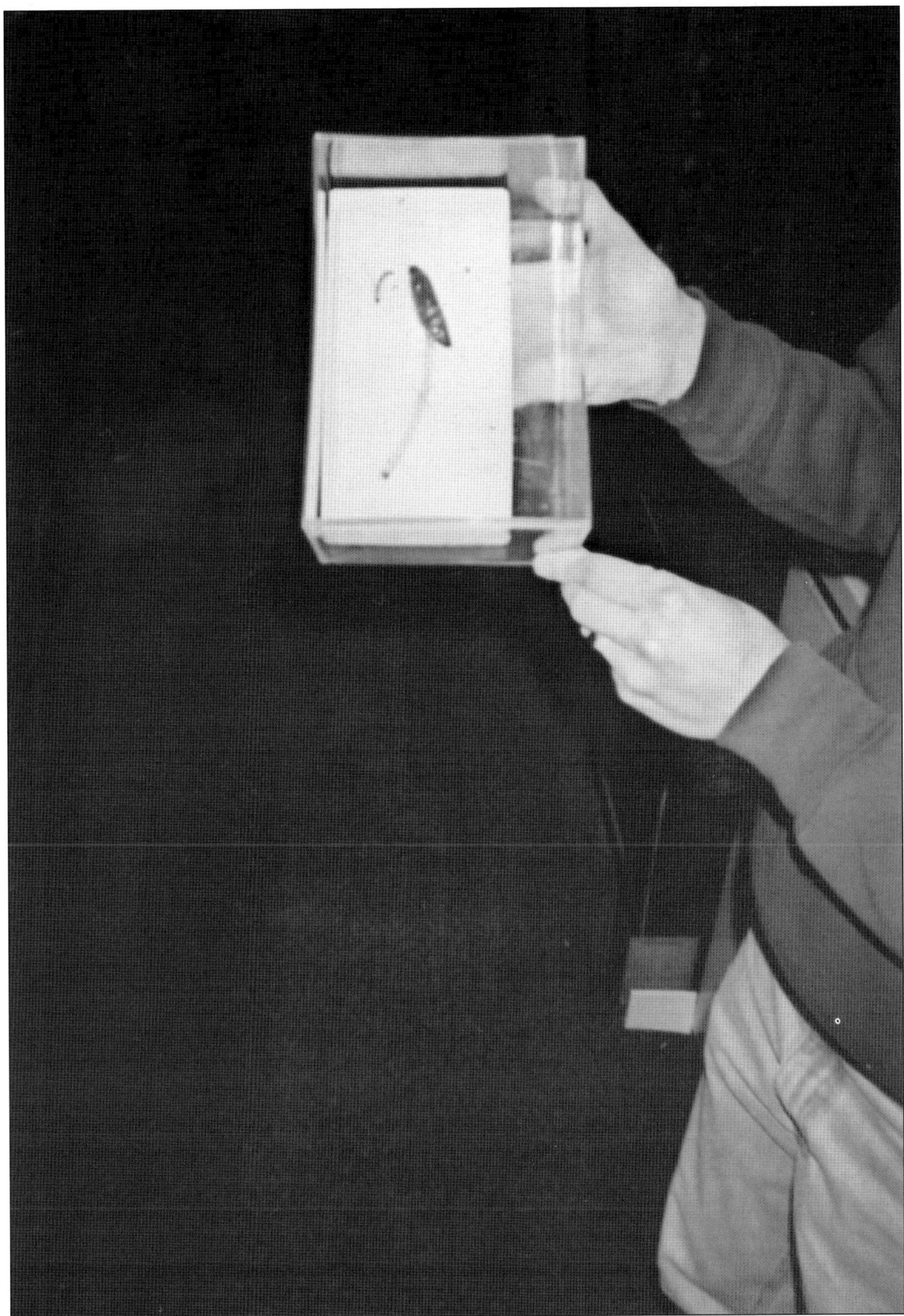

Dr. John Rawlins of the Carnegie Museum of Natural History holds up the moth prop used in *The Silence of the Lambs*. The moth prop was left at the museum once filming at the museum completed. An original script from the movie also resides at the museum.

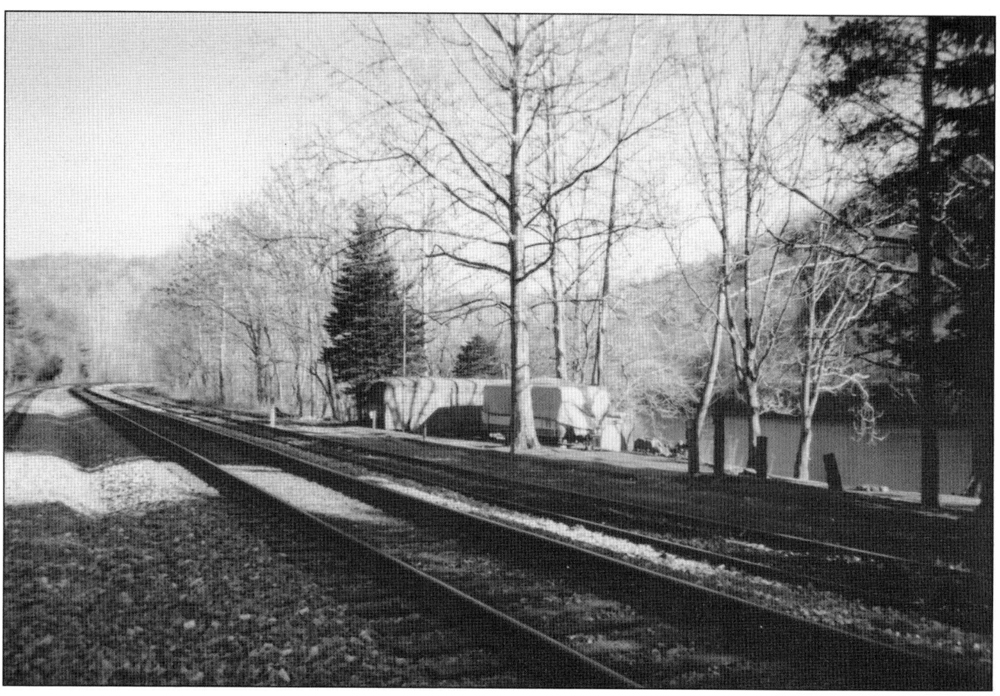

In *The Silence of the Lambs*, a near 180-degree pan by the camera shows the exterior layout of Buffalo Bill's house. Trains actively run on the tracks seen here and had to be worked around in some fashion.

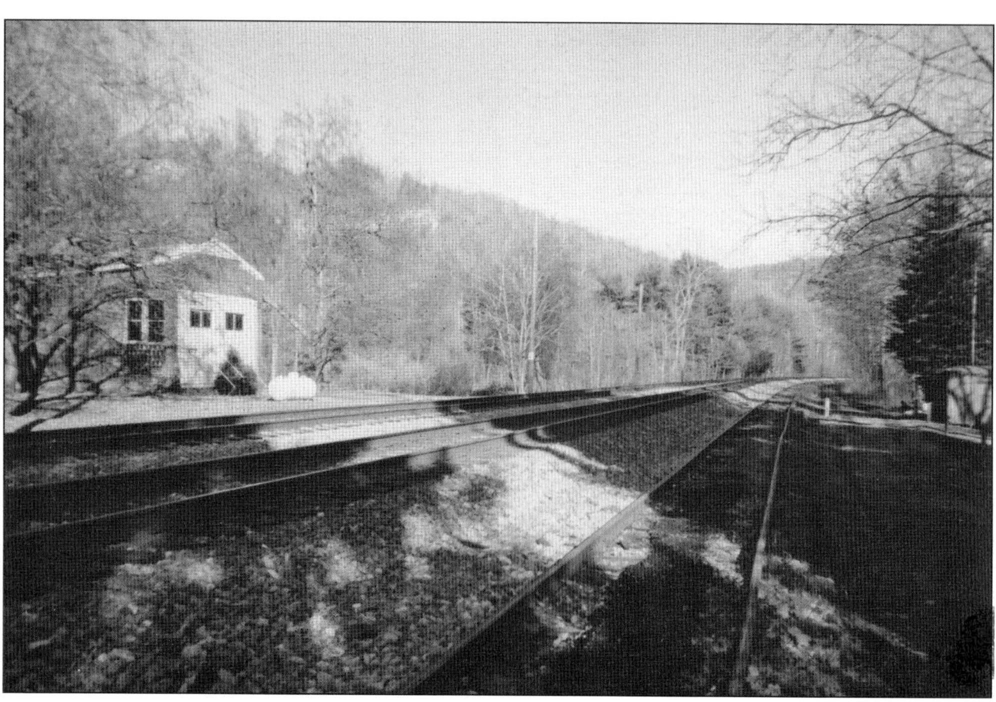

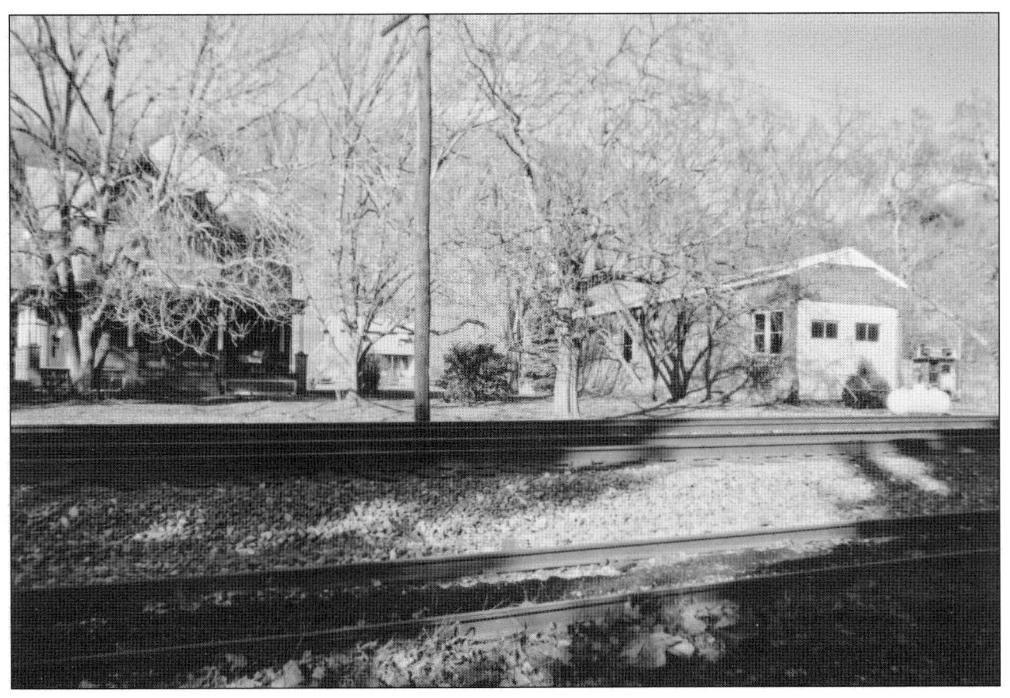

This series of pictures is a continuation of the near 180-degree pan showing Buffalo Bill's house in *The Silence of the Lambs*. The house is actually a private residence in Layton, Pennsylvania.

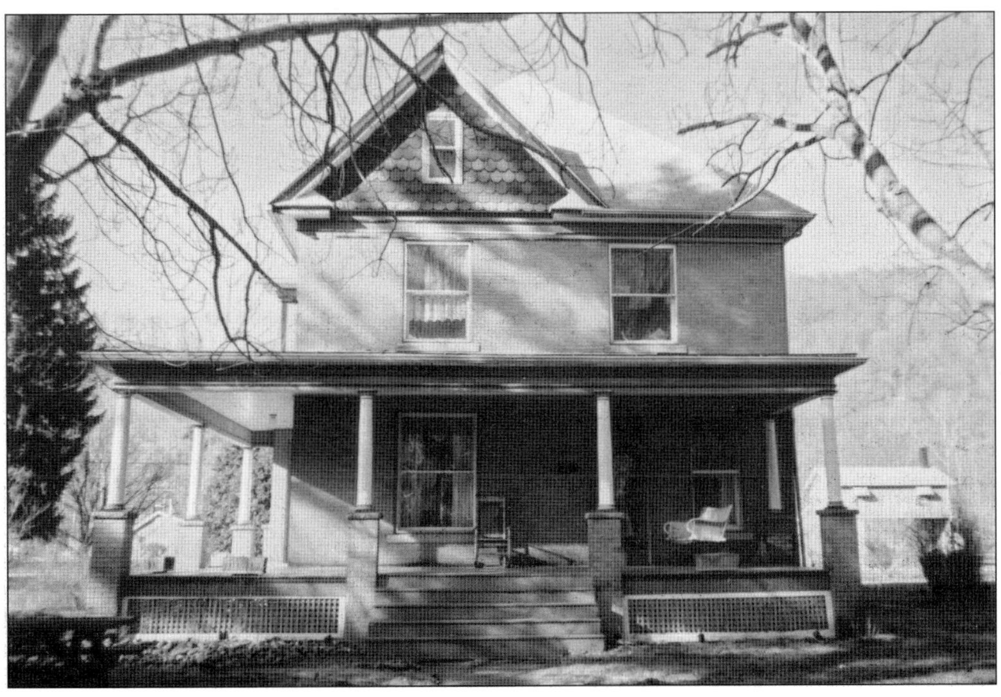

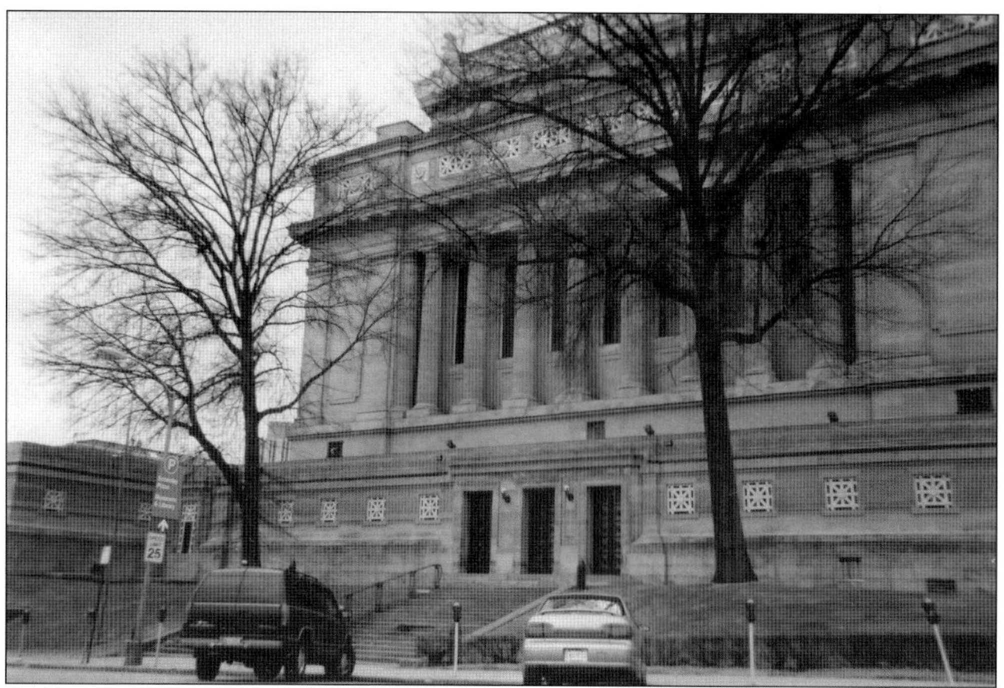

The exterior of the Soldiers & Sailors Memorial Hall and Museum in Pittsburgh can be seen in *The Silence of the Lambs*. The building was substituting for a courthouse in Memphis, Tennessee, in the film.

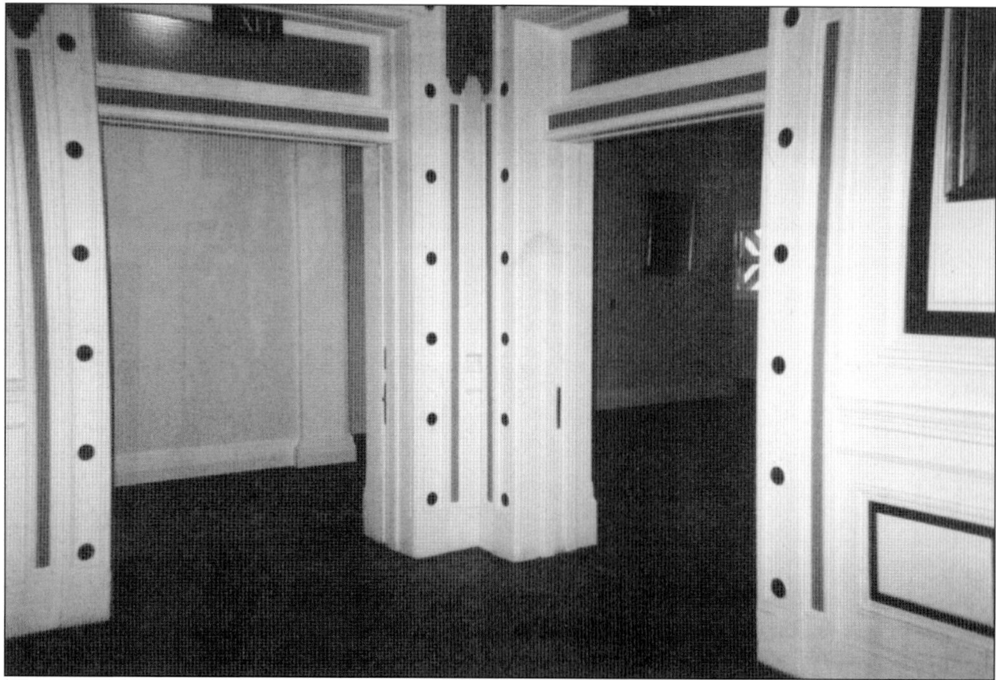

This interior view of the Soldiers & Sailors Memorial Hall and Museum reveals a doorway that can be seen in *The Silence of the Lambs*. This doorway is in the same room as Hannibal Lecter's giant cage.

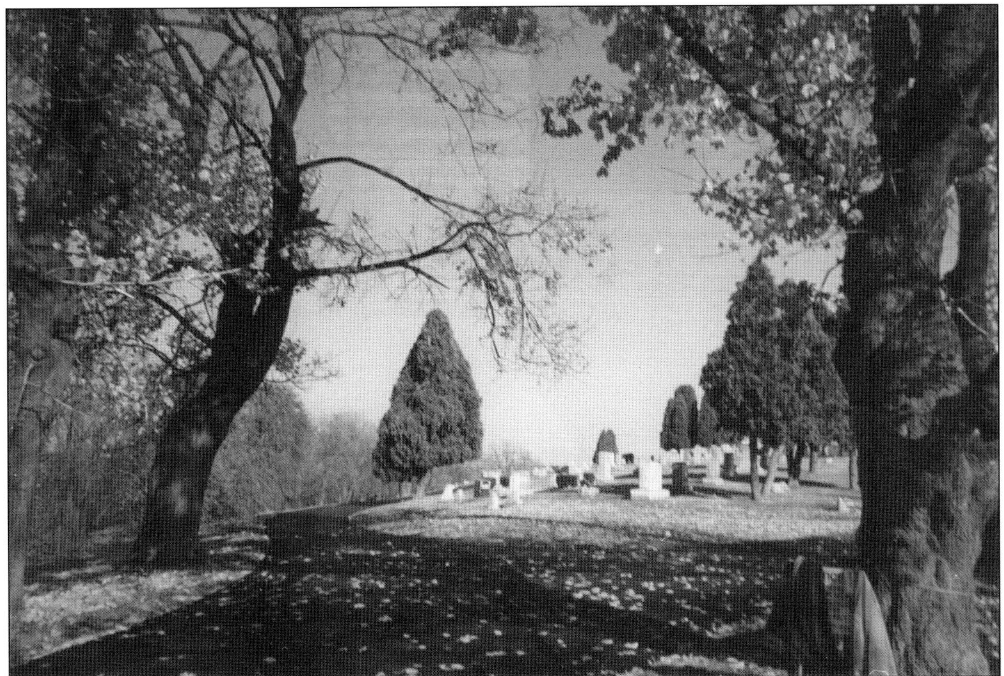

The entrance to the West Middletown Cemetery is seen in the *Night of the Living Dead* 1990 remake. On the set, the production erected a prop archway over the narrow road that identified the cemetery as the Evans City Cemetery, paying homage to the original film.

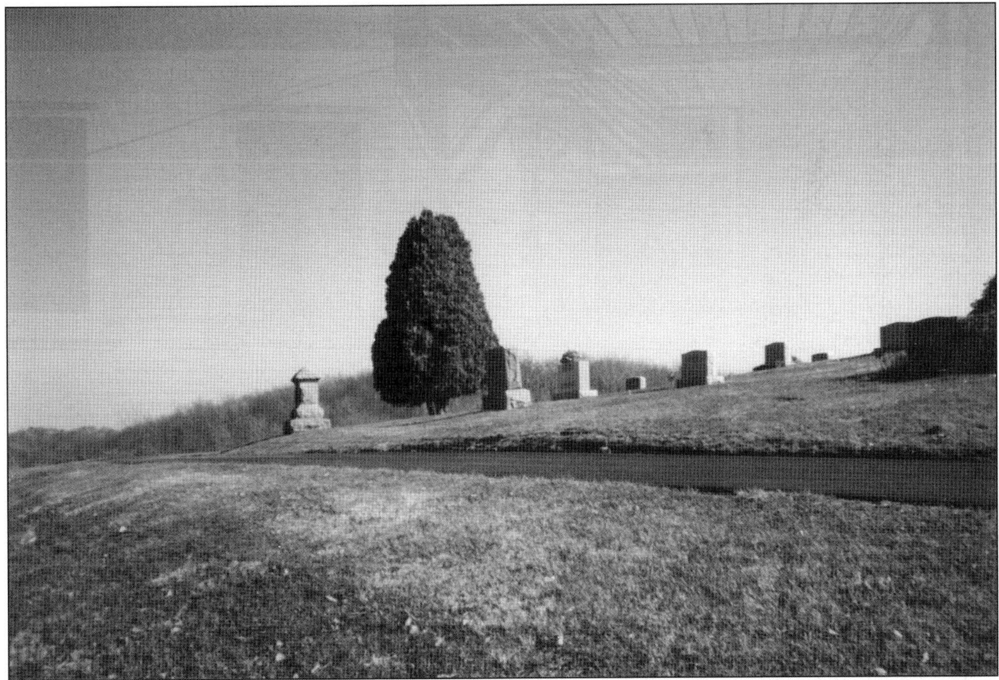

This photograph was taken from a similar camera angle as seen in the *Night of the Living Dead* 1990 remake. This scene in the remake featured actress Patricia Tallman as Barbara and actor Bill Moseley as Johnny circling around the cemetery.

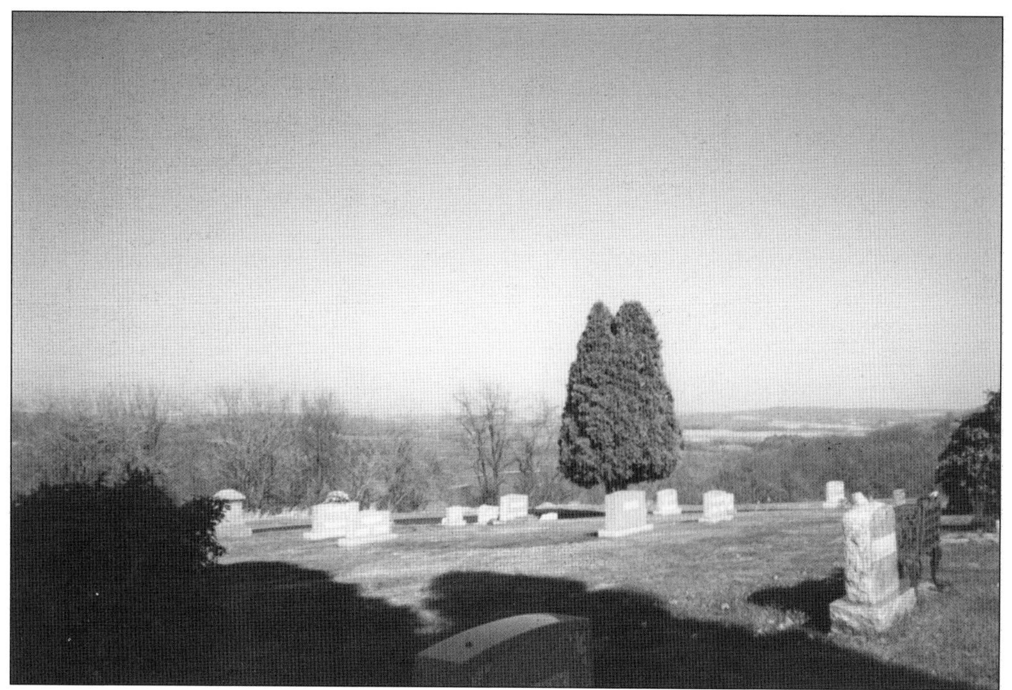

This picture taken from the West Middletown Cemetery shows a view of the countryside. A similar view is seen in the *Night of the Living Dead* 1990 remake.

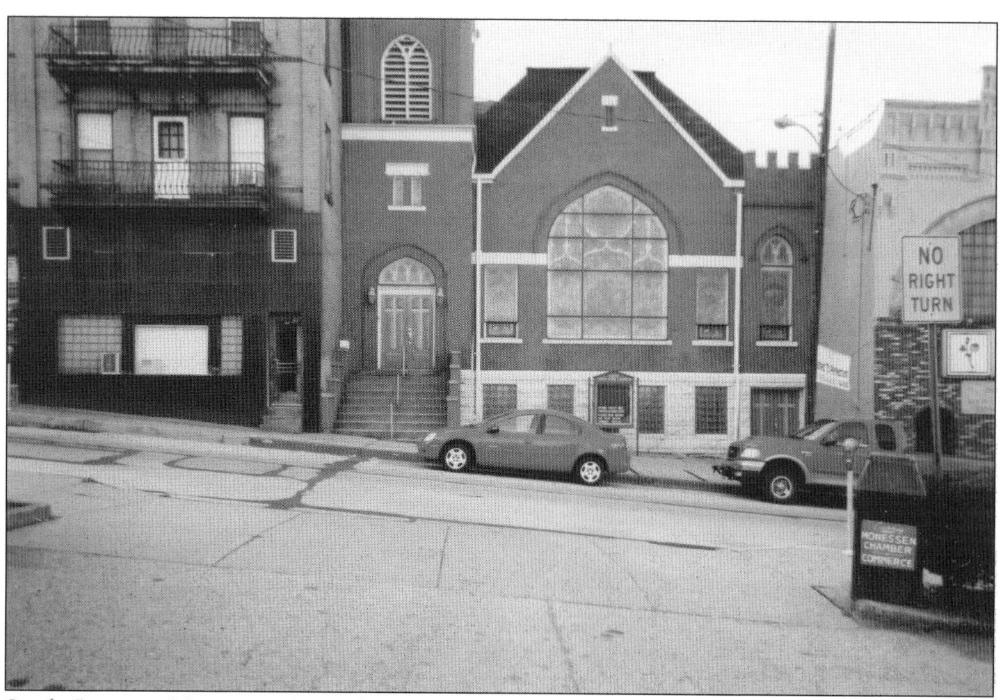

Sixth Street in Monessen, Pennsylvania, was featured in *Striking Distance* during a scene with detective Tom Hardy, played by Bruce Willis, walking up the small hill and into a bar.

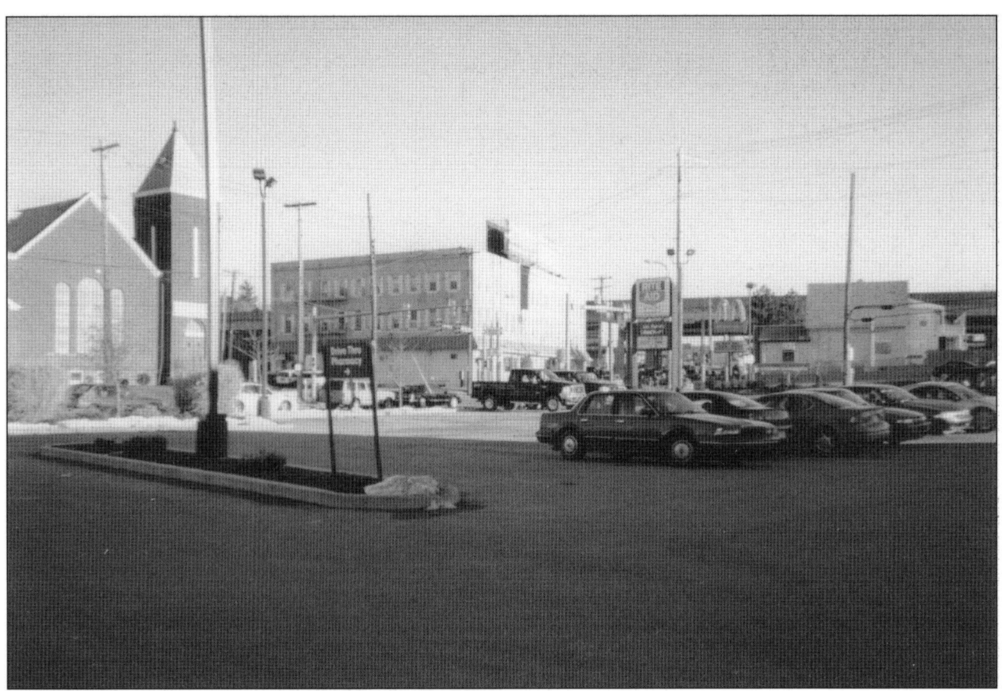

The intersection of East Wylie Avenue and Jefferson Avenue in Washington, Pennsylvania, was featured in George A. Romero's film *The Dark Half.*

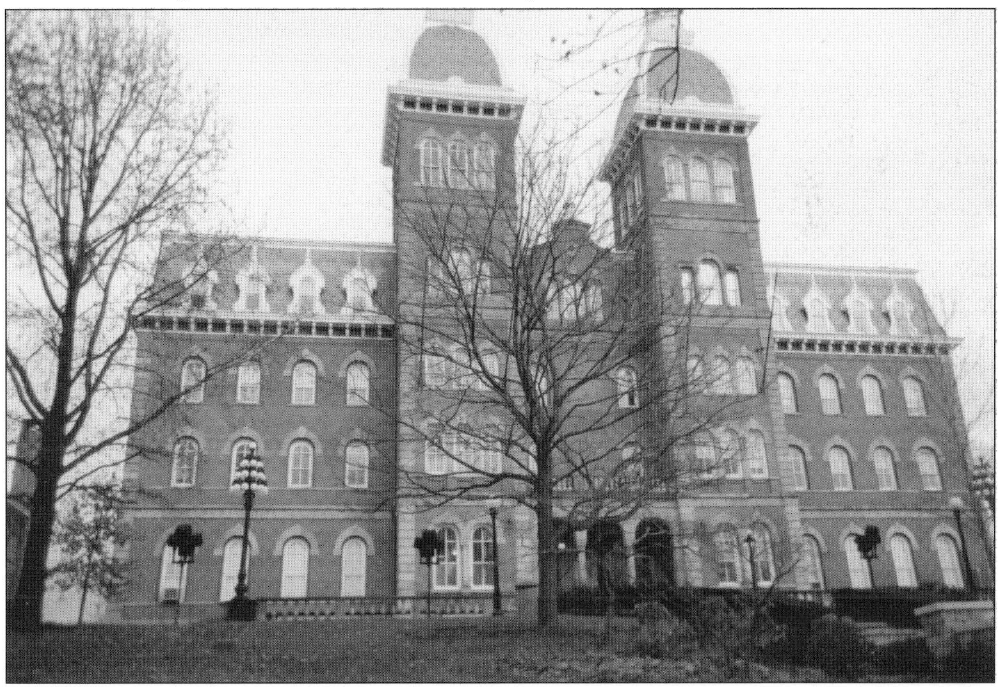

The Old Main building at Washington & Jefferson College is featured in George A. Romero's film *The Dark Half.* The interior and exterior of this building can be seen in the movie. One of the administration offices was used as the office of Thad Beaumont, a character played by Timothy Hutton in the movie.

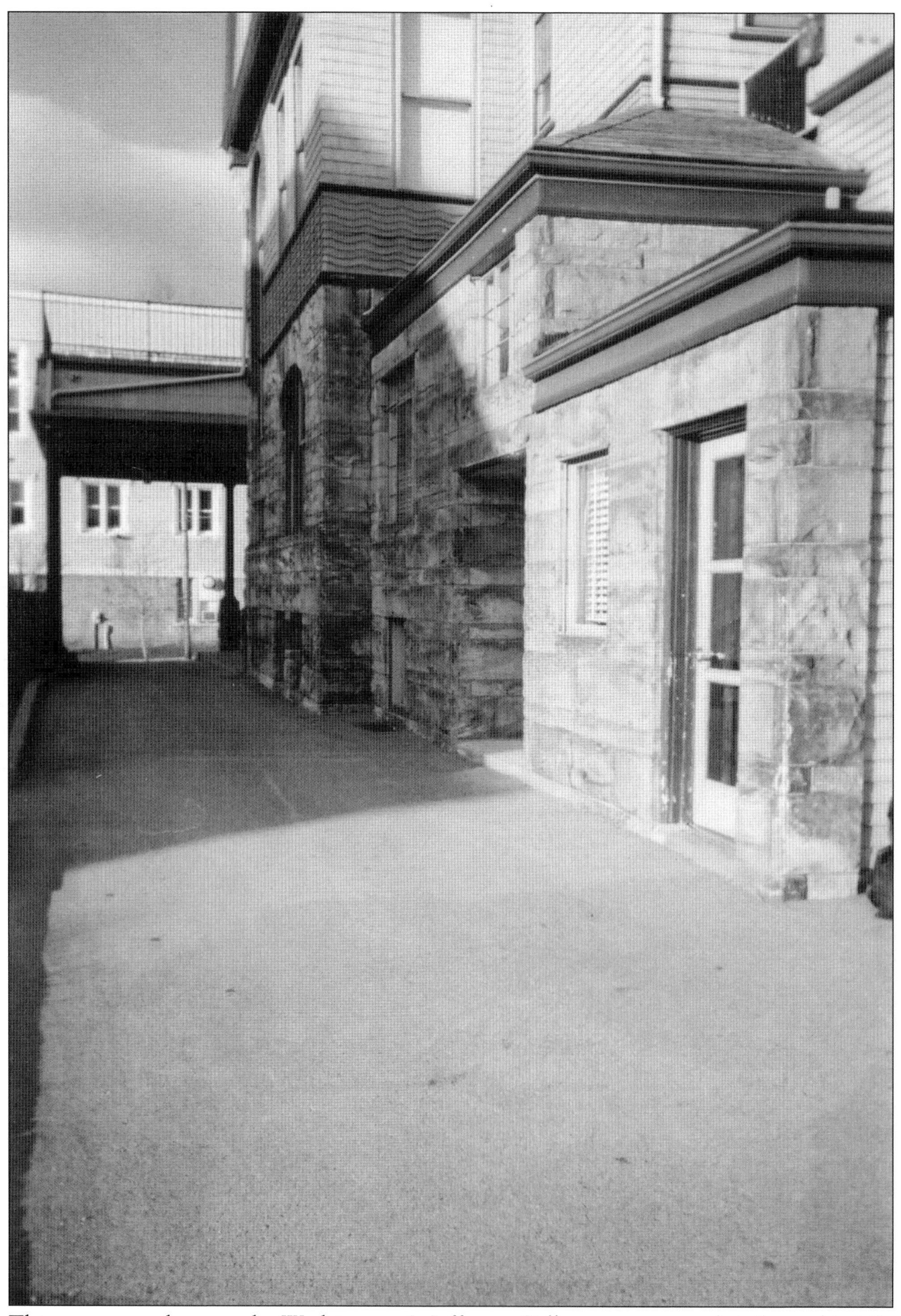

This narrow roadway on the Washington & Jefferson College campus was briefly used in *The Dark Half*. The campus was utilized in October 1990 and was the very first location used for the production.

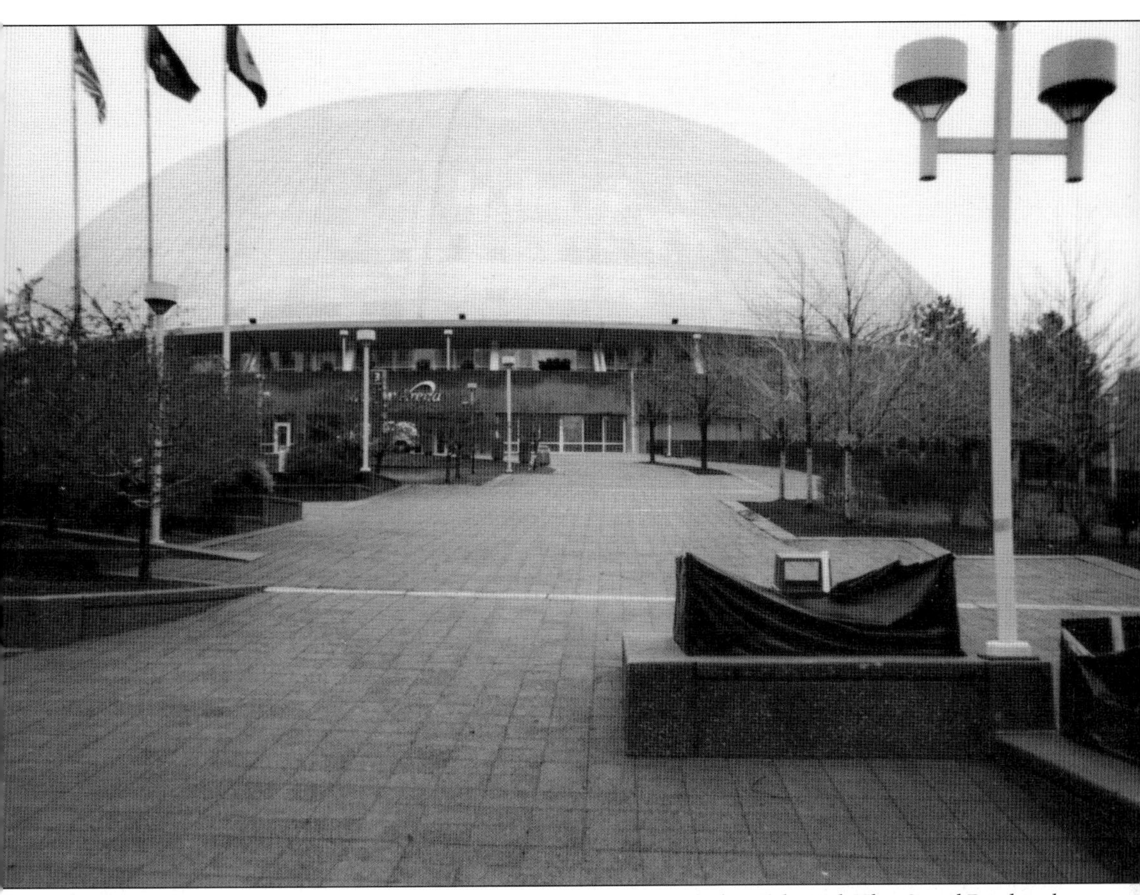

The Mellon Arena has been home to several feature films including *The Fish That Saved Pittsburgh*, *Sudden Death*, and *She's Out of My League*. The arena has since been demolished and replaced with the Consol Energy Center across the street.

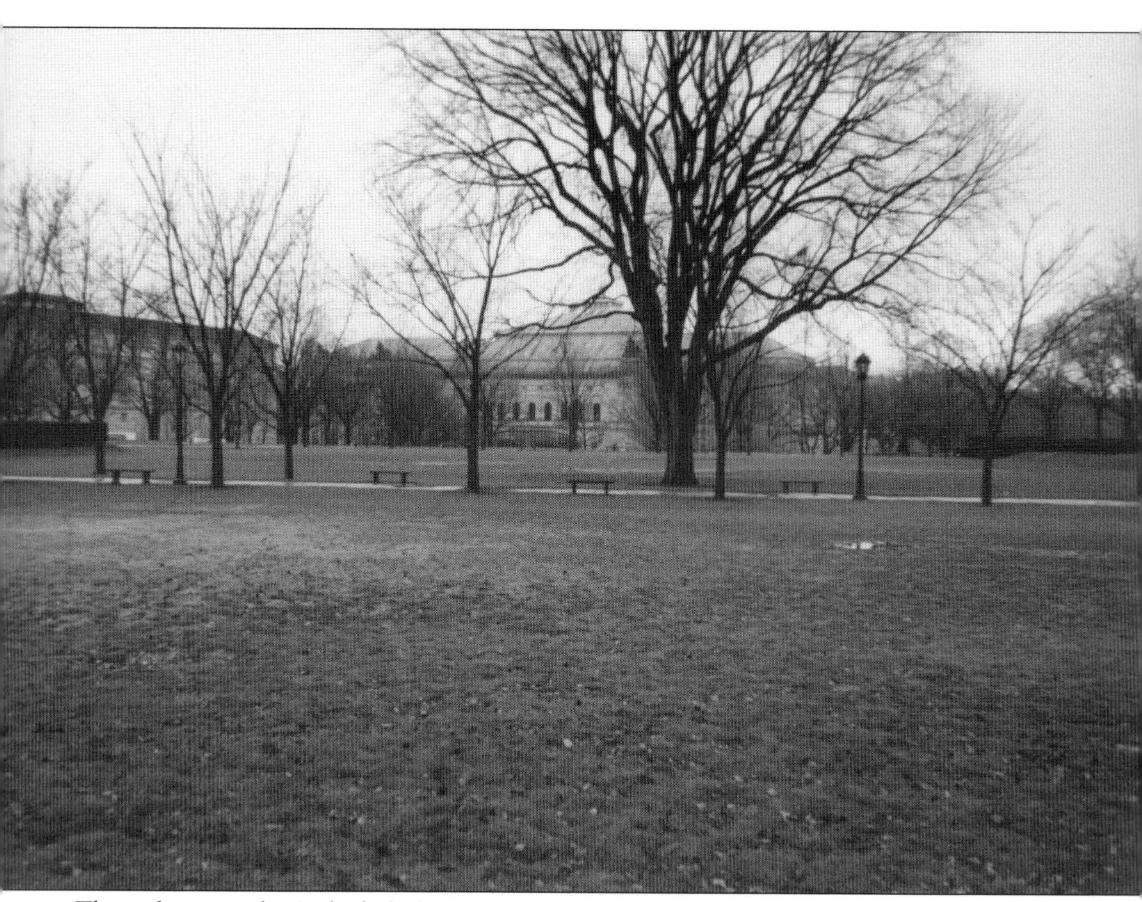

The park next to the Cathedral of Learning, located on the University of Pittsburgh campus, was briefly featured in *The Mothman Prophecies* with Richard Gere as John Klein sitting on a park bench. This section of Pittsburgh has been used in several major films.

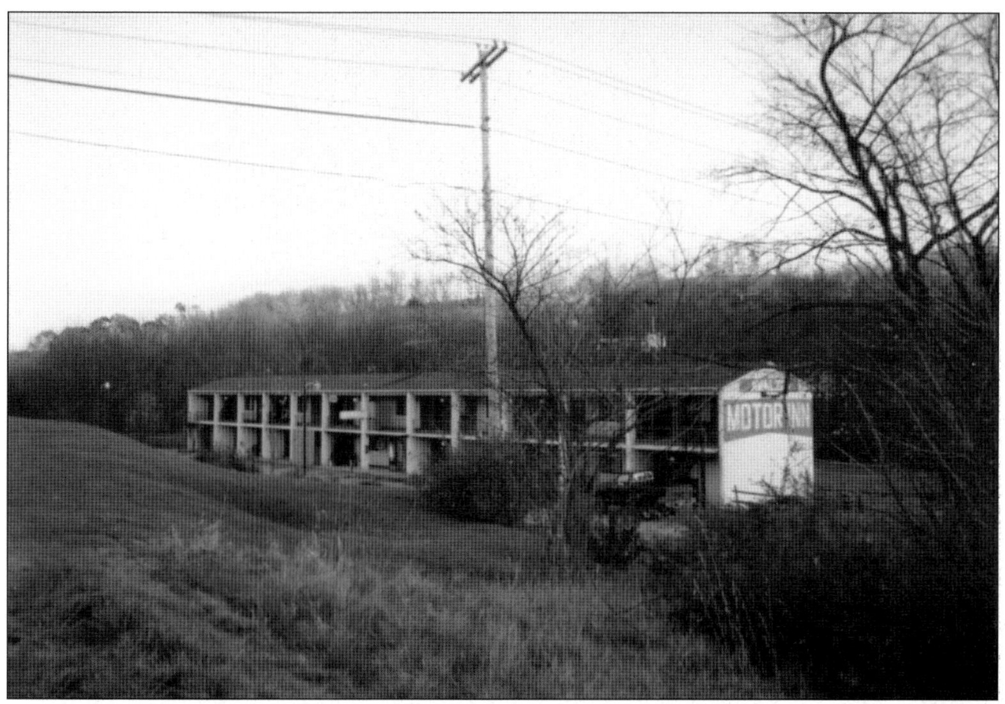

The Avalon Motel along Interstate 70 is featured in the movie *The Mothman Prophecies*. However, a set was constructed for the interior scenes of the motel room because the actual conditions of the motel interior were not satisfactory for the production.

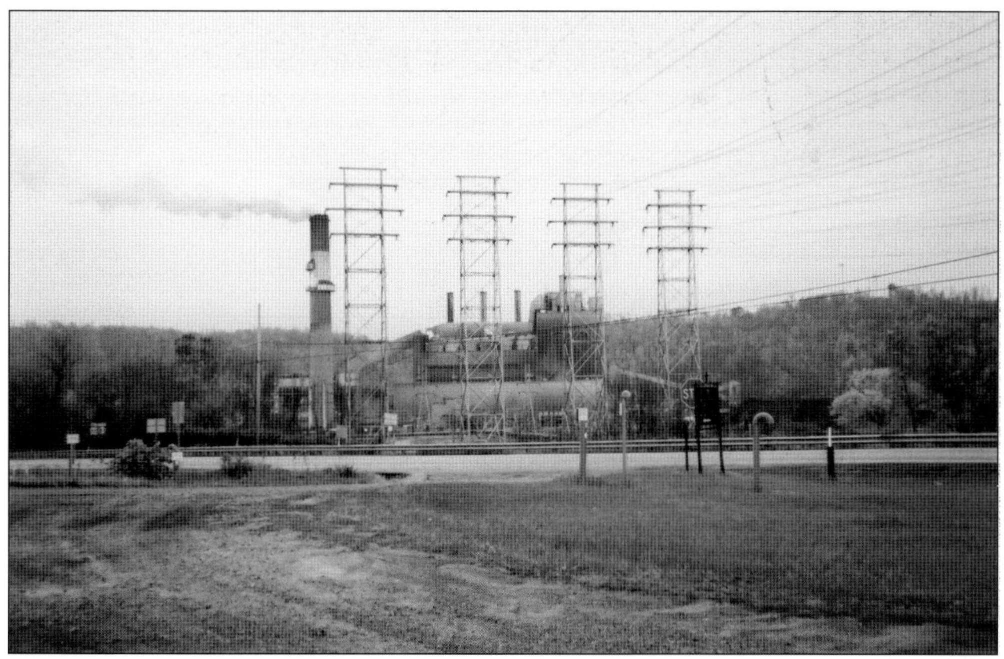

The Elrama Generating Station along the Monongahela River is seen several times in *The Mothman Prophecies*. Director Mark Pellington scouted up and down the Monongahela River and used various locations along the Mon Valley.

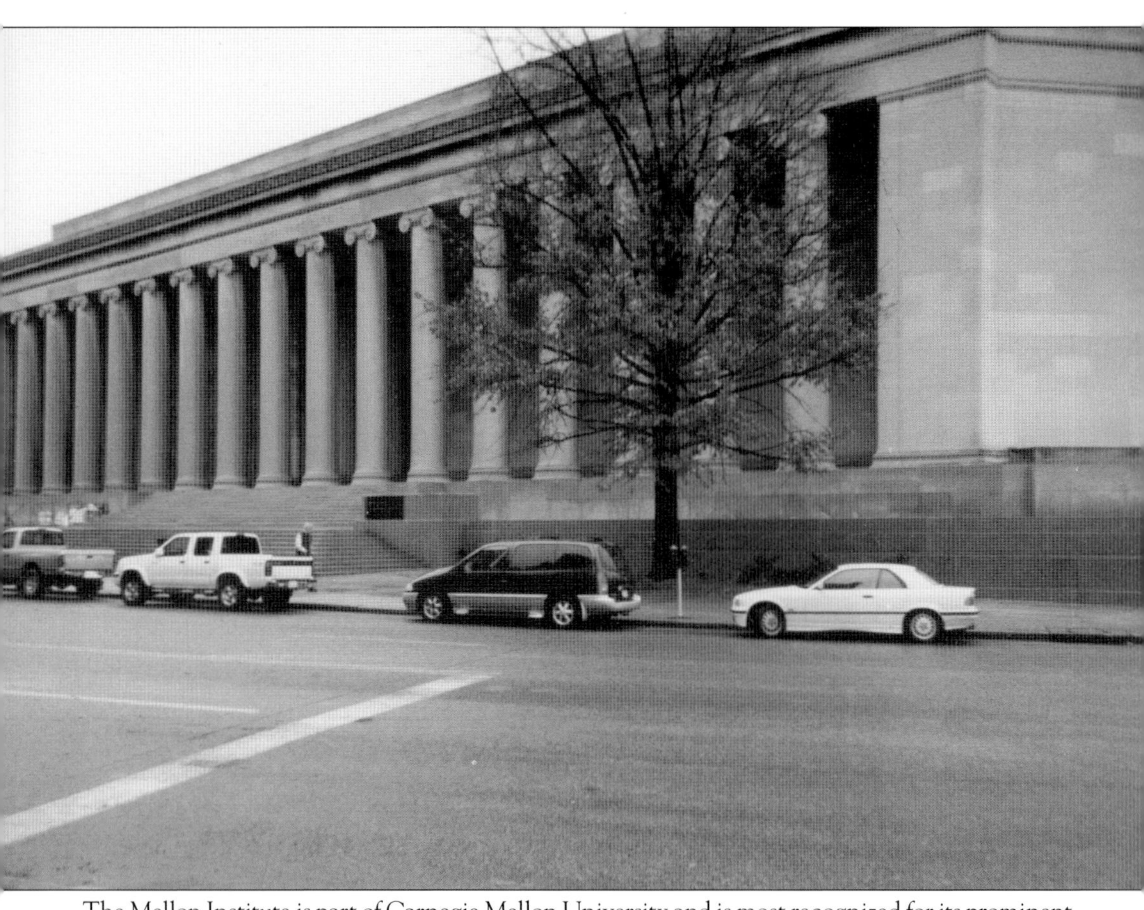

The Mellon Institute is part of Carnegie Mellon University and is most recognized for its prominent role in *The Dark Knight Rises* as Gotham City Hall. The building was also used in the movies *Citizen Cohn*, *Hoffa*, and *The Mothman Prophecies* as well as the television show *Smith*.

Four

Behind the Scenes of Modern Pittsburgh Filmmaking

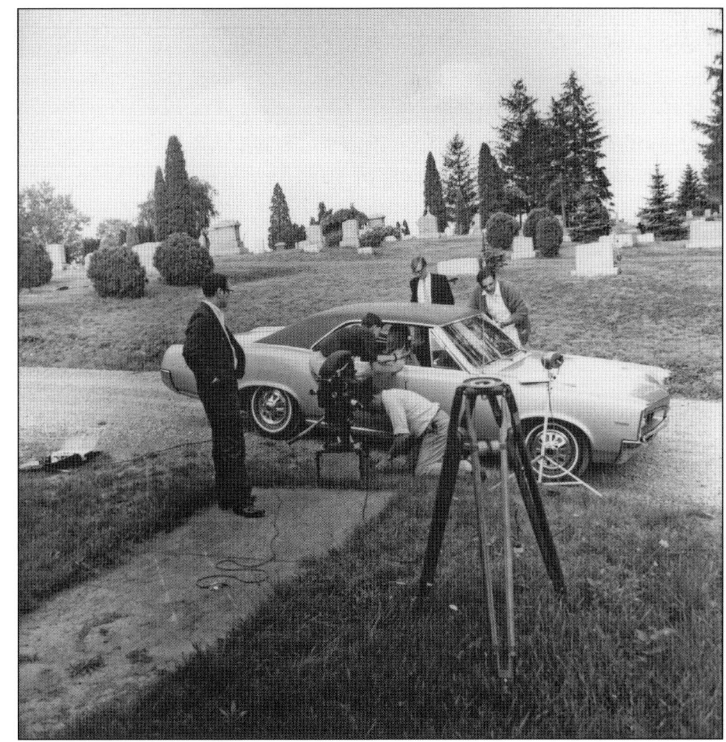

George A. Romero directs Russ Streiner and Judy O'Dea at the Evans City Cemetery in 1967. They are accompanied by a few crew members who are setting up a shot for the classic *Night of the Living Dead*. (NIGHT of the LIVING DEAD™ images © 1968-2011 Image Ten, Inc. All Rights Reserved. Photo restoration: Jim Cirronella.)

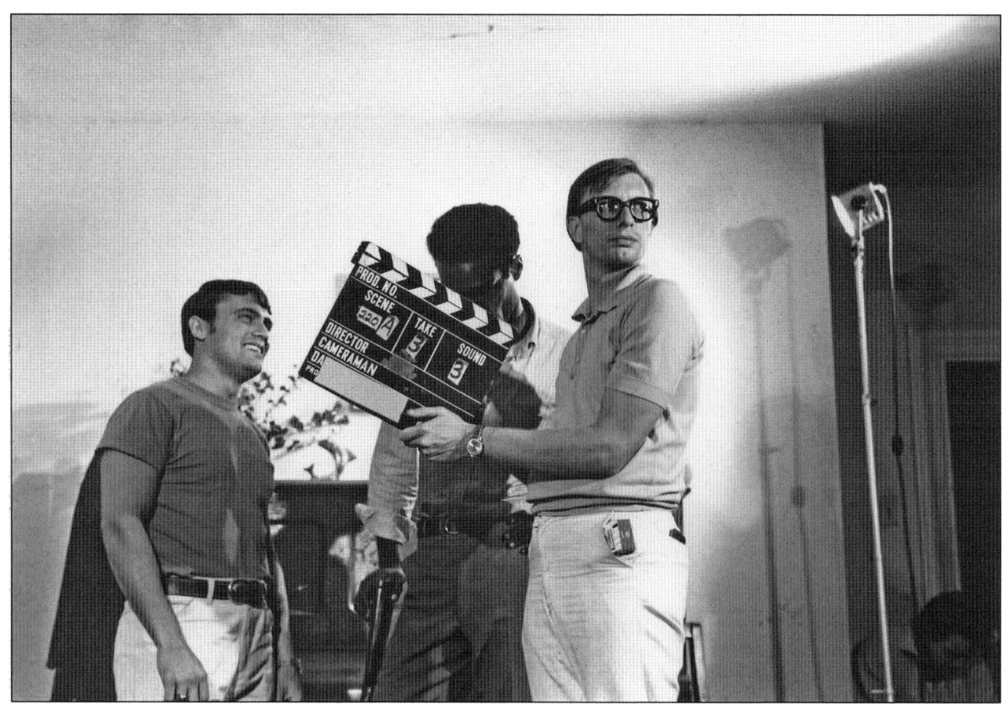

Keith Wayne and Duane Jones prepare to film a scene in a farmhouse for *Night of the Living Dead* with Russ Streiner holding the clapper board. (NIGHT of the LIVING DEAD™ images © 1968-2011 Image Ten, Inc. All Rights Reserved. Photo restoration: Jim Cirronella.)

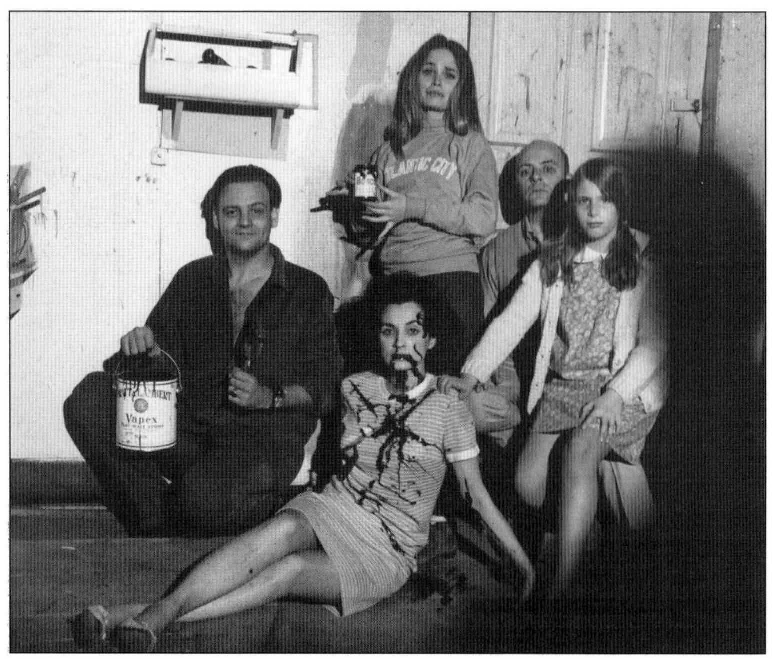

From left to right, George A. Romero, Marilyn Eastman, Judith Ridley, Karl Hardman, and Kyra Schon pose on the *Night of the Living Dead* set. (NIGHT of the LIVING DEAD™ images © 1968-2011 Image Ten, Inc. All Rights Reserved. Photo restoration: Jim Cirronella.)

At Carnegie Mellon University, the cast and crew prepare between takes on the television movie *Against Her Will: An Incident in Baltimore* in 1991.

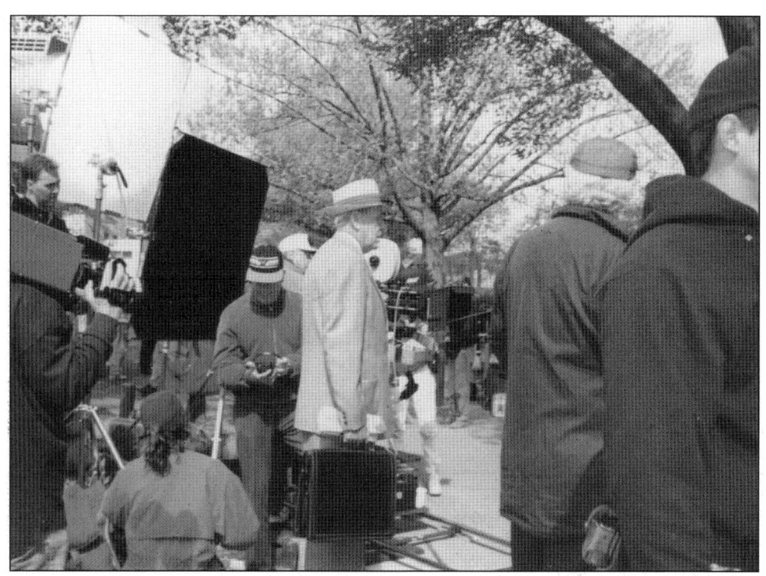

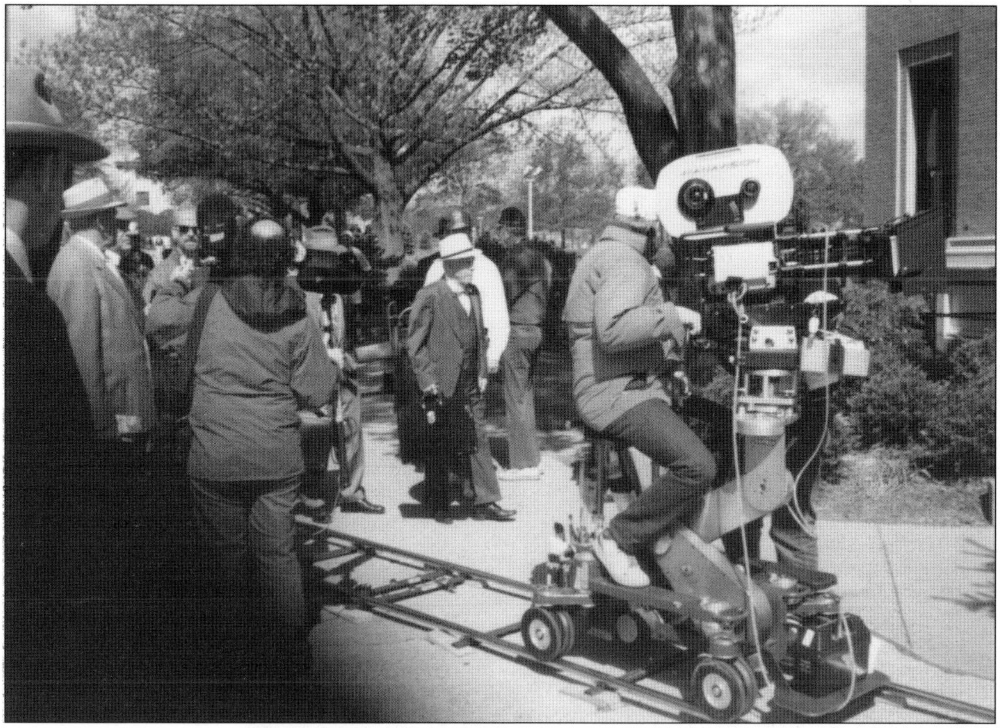

Legendary actor Harry Morgan prepares to film a scene for *Against Her Will*. He is best known for his work on television shows such as *M*A*S*H* and *Dragnet*. In *Against Her Will*, Morgan reprised his role as Judge Bell from a television movie made two year prior called *The Incident*, a movie that did not film in Pittsburgh. Morgan played Judge Bell one more time in a movie called *Incident in a Small Town*, which also was not shot in Pittsburgh. *Against Her Will* was the only time Morgan worked on a production in Pittsburgh.

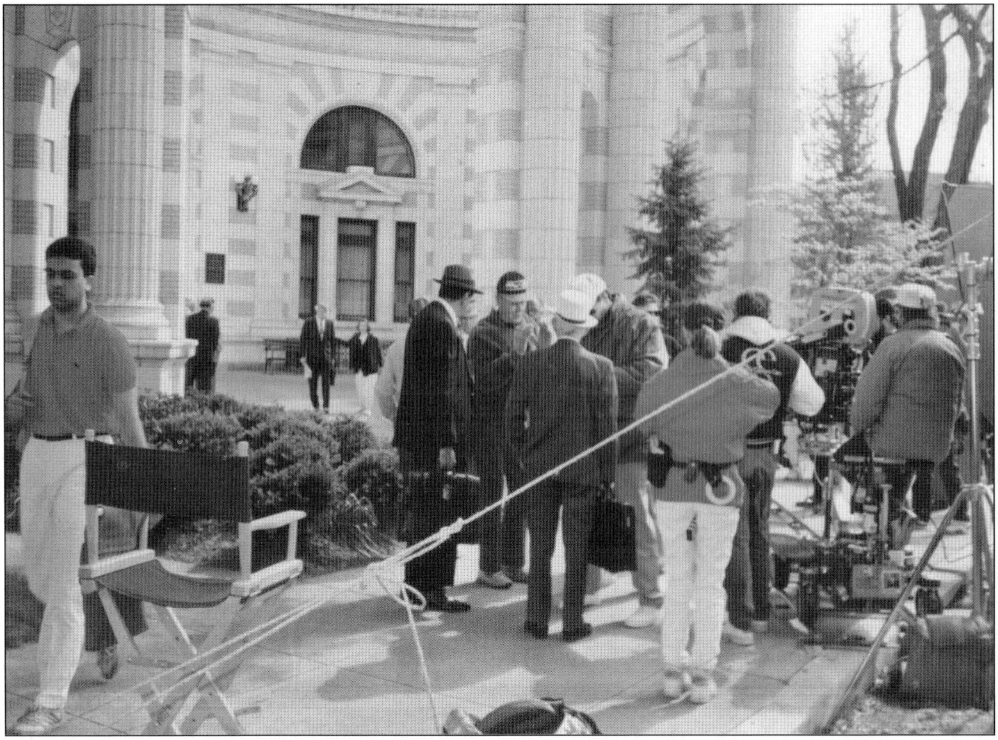

Harry Morgan and Walter Matthau discuss their next scene for *Against Her Will* with director Delbert Mann on the Carnegie Mellon University campus in front of Margaret Morrison Carnegie Hall. Matthau reprised his role as Harmon Cobb from *The Incident*. He played Cobb one more time in *Incident in a Small Town*. Like Morgan, *Against Her Will* was the only time Matthau worked on a production in Pittsburgh.

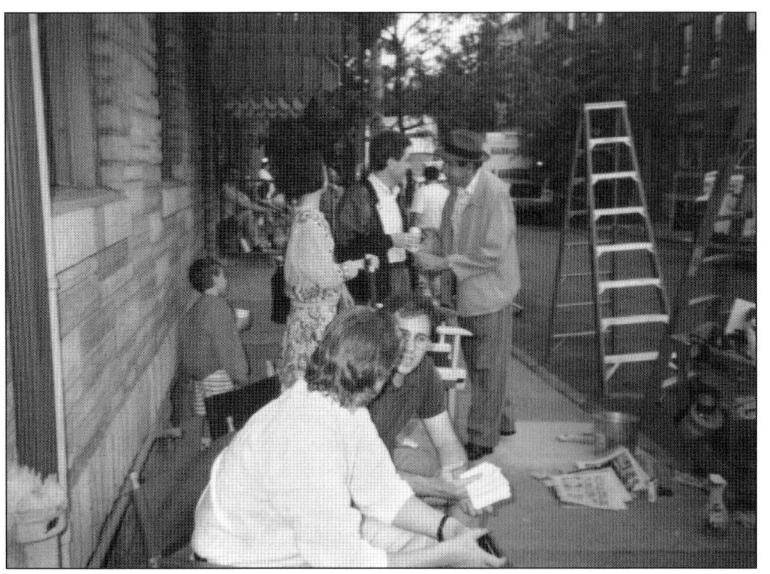

Walter Matthau chats with locals on the set of *Against Her Will*. Working on movies will teach the everyday person that many actors and actresses are just like them, while a few are not. Sometimes, actors and actresses are wrongly accused of not being social when in reality, they are trying to stay in character.

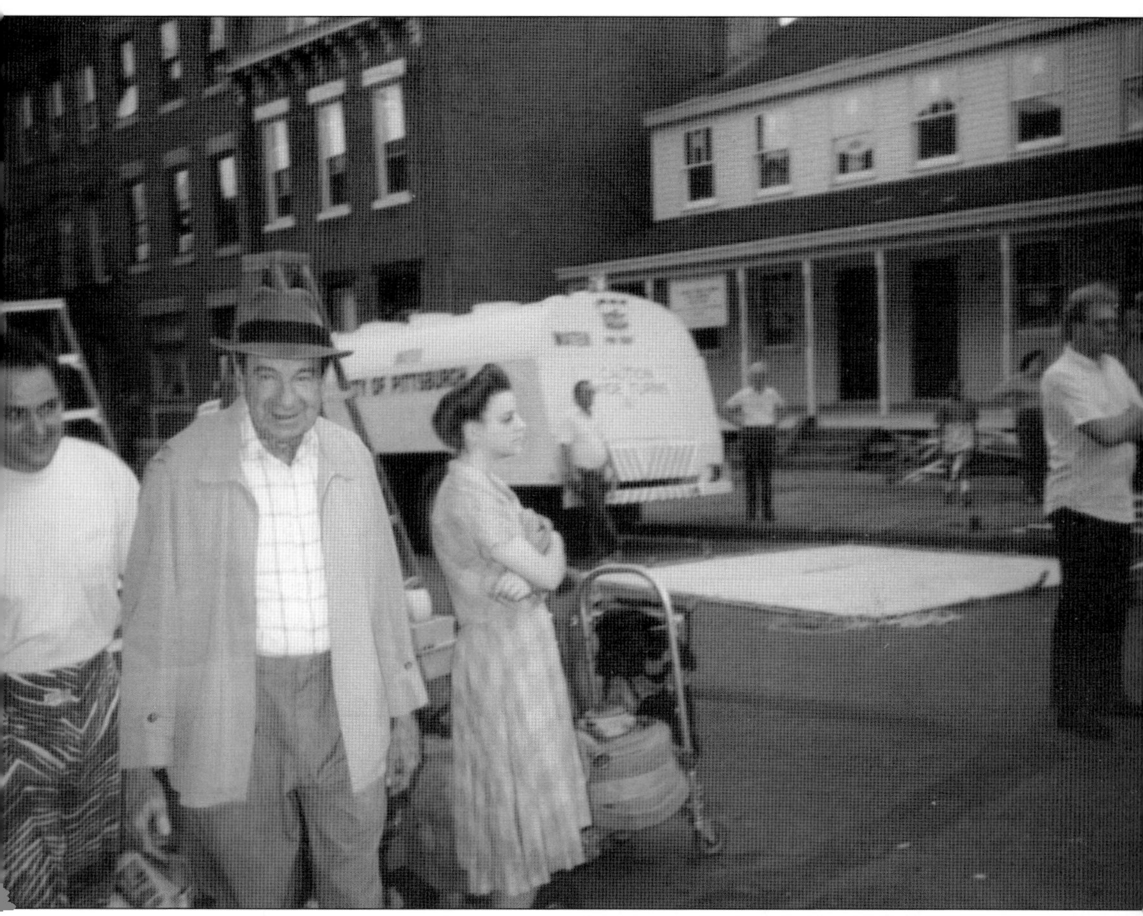

Walter Matthau poses while making *Against Her Will*. Those who had the pleasure of working with Matthau described him to be as funny and personable off camera as he was on camera. Because this movie was a sequel to *The Incident*, many plot elements from that film rolled over into this one. One of the more notable plot elements involves Matthau's character Harmon Cobb moving to Baltimore.

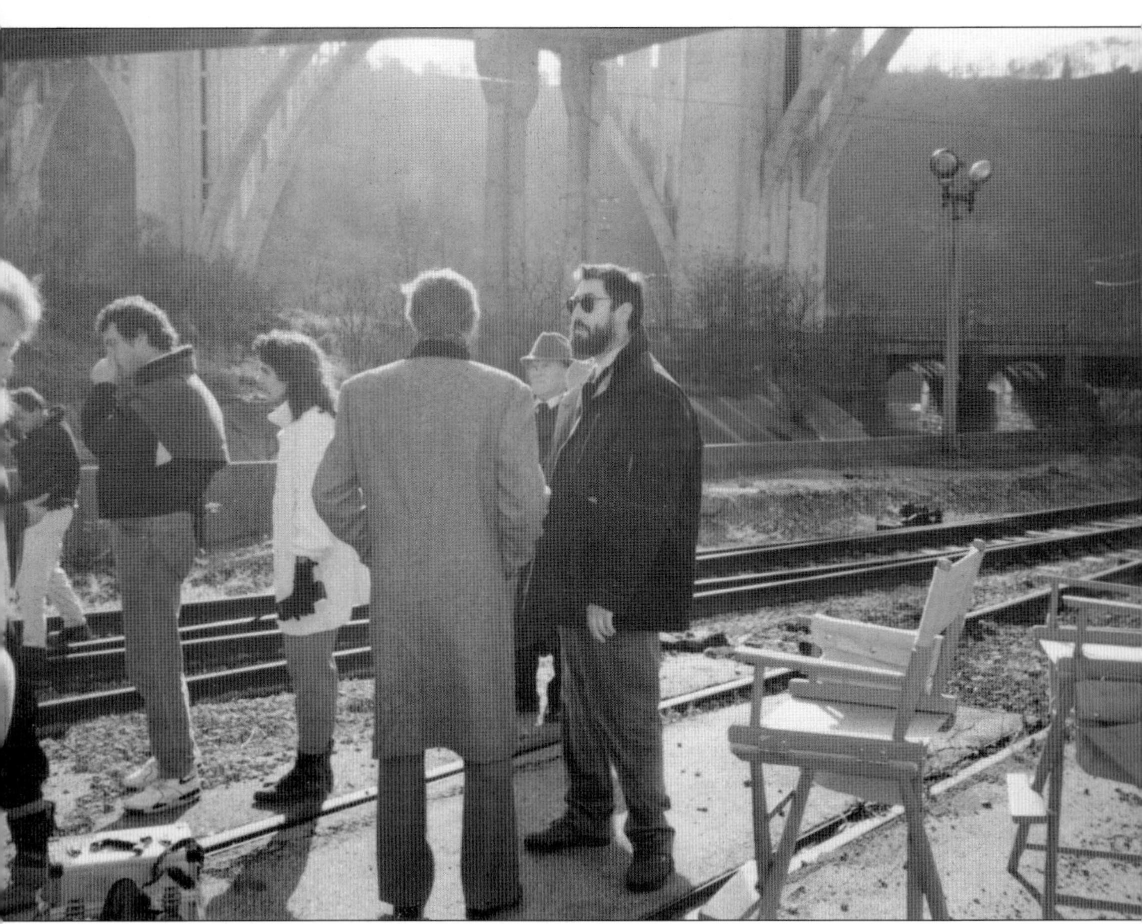

John Landis (right) has a discussion between takes while directing *Innocent Blood*, a movie about a vampire with morals who feeds off of the criminals in Pittsburgh. To date, this is the only movie Landis directed in Pittsburgh.

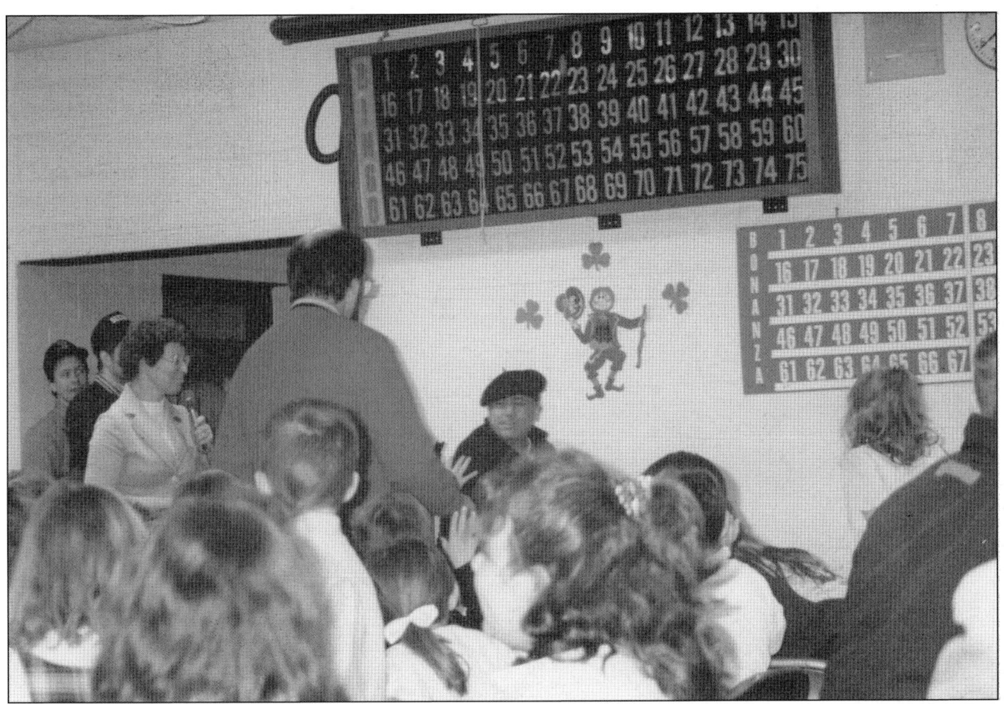

Danny DeVito (center) entertains locals during the filming of *Hoffa* in 1992. *Hoffa* was essentially a biography of the Teamsters leader Jimmy Hoffa, played by Jack Nicholson. This was the only time DeVito and Nicholson worked on a production in Pittsburgh.

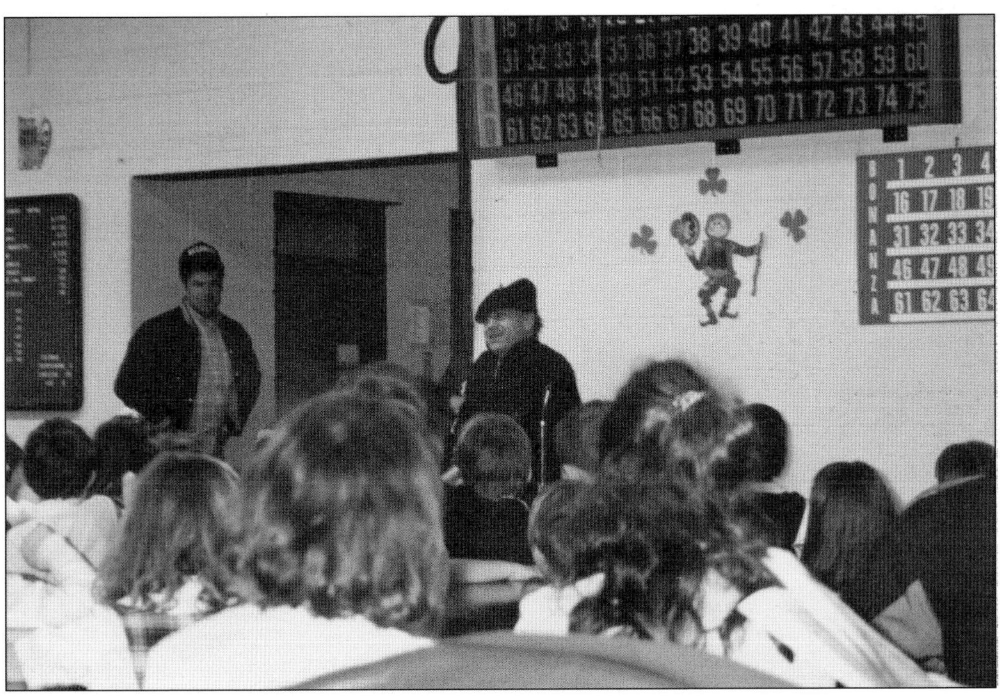

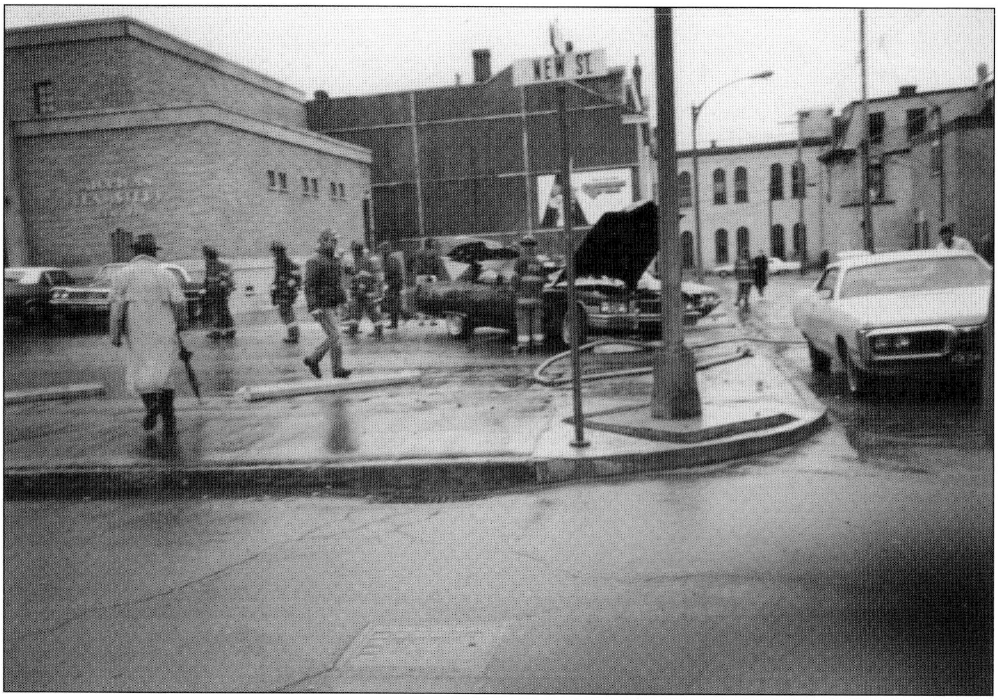

A controlled fire is burning on the *Hoffa* production. Film crews usually take a lot of precautions when it comes to staging fires. Local fire departments are usually brought in to assist with the safety measures.

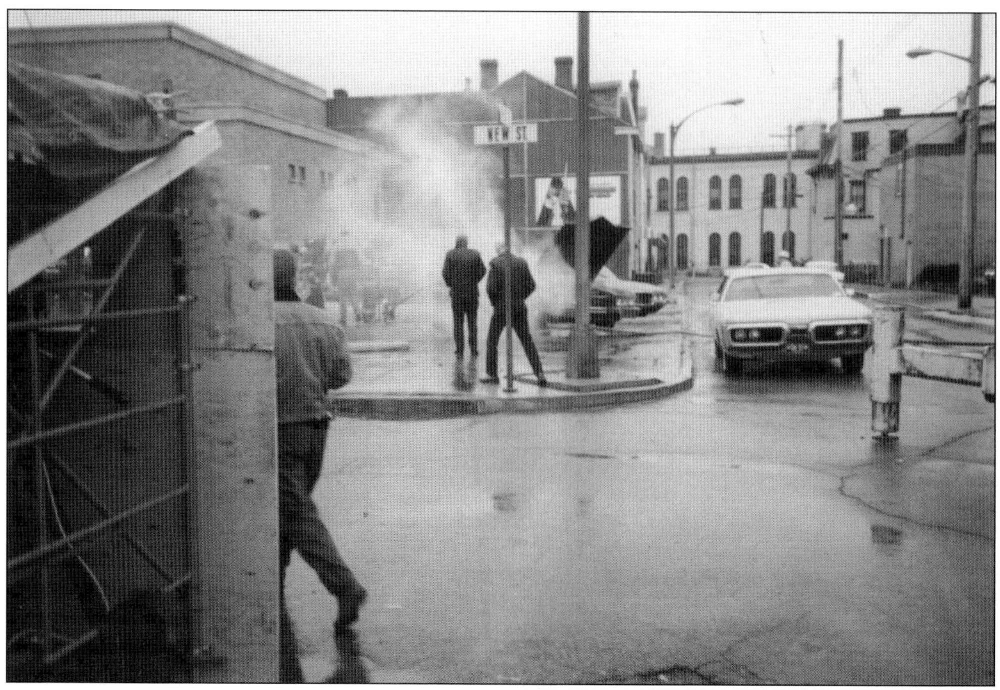

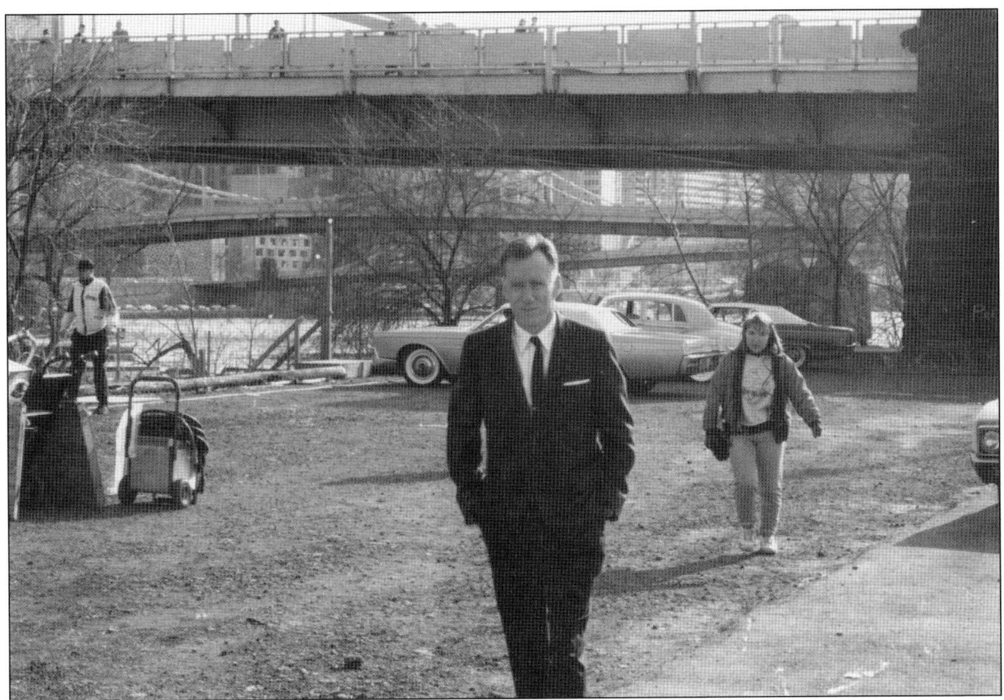

James Woods walks on the set of the television movie production for *Citizen Cohn*, which was filmed around Pittsburgh in 1992. *Citizen Cohn* is essentially a biography of Roy Cohn, the controversial chief counsel to Joseph McCarthy.

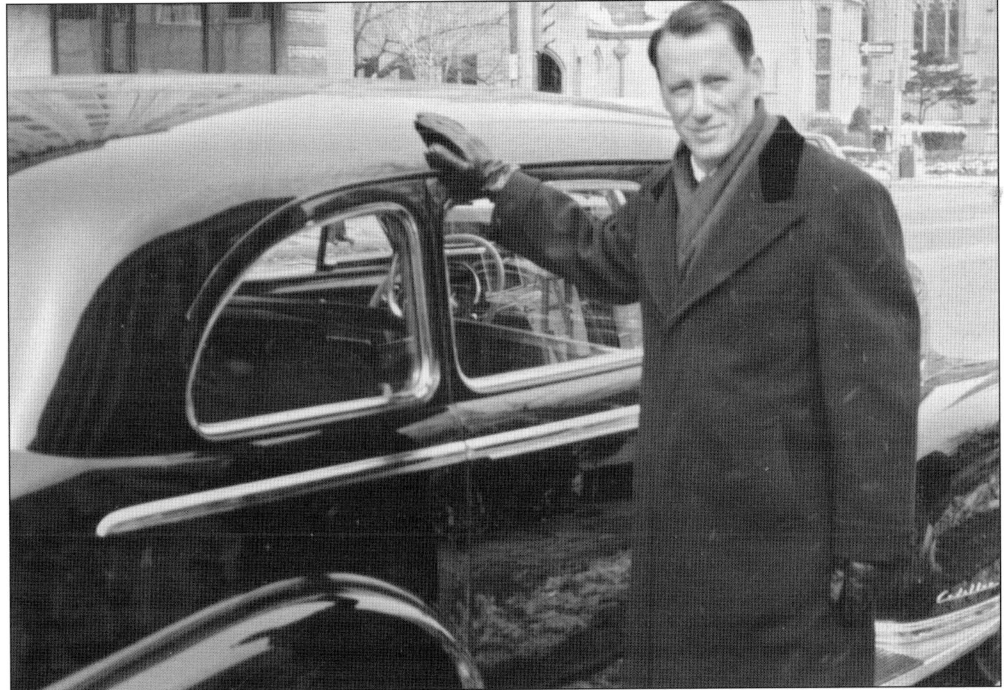

This photograph shows James Woods posing for a picture between takes while filming *Citizen Cohn*. Woods plays the title role of Roy Cohn in the movie.

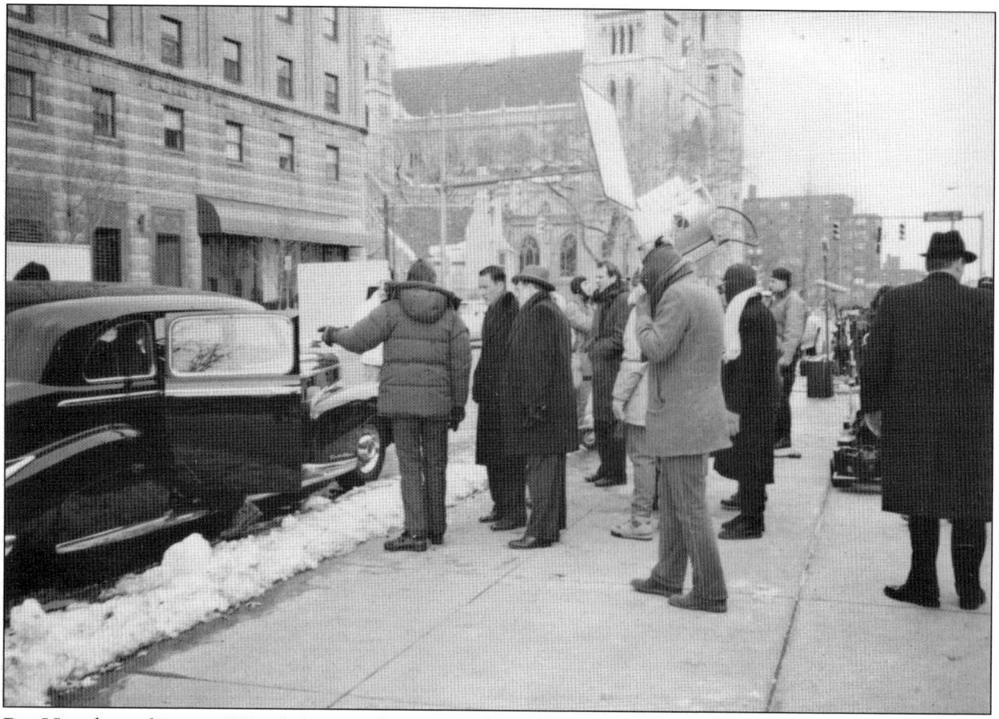

Pat Hingle and James Woods have a discussion between takes on *Citizen Cohn*. This was the only time Hingle and Woods worked on a production in Pittsburgh.

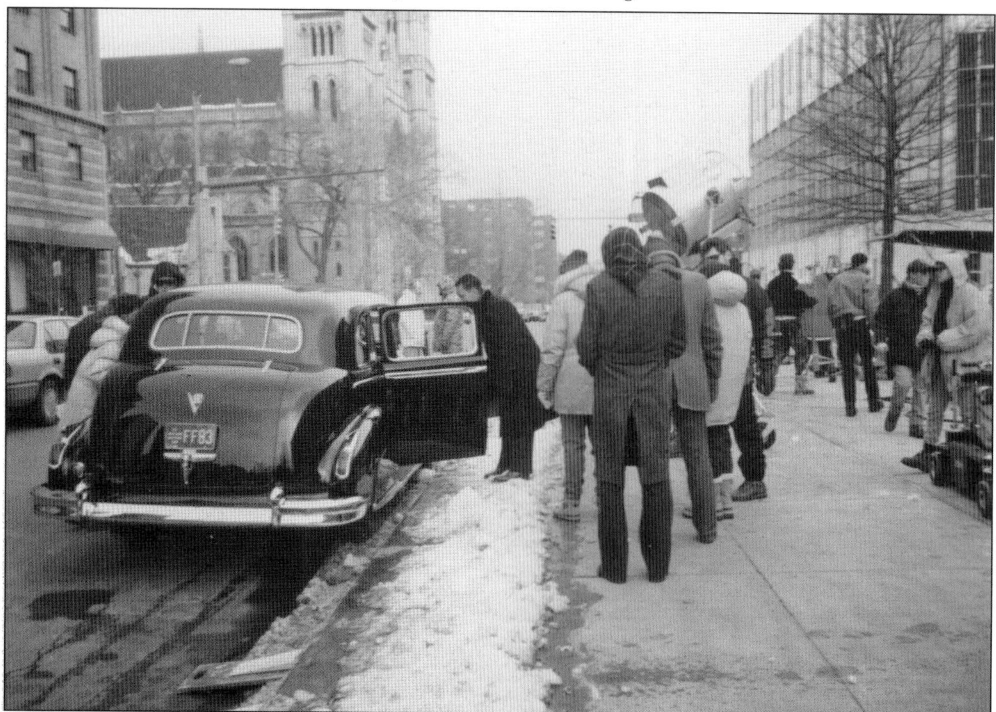

The cast and crew work on the set of *Citizen Cohn* at the intersection of Fifth Avenue and Dithridge Street in Oakland.

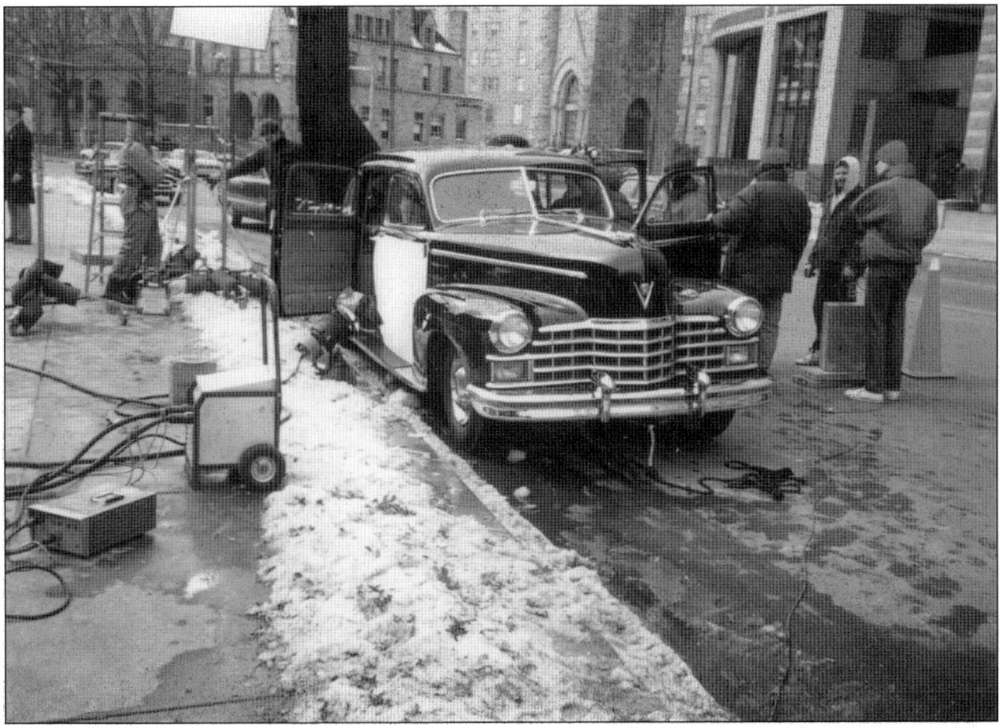

The *Citizen Cohn* crew works around cars on the set. Filming a movie or television show can be very time consuming, with more time spent working behind the scenes on the set rather than filming the actual movie or television show.

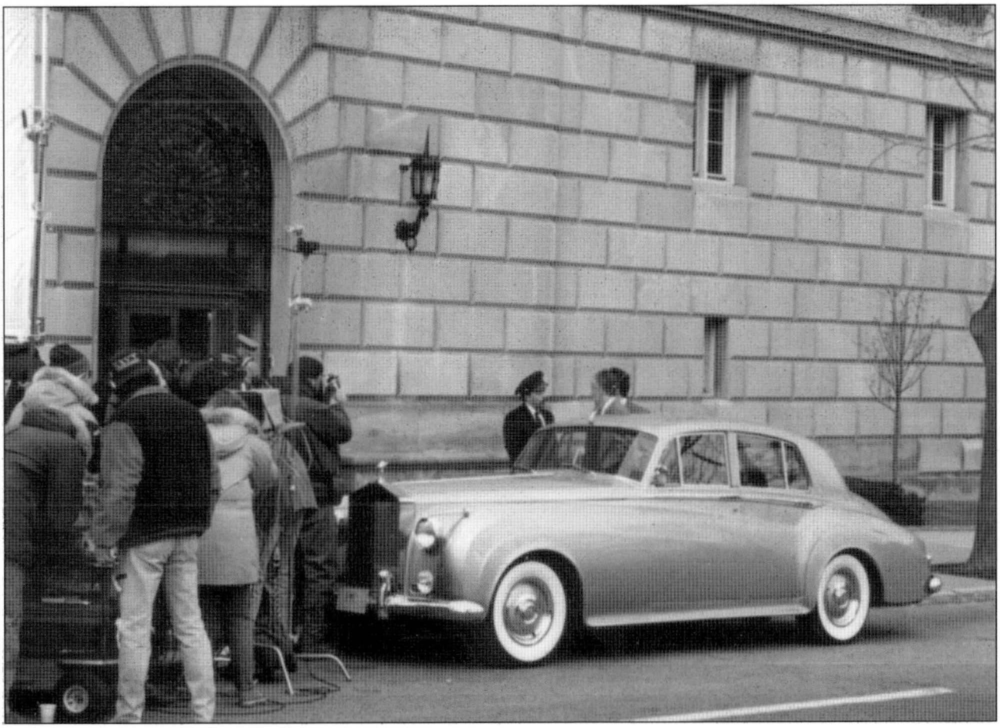

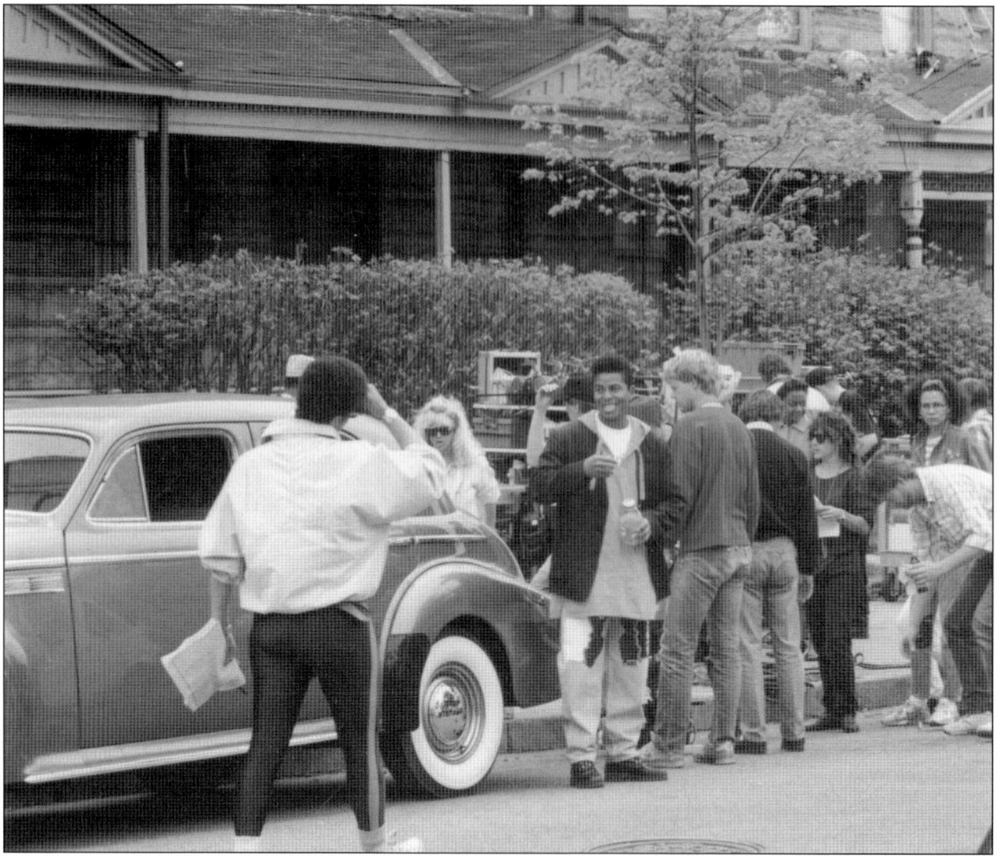

These are set pictures from the television miniseries *The Jacksons: An American Dream* in 1992. The successful miniseries was a biography of the Jackson family as well as The Jackson Five. Although the movie was meant to be a biography, it deviated in some respects from the actual events that transpired.

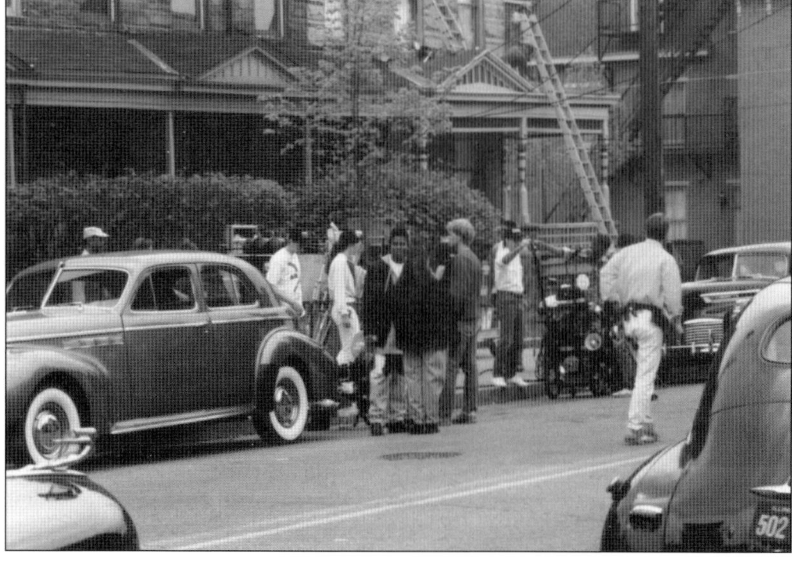

Cast, crew, and security stand around on the set of *The Jacksons: An American Dream*, with production trucks populating the street. A few members of the Jackson family appeared on the set with popular actors and actresses such as Vanessa Williams, Angela Bassett, and Billy Dee Williams, who were appearing in the miniseries.

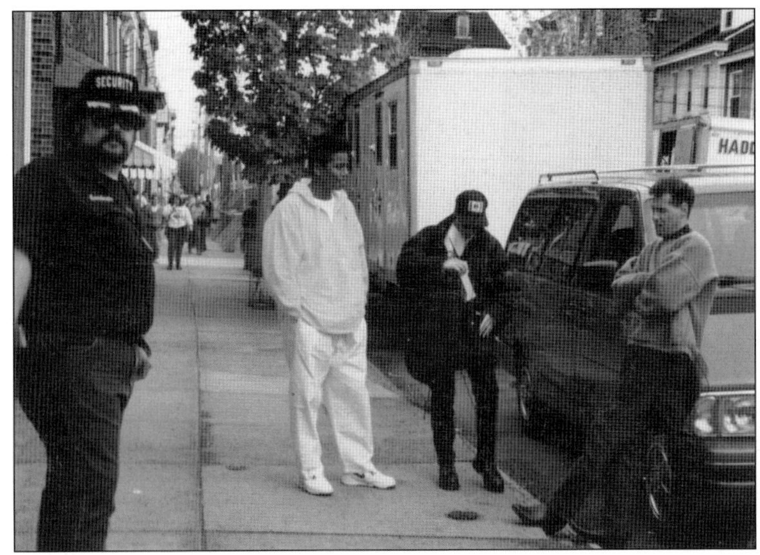

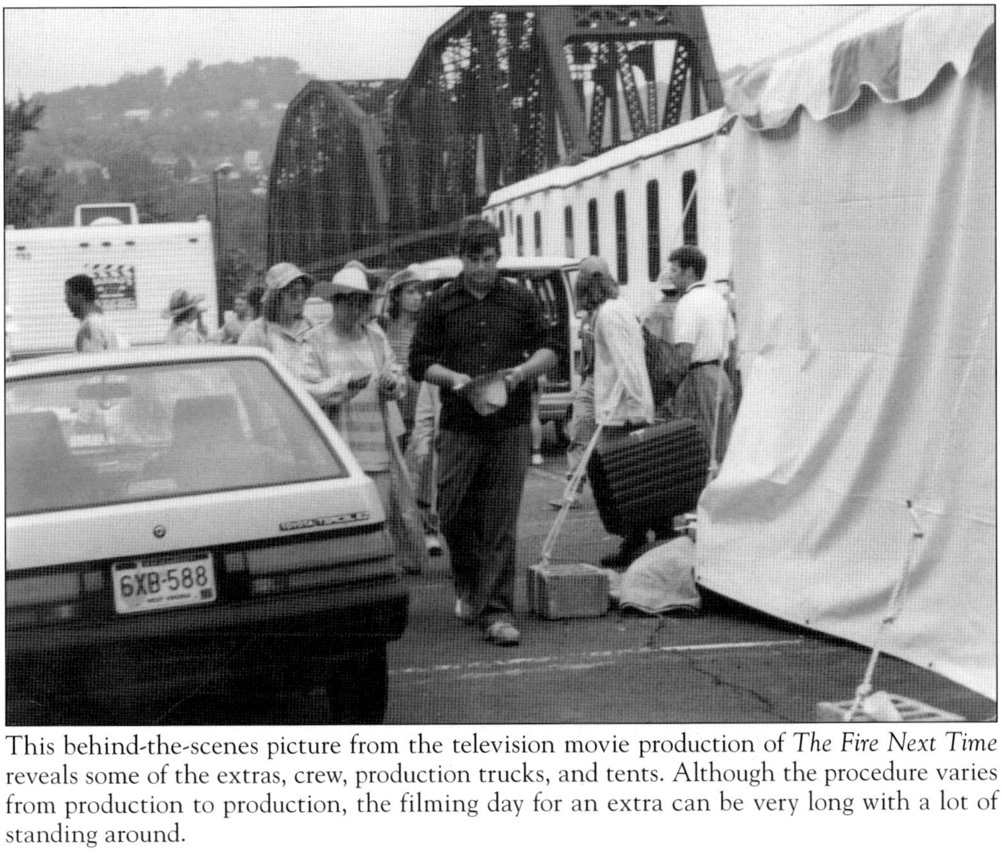

This behind-the-scenes picture from the television movie production of *The Fire Next Time* reveals some of the extras, crew, production trucks, and tents. Although the procedure varies from production to production, the filming day for an extra can be very long with a lot of standing around.

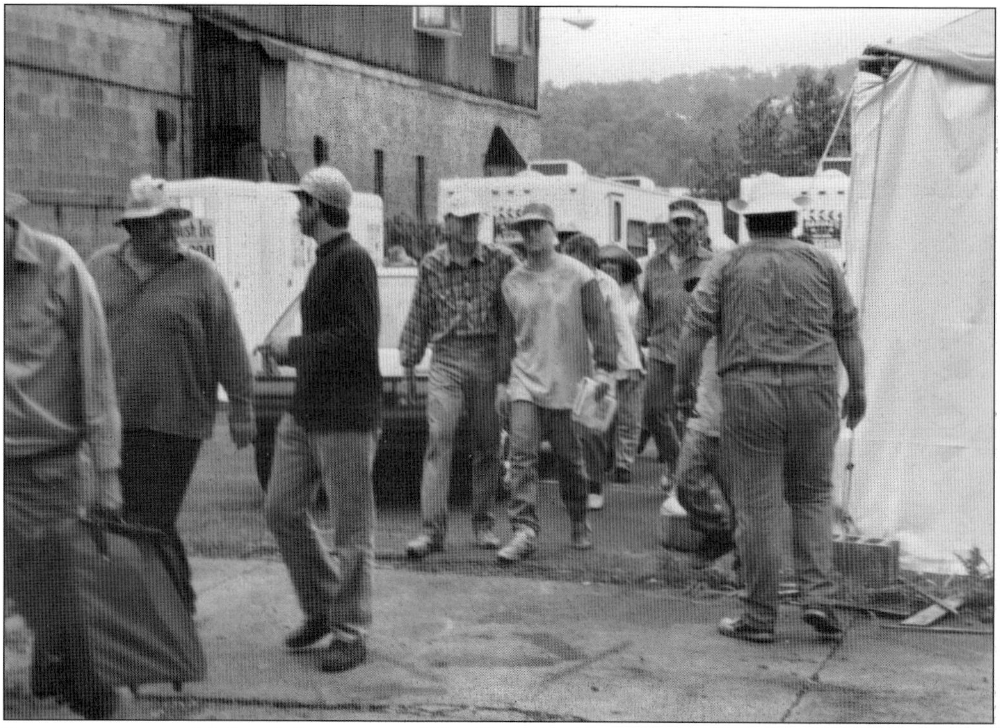

Extras are pictured behind the scenes of *The Fire Next Time*. Typically, extras are instructed to park at a certain place and a certain time (known as the call time). From there, they are usually shuttled to the set where they will go through a check-in, as well as a makeup and wardrobe check. Until extras are called onto the actual set being filmed, they remain in the holding area. During this time, extras usually meet each other and converse; sometimes, the extras are from the Pittsburgh region, and sometimes they are not. Extras also get to know the local production assistants better.

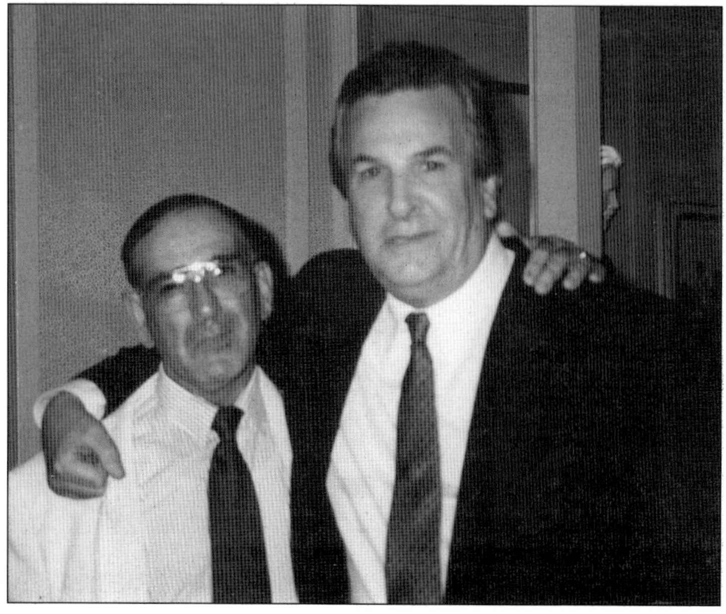

Background actor and Pittsburgh native Tony Amen (left) poses with actor Danny Aiello during the 1992 movie production *The Cemetery Club*. This was the only production Aiello ever worked on in Pittsburgh.

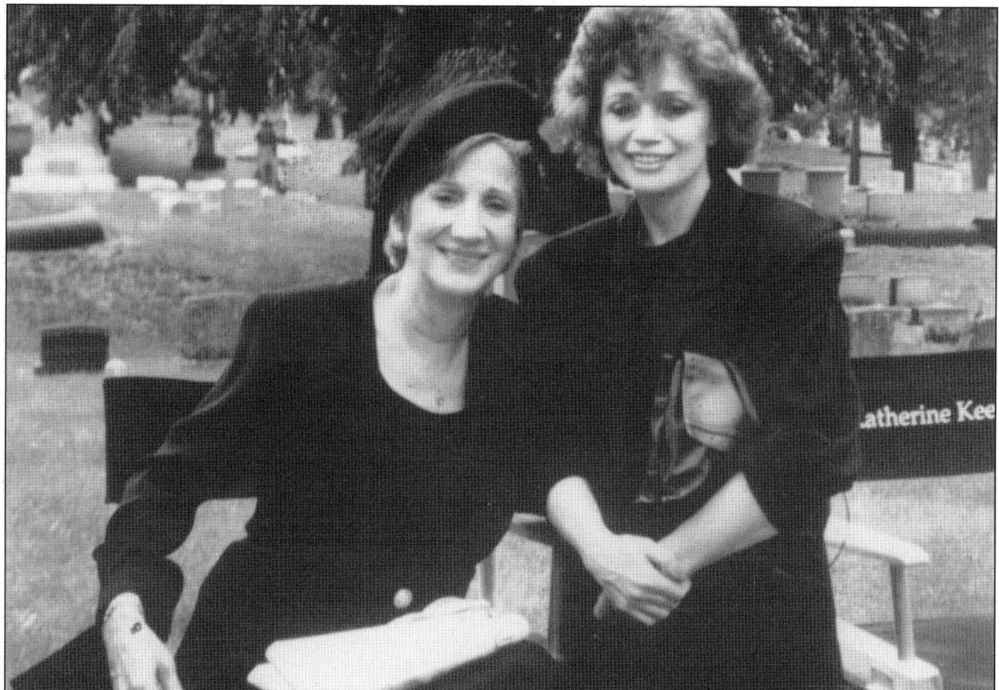

Olympia Dukakis and Pittsburgher Virgie Harbreth pose during the filming of *The Cemetery Club*. The cemetery set is an actual cemetery in Allegheny County. Location filmmaking can be difficult in situations such as this, as the cast and crew have to work around graves, respecting the property.

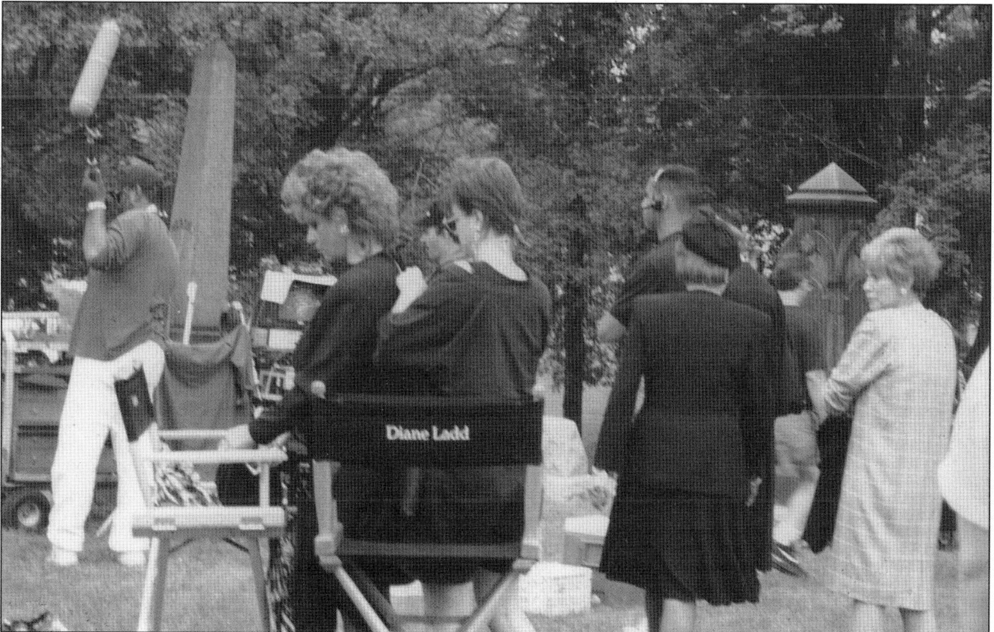

This photograph shows the cast and crew working on the set of *The Cemetery Club*. One of the prominent members of the crew was the film's director Bill Duke, who is better known for his acting work.

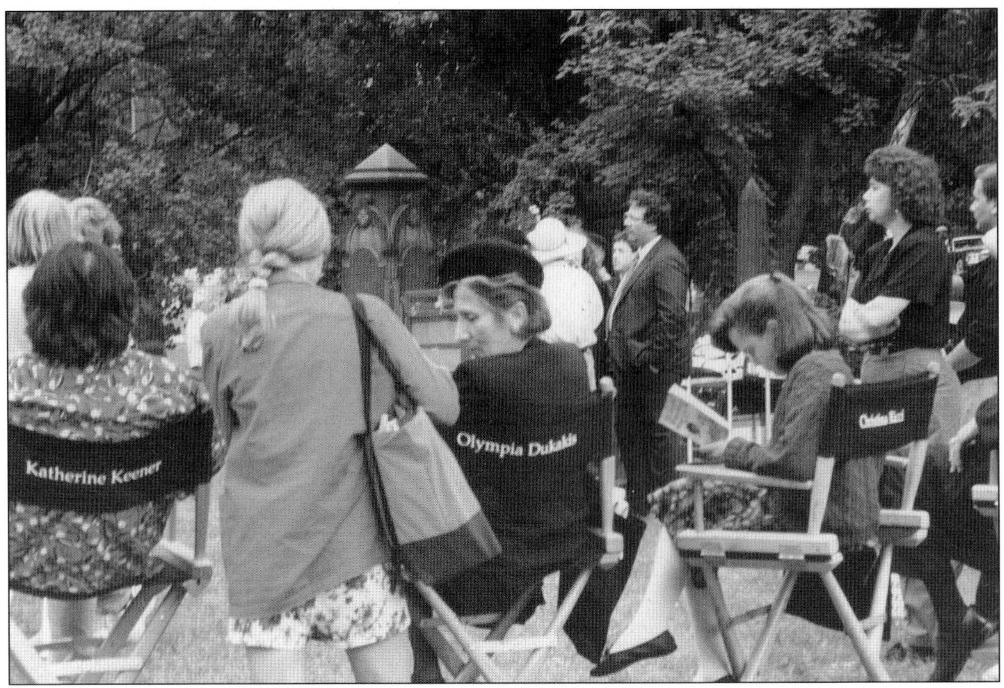

Olympia Dukakis and Christina Ricci sit in their chairs between takes while working on *The Cemetery Club*. Currently, this is the only Pittsburgh production Dukakis and Ricci have worked on.

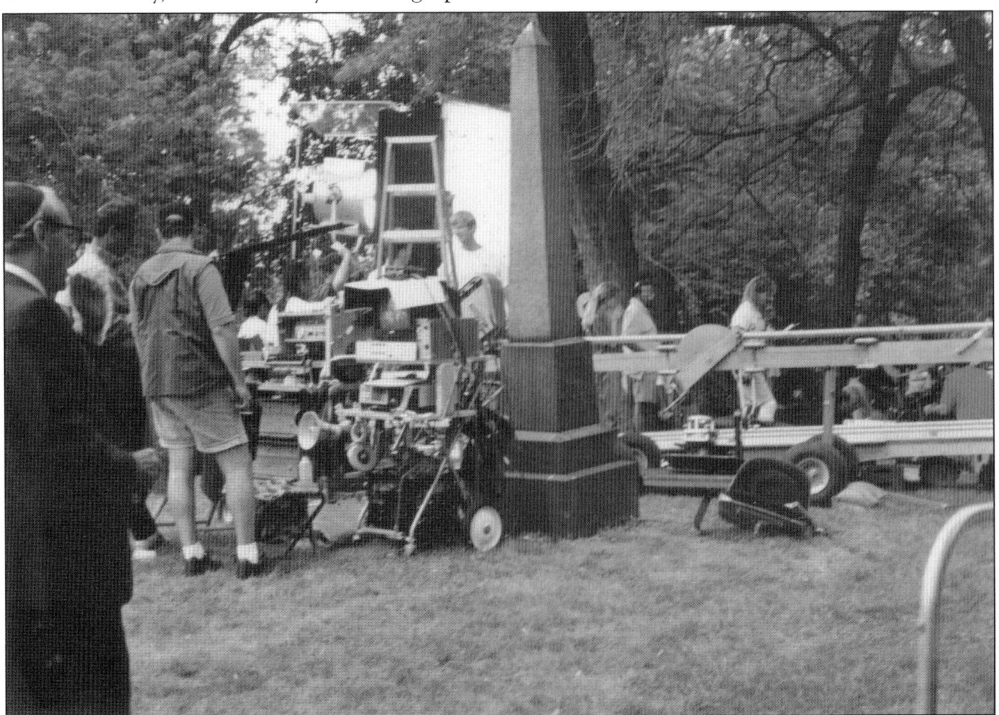

The crew works on *The Cemetery Club*. This image also shows the large equipment that was being used on the production. This equipment had to be carefully maneuvered around the gravestones in the cemetery.

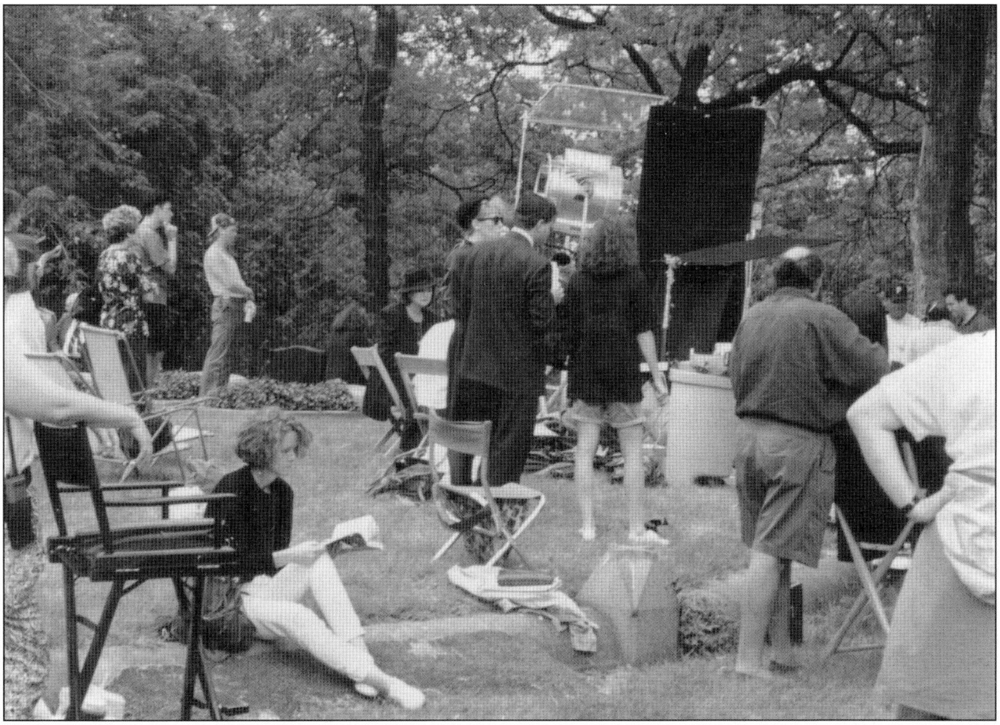

These photographs show the cast and crew relaxing between takes on *The Cemetery Club*.

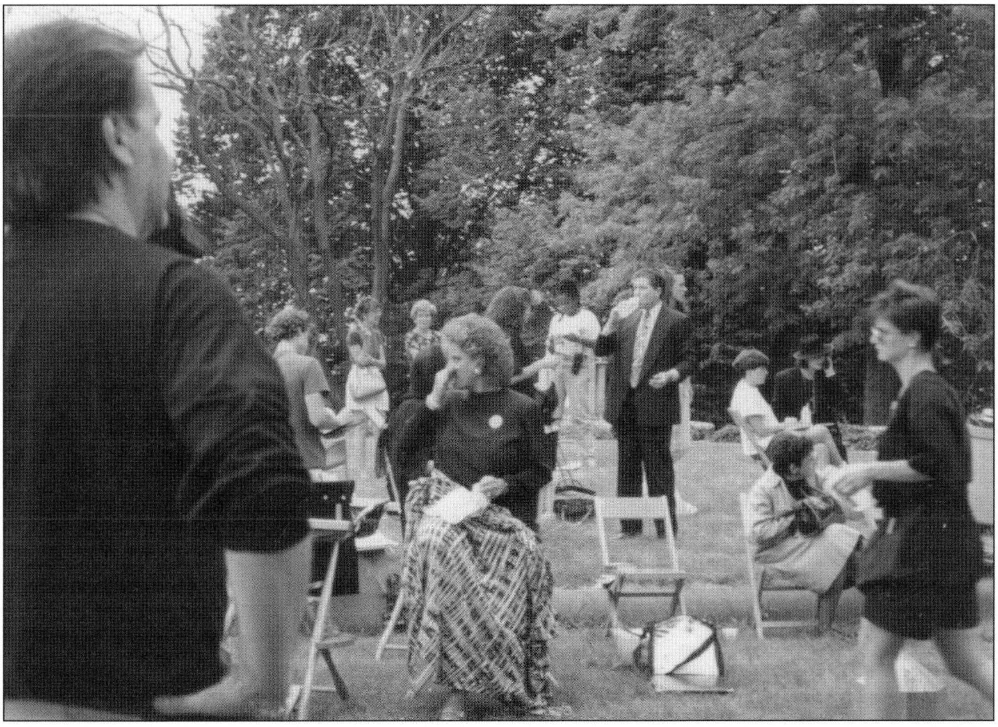

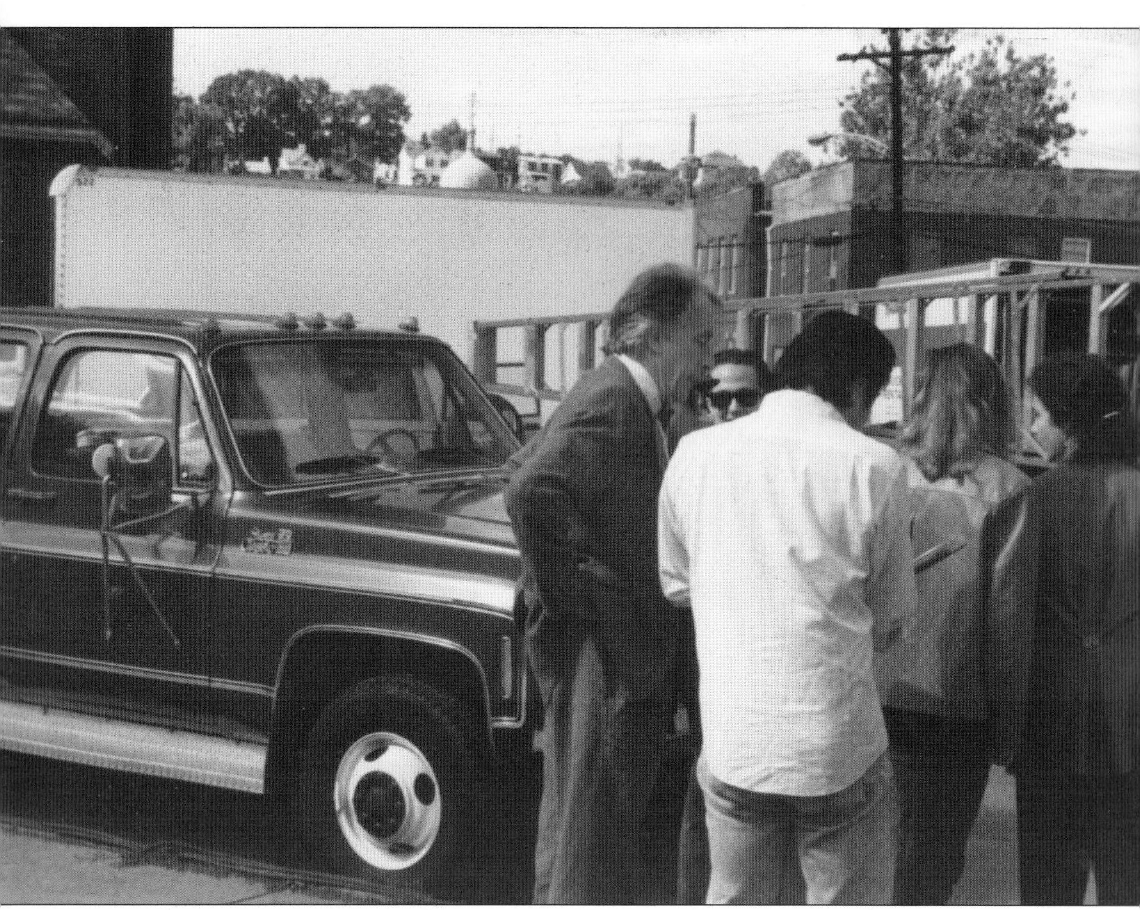

Veteran actor Fritz Weaver (left) is having a discussion with a member of the crew on the *Blind Spot* set in 1992. In the movie, Weaver and Joanne Woodward play the parents of actress Laura Linney, who plays a cocaine addict. Linney has worked extensively in Pittsburgh, being involved with productions such as *Lorenzo's Oil*, *Blind Spot*, and *The Mothman Prophecies*. Weaver previously worked on *Citizen Cohn* and *Creepshow*, making *Blind Spot* his third movie made in the city.

Joanne Woodward walks on the set of the *Blind Spot* television movie production. Woodward's husband, Paul Newman, was also in Pittsburgh while she was making this movie; however, this wasn't Newman's first time in the region. In 1976 he starred in the cult classic *Slap Shot*, which was filmed in Johnstown, Pennsylvania.

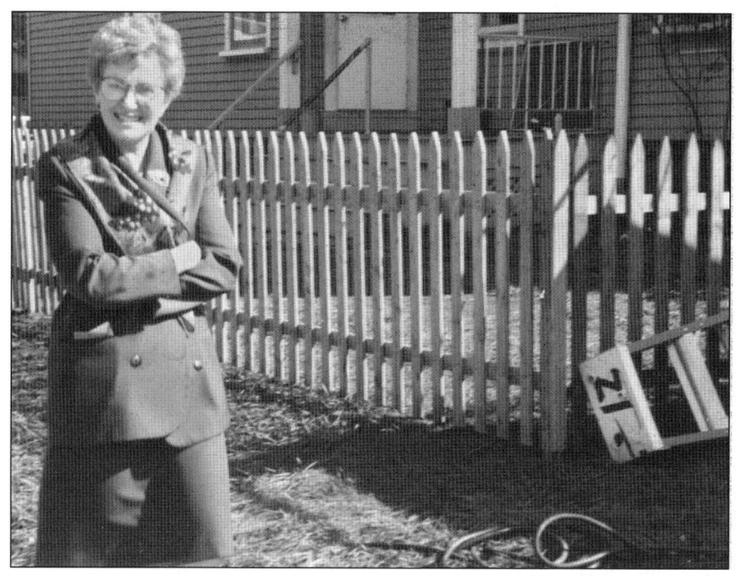

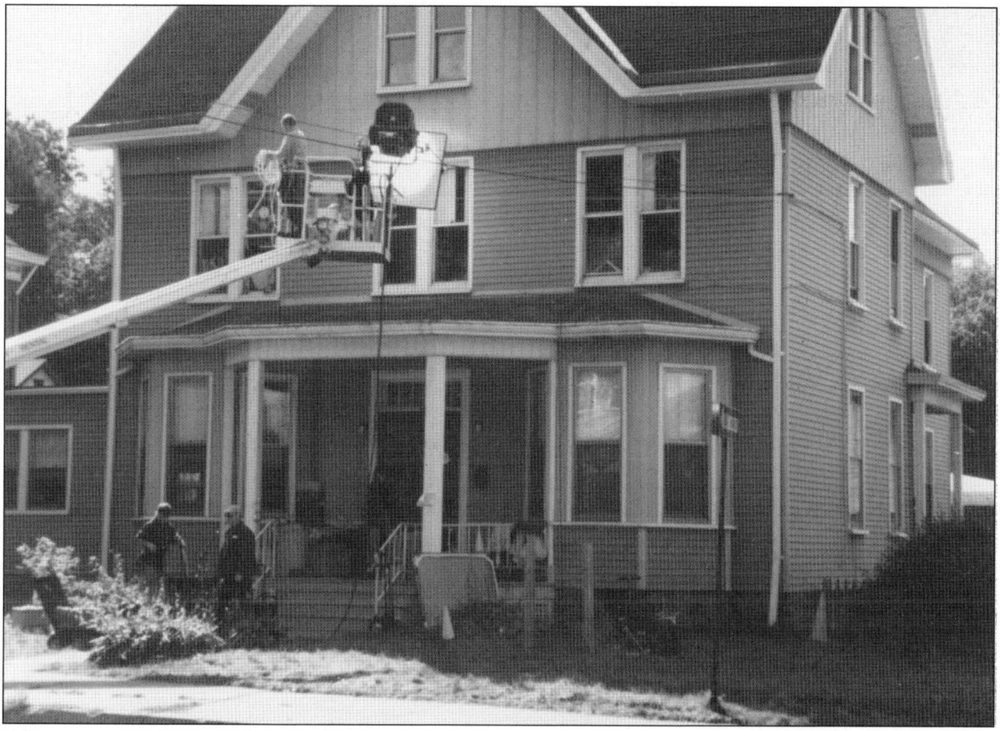

Film crews work around a Pittsburgh area home that was selected to be used for *Blind Spot*. It is not uncommon for movie productions to approach private homeowners in the hopes of using their house. Over the decades, several homes in the Pittsburgh area have been used for movies.

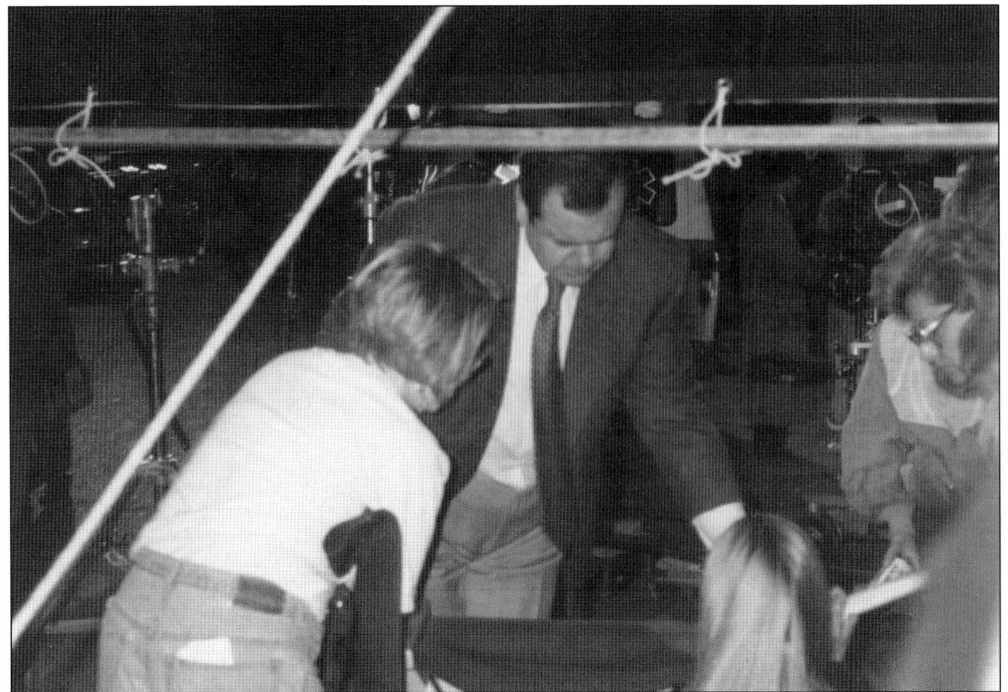

Paul Sorvino appears behind the scenes of the 1993 crime drama *Backstreet Justice*. This was the only production Sorvino worked on in Pittsburgh.

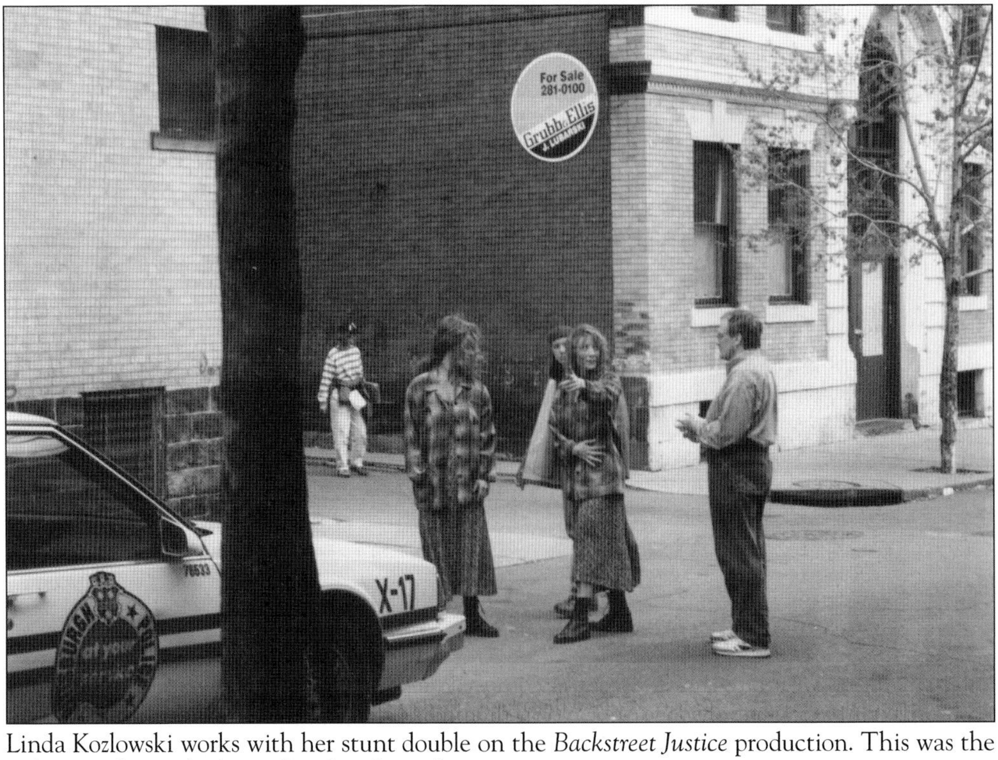

Linda Kozlowski works with her stunt double on the *Backstreet Justice* production. This was the only time she worked on a Pittsburgh production.

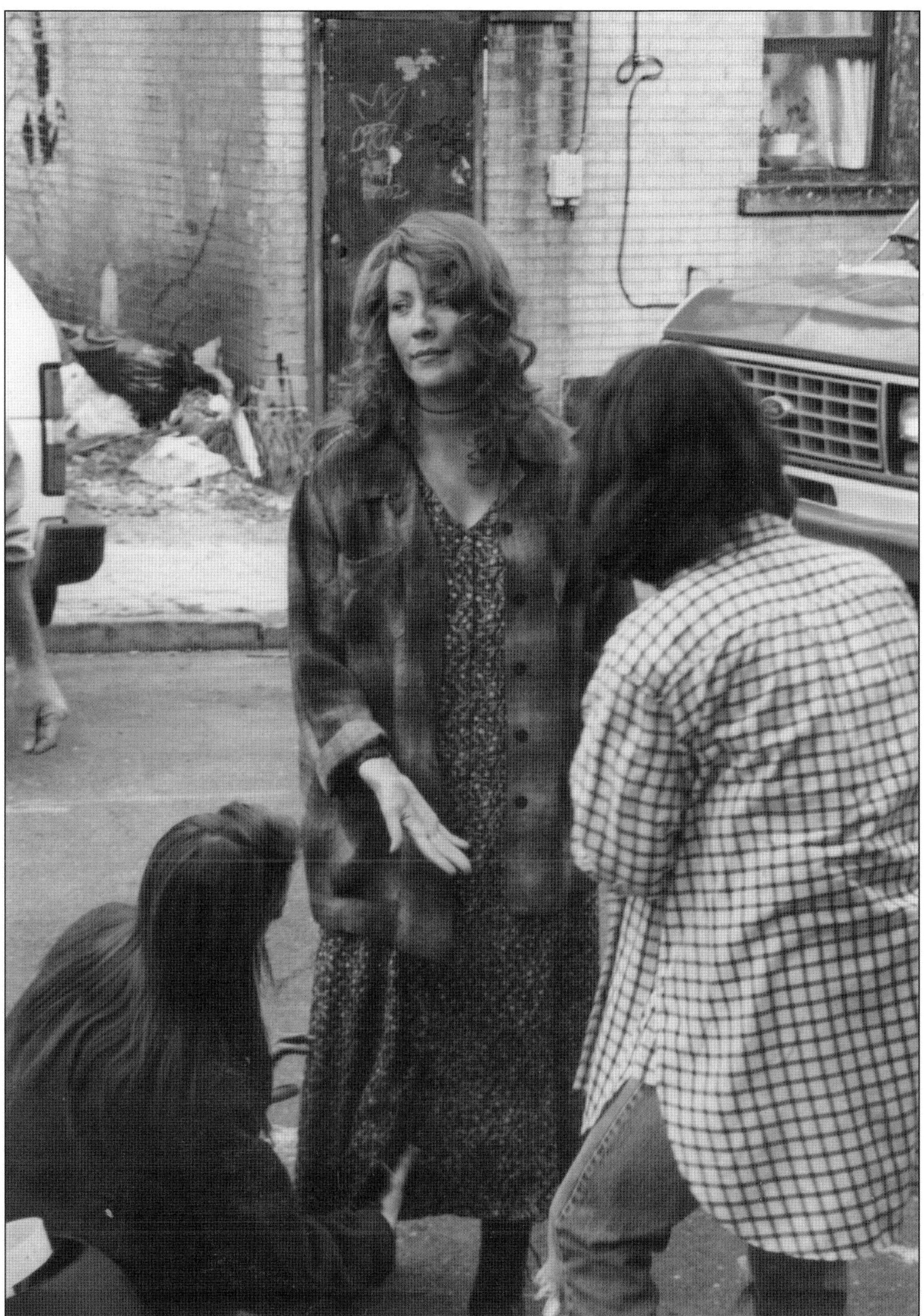

On the set of *Backstreet Justice*, the wardrobe crew works on actress Linda Kozlowski. It is important to have members of the hair, makeup, and wardrobe crew around the actors and actresses to preserve continuity on-camera. Because of the quantity of takes, hair, makeup, and wardrobe have the potential of being messed up over time.

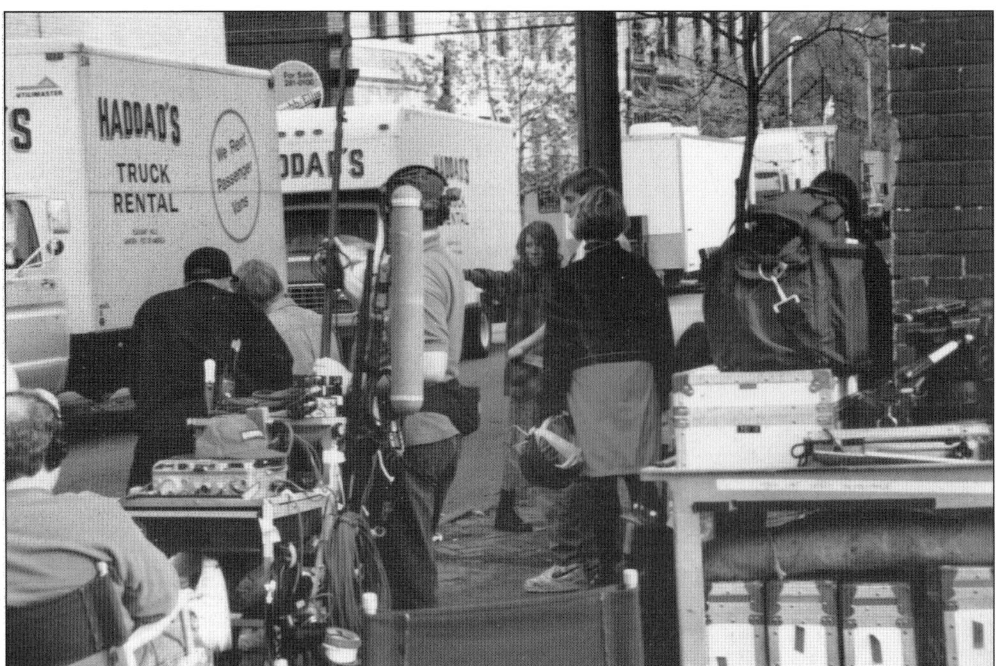

Linda Kozlowski and the film crew work behind the scenes on the *Backstreet Justice* production. Trucks from Haddad's, a Pittsburgh truck rental service for film productions, are lined up and down the street in the background.

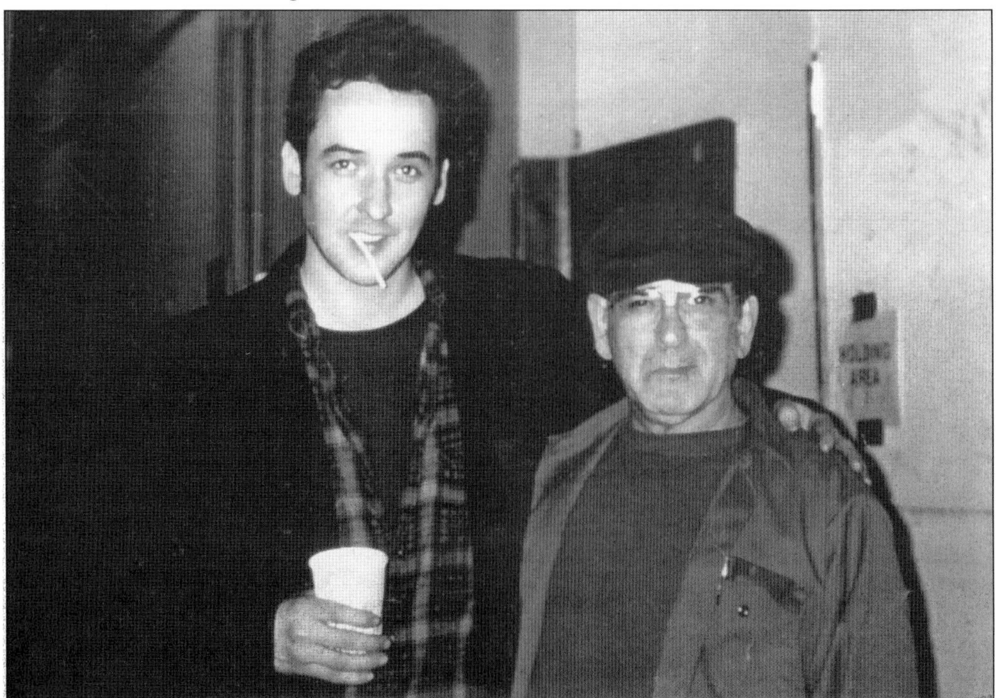

Hollywood actor John Cusack and veteran Pittsburgh background actor Tony Amen pose on the set of 1993's *Money for Nothing*, which was Cusack's second movie production in Pittsburgh; his first was *Bob Roberts*.

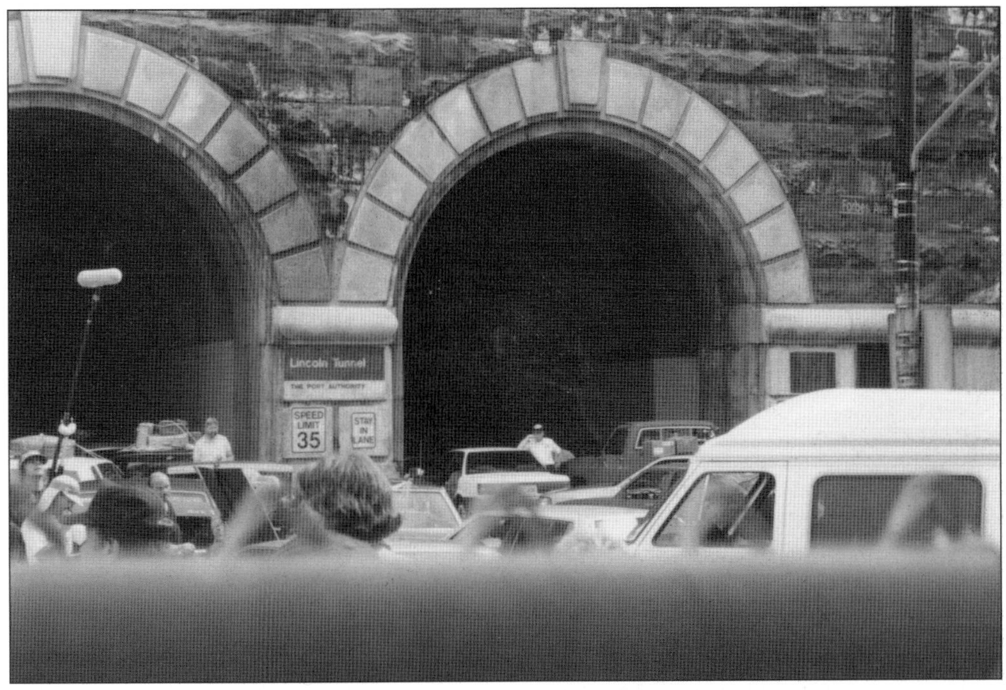

Film crews work in front of the Armstrong Tunnels in Pittsburgh for the 1993 production of the Stephen King miniseries *The Stand*. The Armstrong Tunnels are substituting for the Lincoln Tunnel in New York.

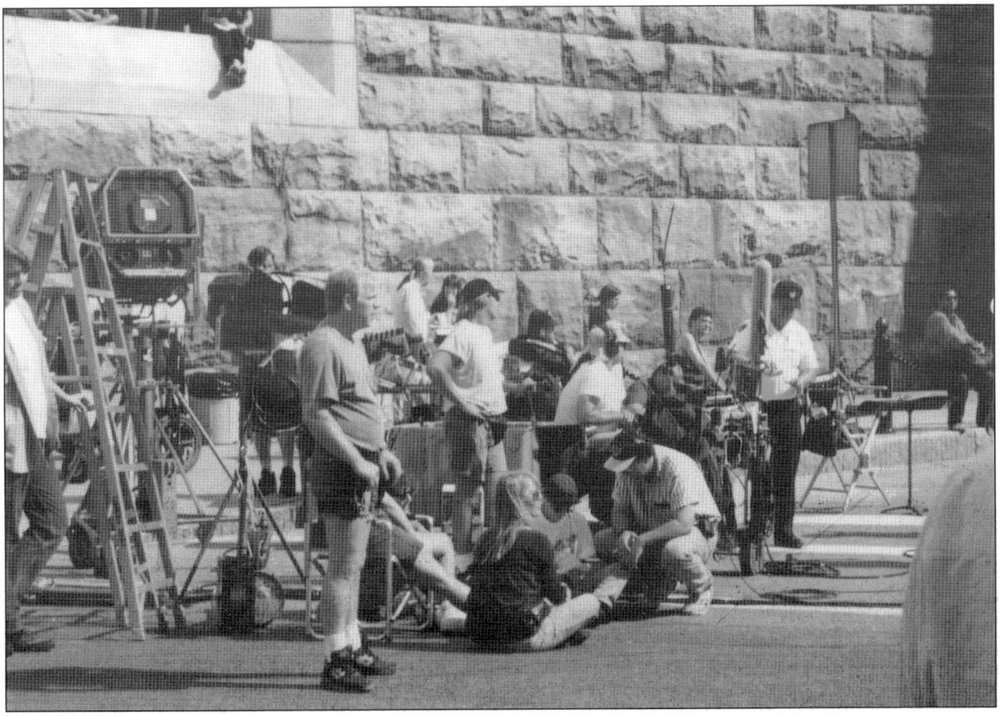

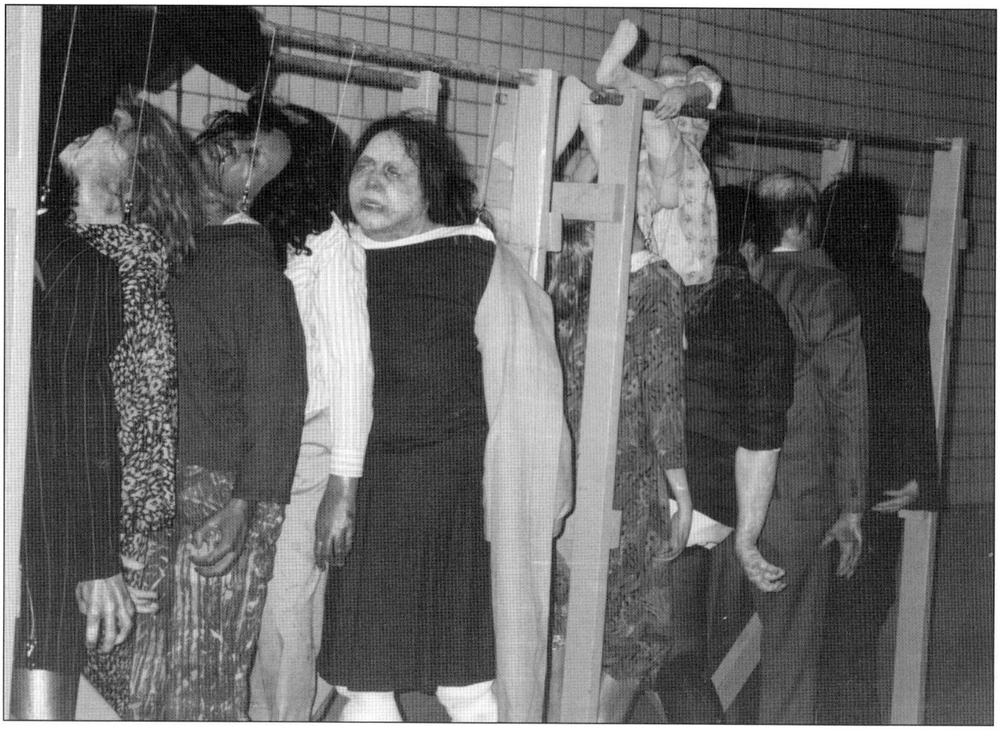

Mannequin props of dead people hang behind the scenes of *The Stand*. As the pictures show, the mannequins were meant to be extraordinarily lifelike.

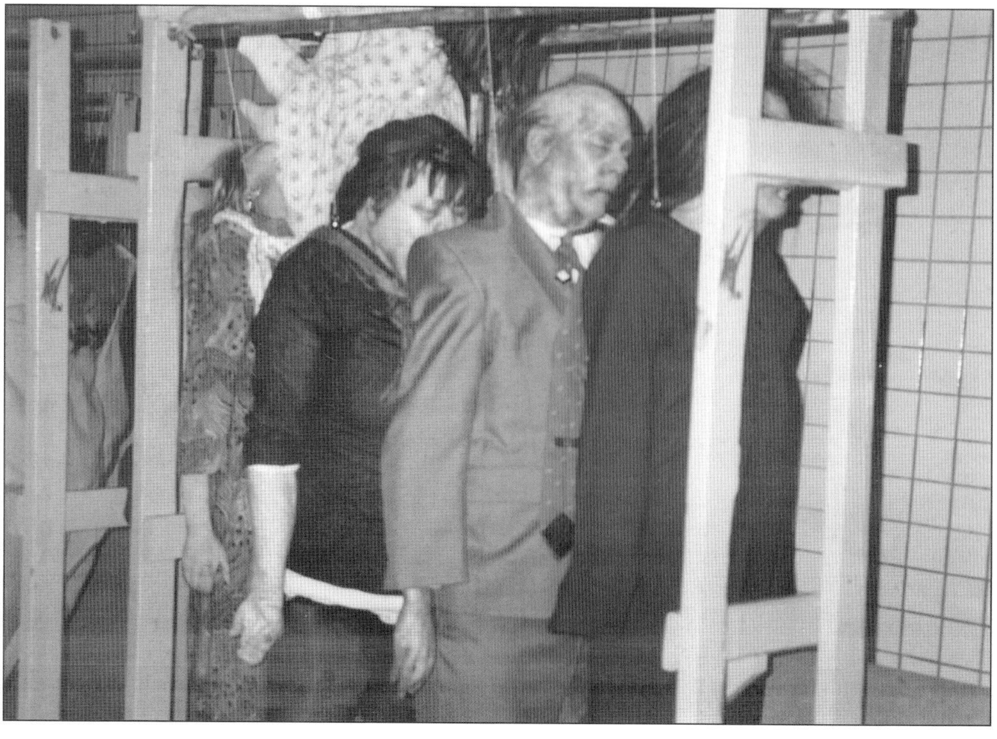

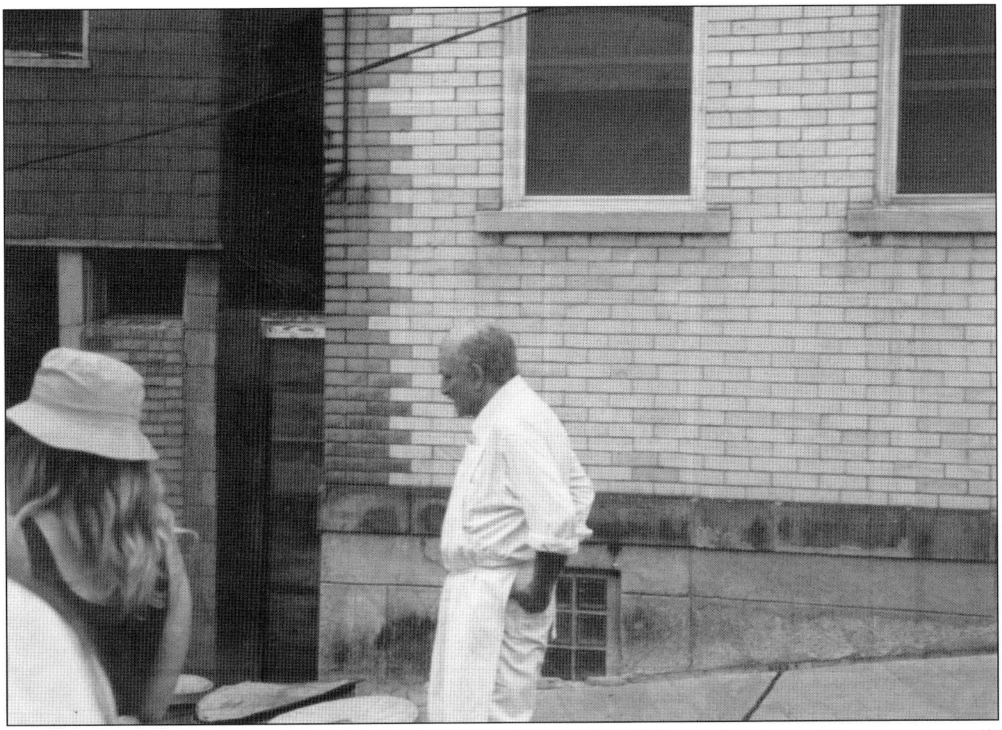

Peter Falk walks down the street in full makeup during the 1993 production of *Roommates*. Falk found *Roommates* to be a very exhausting shoot, given the hours he had to spend in the makeup chair as well as his advanced age at the time.

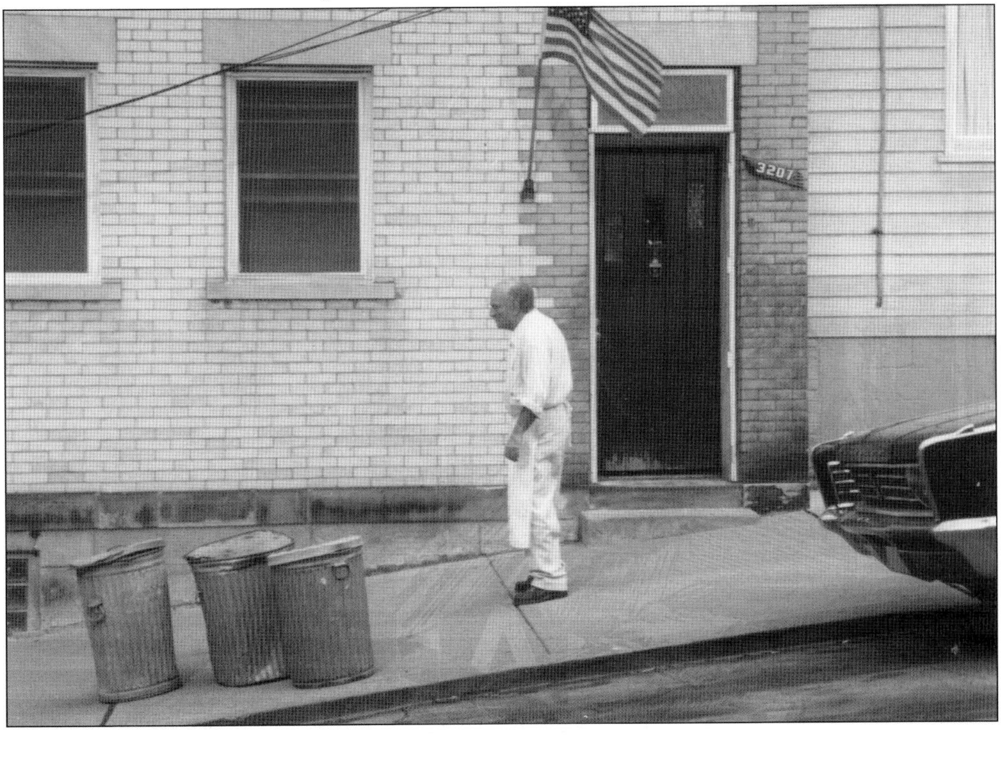

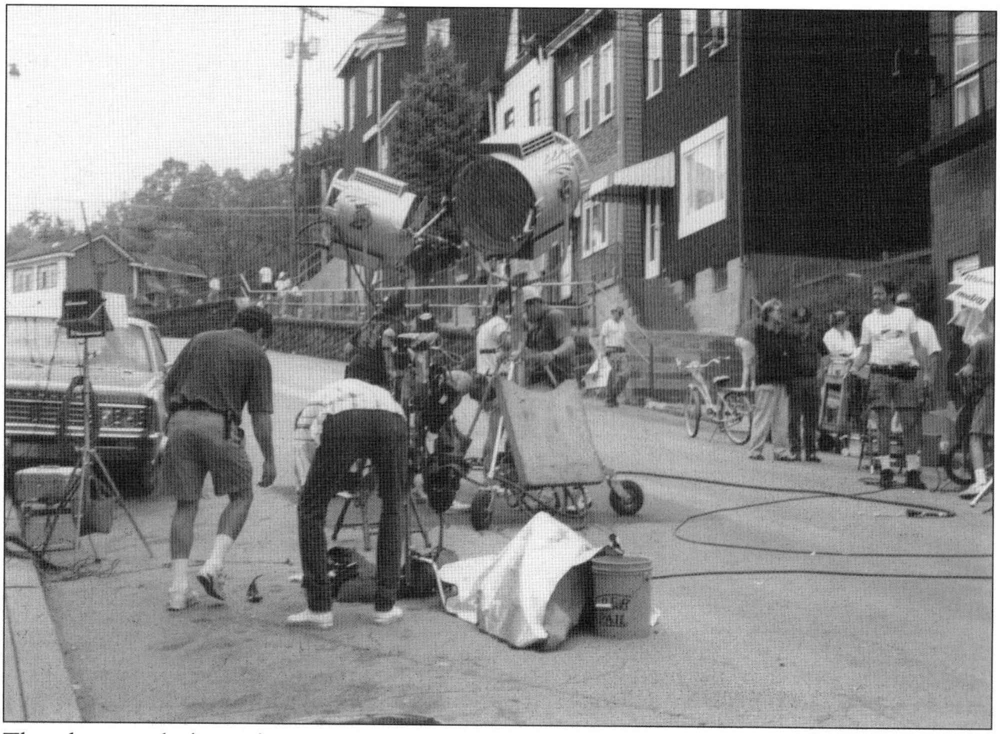

This photograph shows the crew of *Roommates* working on Brereton Street in Pittsburgh's Polish Hill neighborhood.

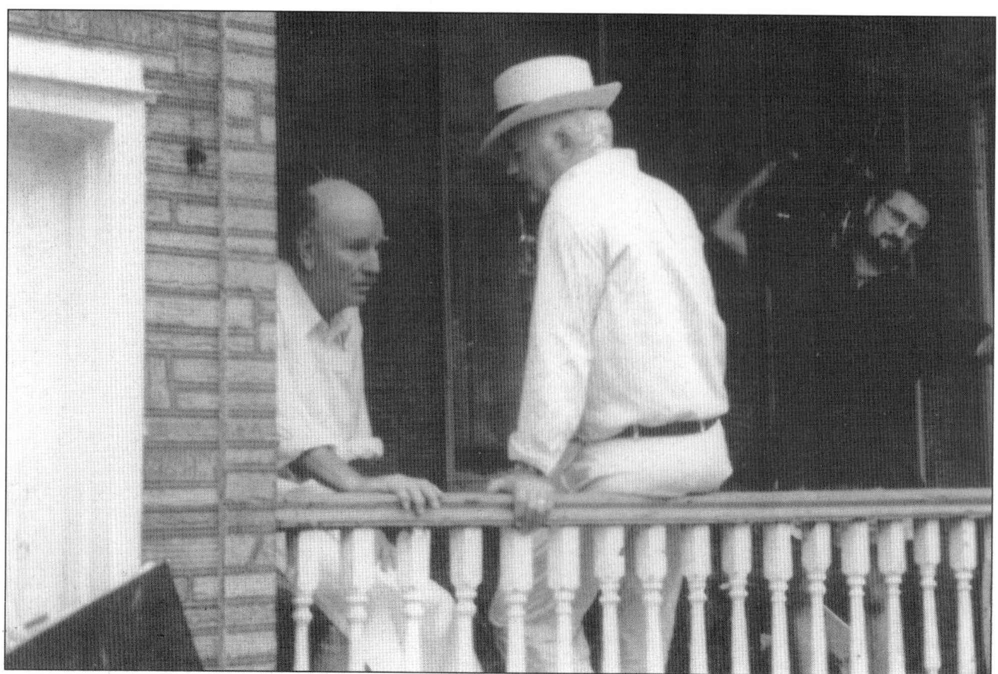

Director Peter Yates and star Peter Falk have a discussion while making *Roommates*. This was the only production Yates and Falk worked on in Pittsburgh.

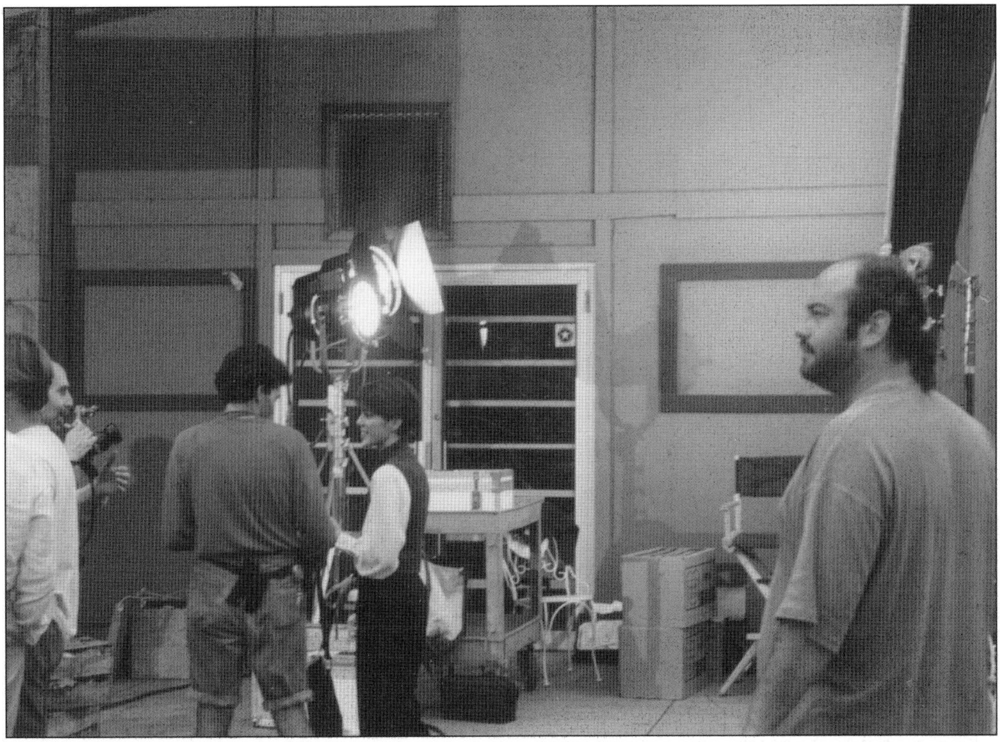

Actress Marisa Tomei has a discussion on the 1993 Pittsburgh set of *Only You*. Most of the scenes filmed in Pittsburgh centered on Tomei. This was the only production she worked on in Pittsburgh, but Robert Downey Jr. returned to the city years later to make *Wonder Boys*.

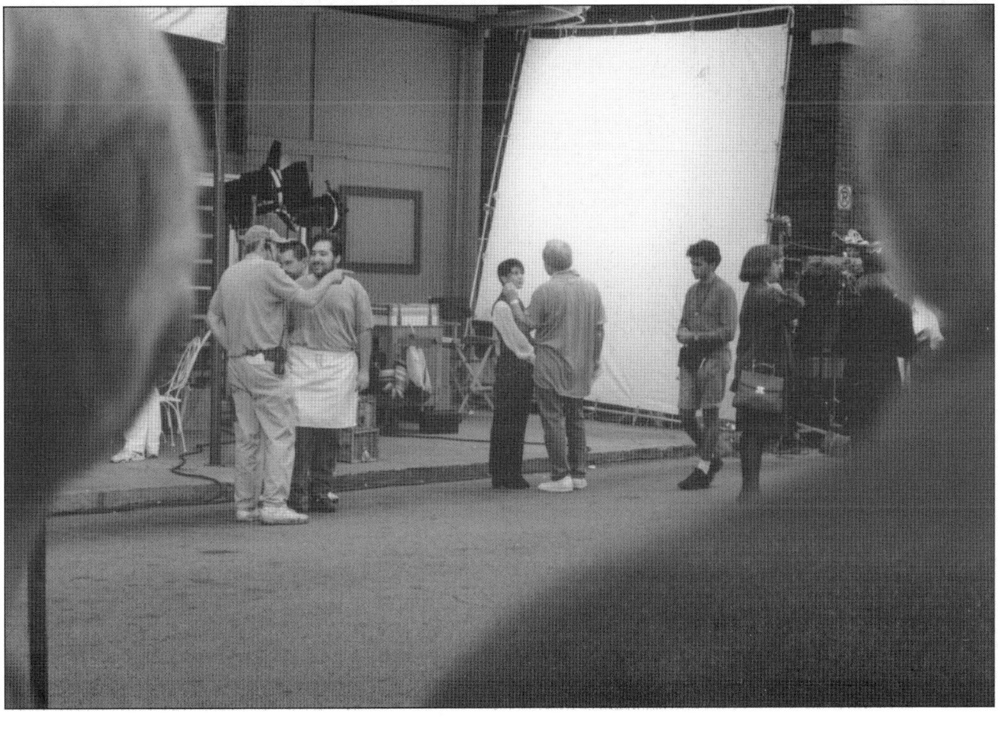

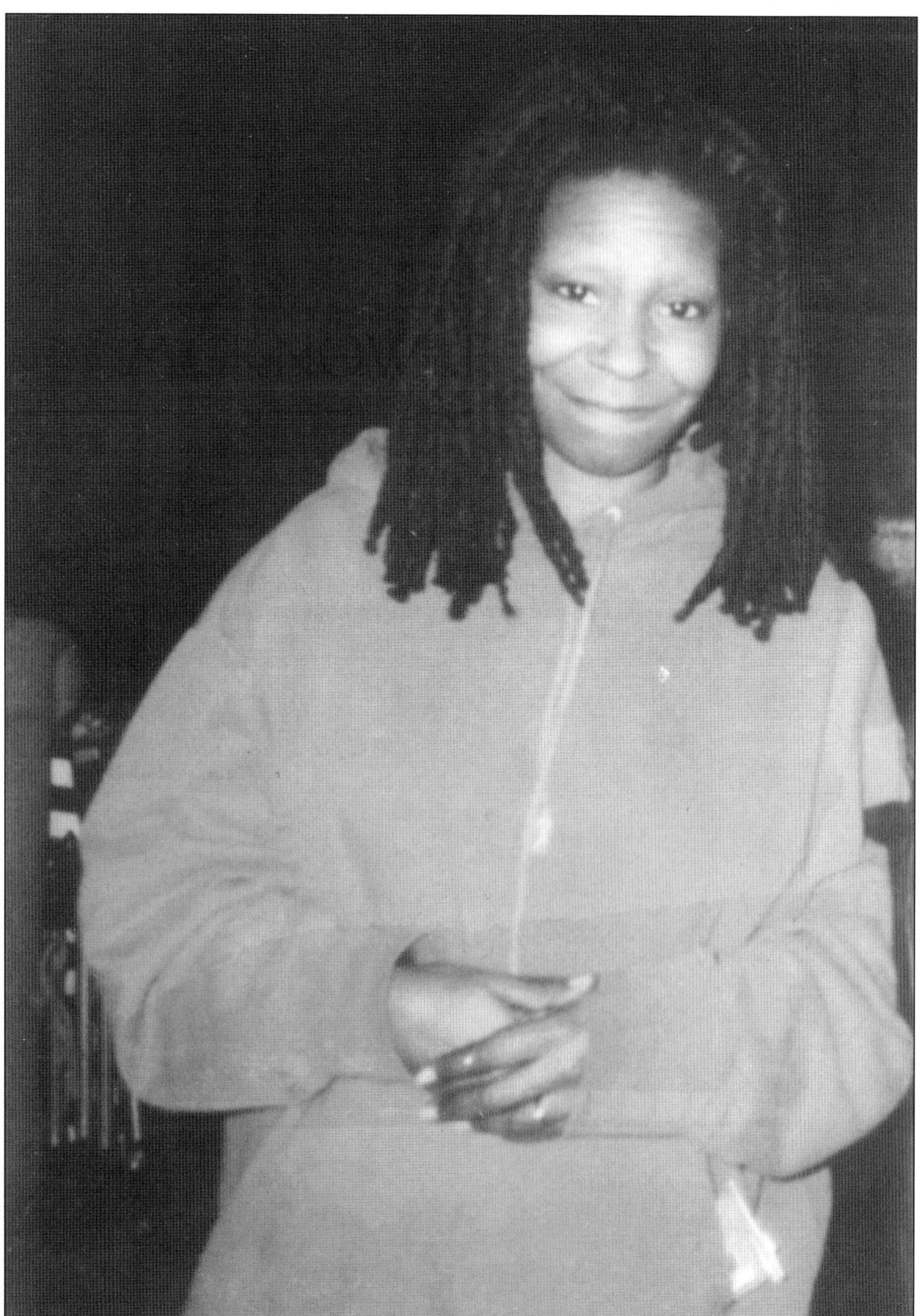

Actress Whoopi Goldberg poses while making the movie *Boys on the Side* in February 1994. Goldberg was only in town for five days, working 8–14 hour days. Many locals didn't get to see her unless they were on set. This is one of the rare photographs of the actress in Pittsburgh. What makes it even more special is that this was the only production Goldberg worked on in Pittsburgh.

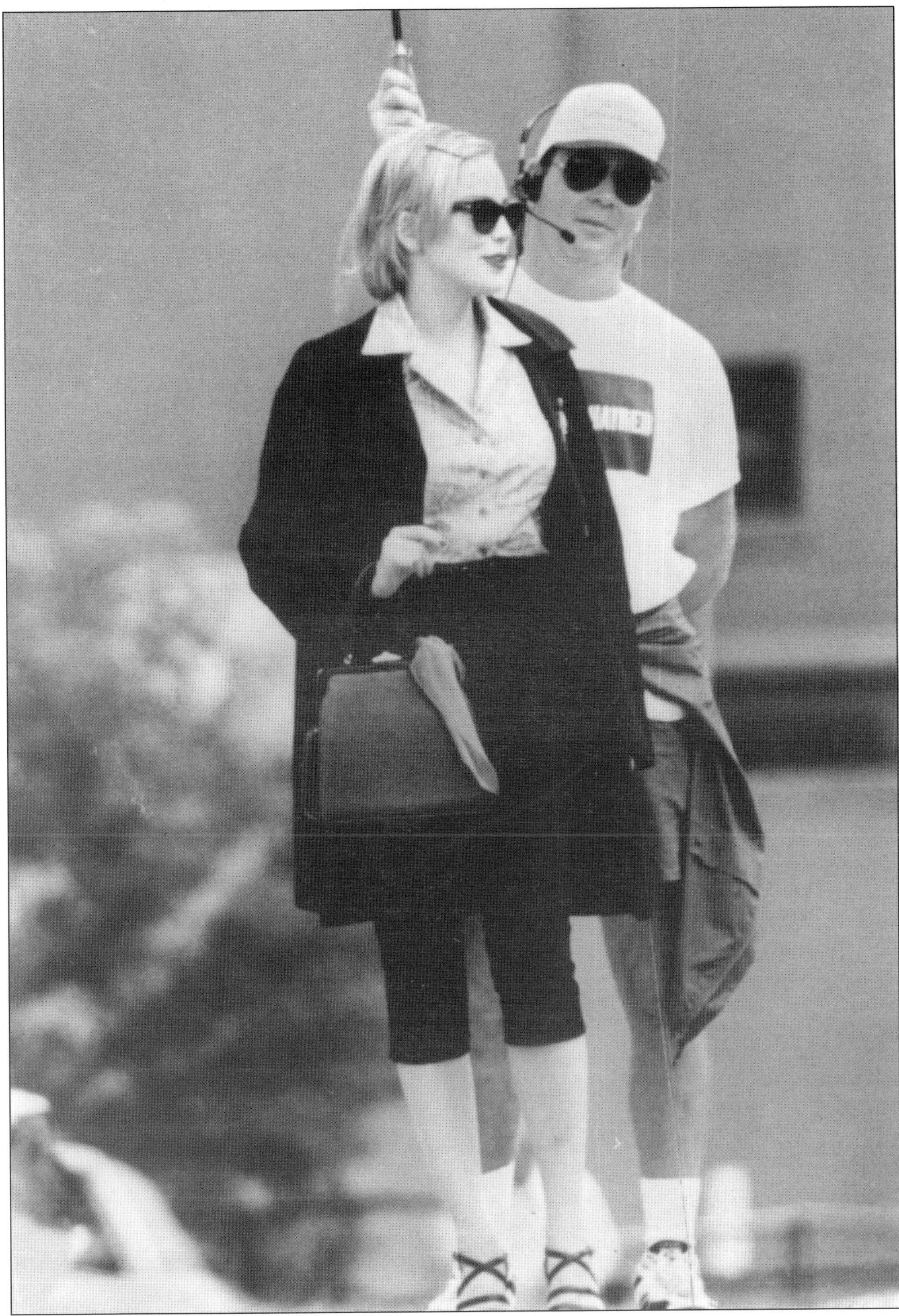
Actress Sharon Stone stands on the set of the 1995 production of *Diabolique* with a crew member. *Diabolique* is the only movie Stone has made in Pittsburgh.

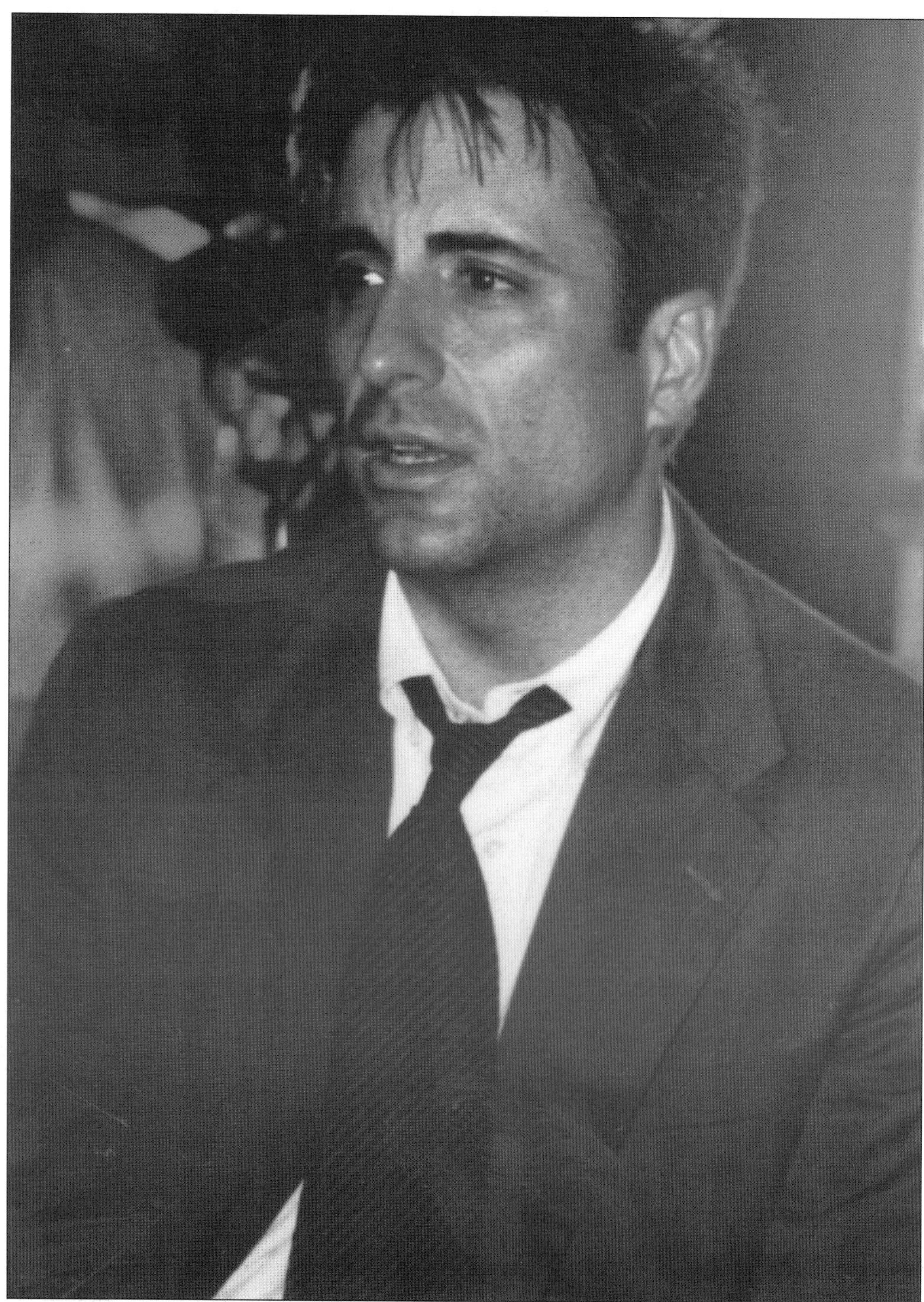

Andy Garcia appears behind the scenes of the 1996 production of *Desperate Measures*. Pittsburgh's very own hometown Hollywood actor Michael Keaton also stars in this movie. During the production in Pittsburgh, Keaton was awarded with a plaque and a day—September 10—named in his honor.

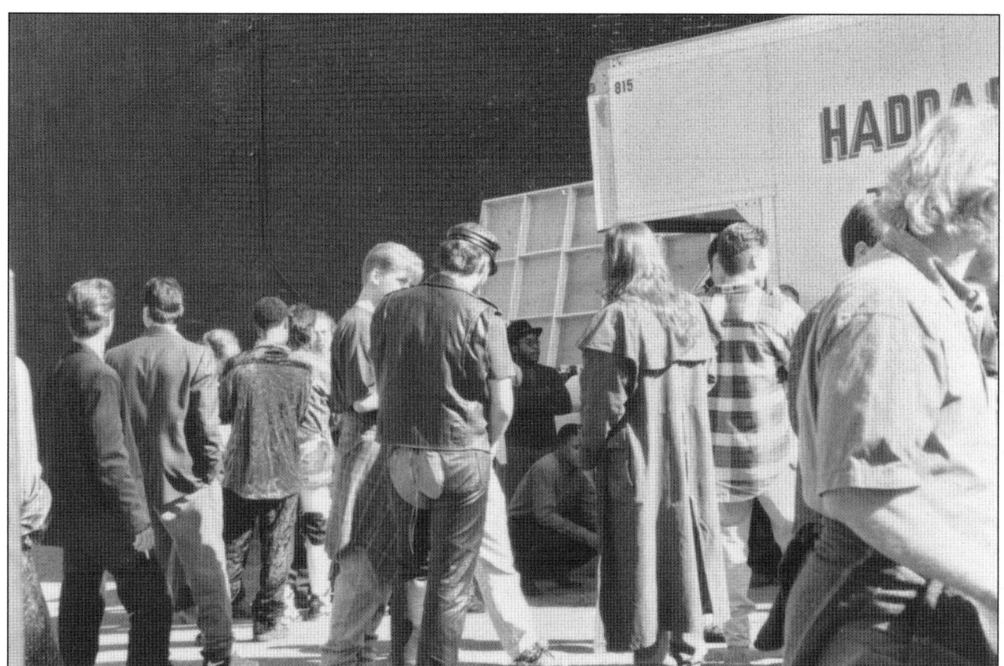

Crew members work on the 1995 *Kingpin* production. *Kingpin* brought actors such as Woody Harrelson and Bill Murray to work in Pittsburgh for the first and only time in their careers.

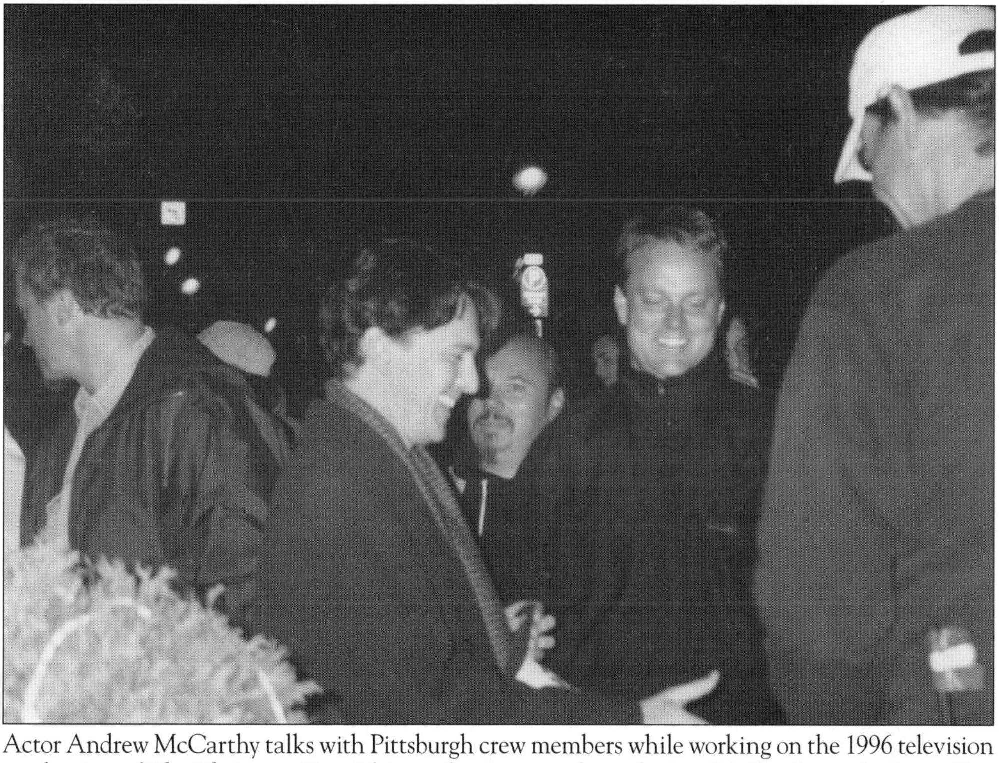

Actor Andrew McCarthy talks with Pittsburgh crew members while working on the 1996 television production of *The Christmas Tree*. This production was the only time McCarthy worked on a film or television show in Pittsburgh.

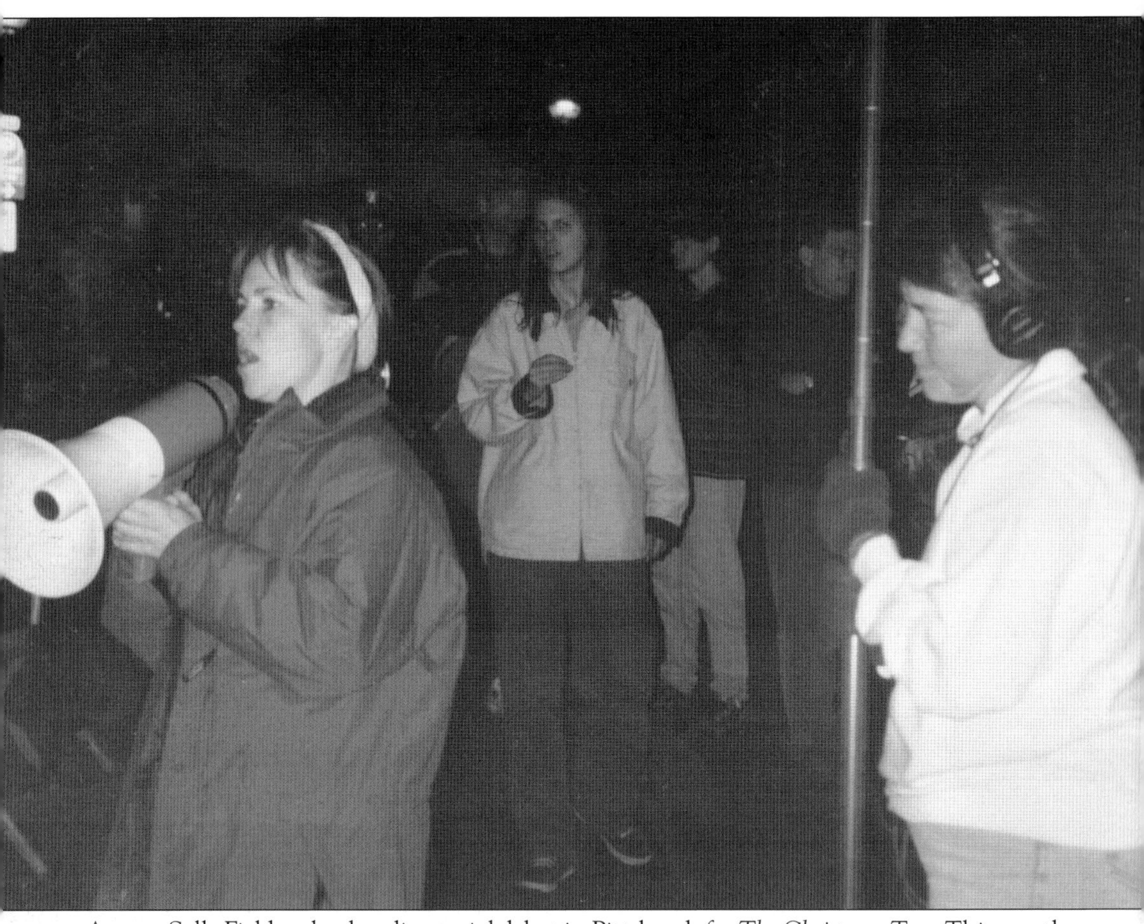

Actress Sally Field makes her directorial debut in Pittsburgh for *The Christmas Tree*. This was the only time Sally Field worked on a movie in Pittsburgh.

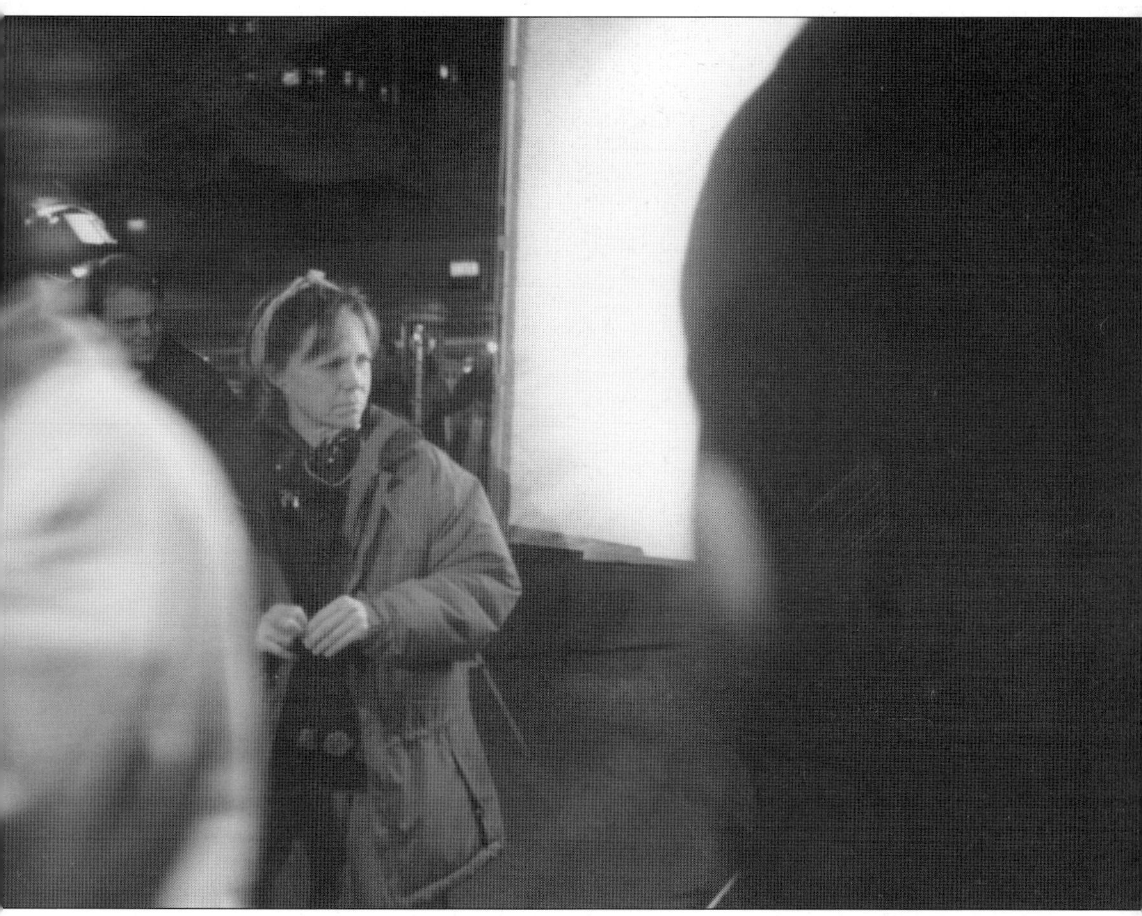

Sally Field works behind the scenes on *The Christmas Tree*, directing her cast and crew. Most of the cast and crew was comprised of local Pittsburghers, such as actresses Suzi Hofrichter and Betty Aberlin of *Mister Rogers' Neighborhood* fame.

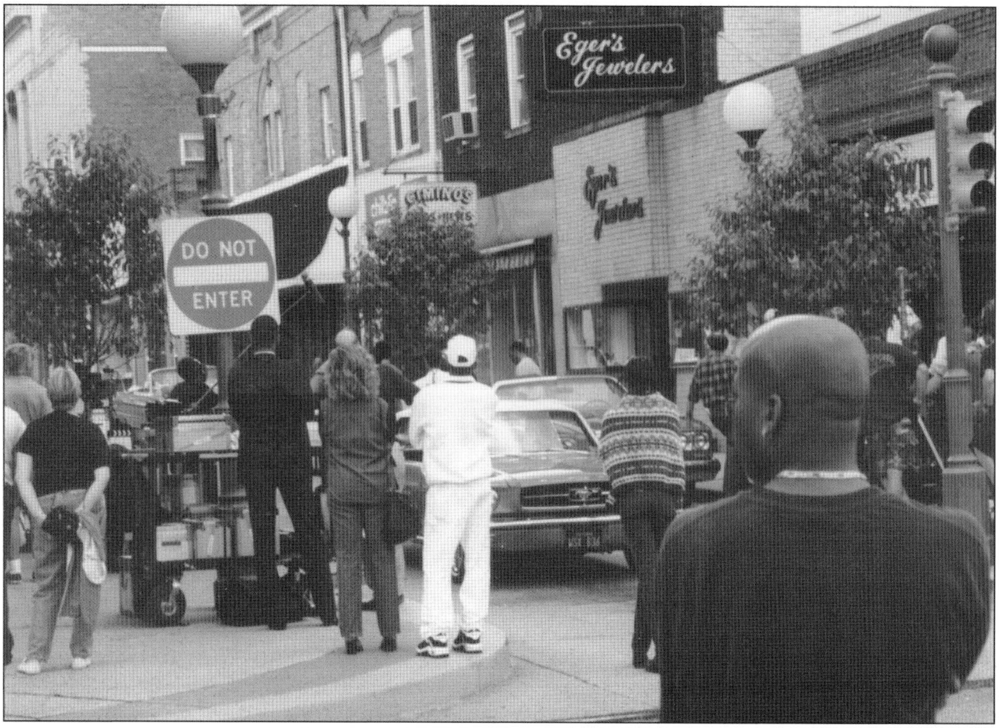

Crew members and extras look toward the set of the 1998 television movie *The Temptations*. Local Pittsburghers usually get excited to see a movie being made in their neighborhood.

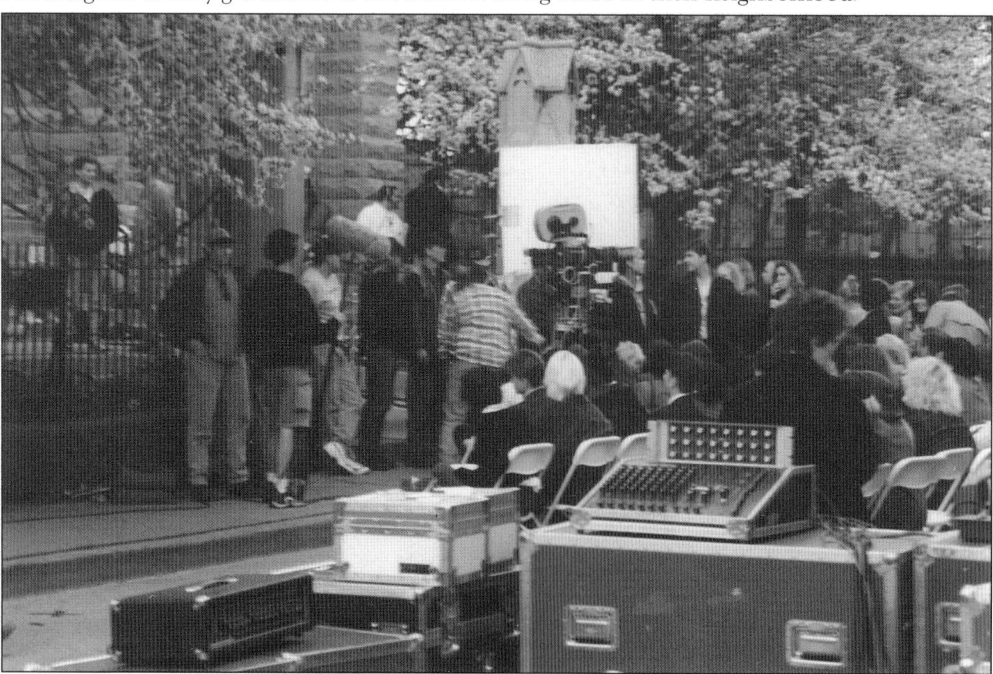

In downtown Pittsburgh, Matt Damon and Ben Affleck are surrounded by the crew of the 1998 film *Dogma*. Damon returned to the Pittsburgh area in the spring of 2012, filming the movie *Promised Land*.

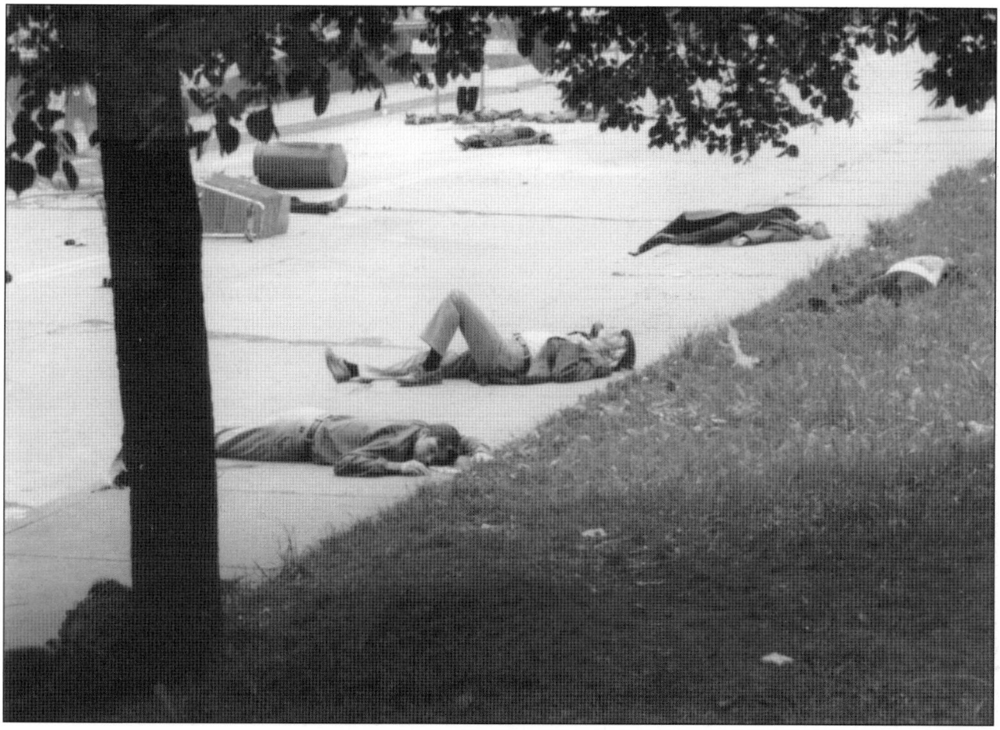

In *Dogma*, Ben Affleck plays Bartleby and Matt Damon plays Loki. When they arrive at a church, Bartleby kills everyone. This photograph shows the Pittsburgh extras pretending to be dead on the street after being killed by Bartleby.

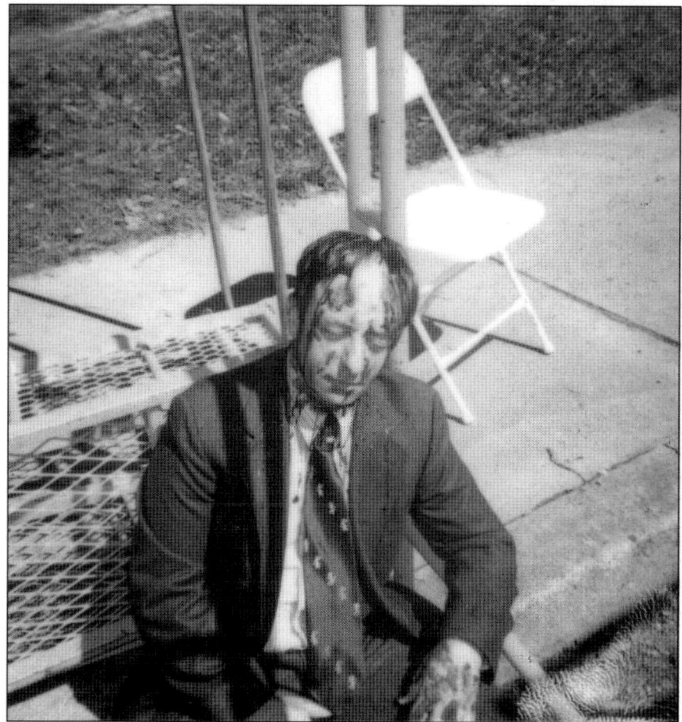

Background actor Phil Nardozzi takes a rest in full makeup on the *Dogma* set. Nardozzi has been involved in over a dozen Pittsburgh movie productions over the past 15 years as an extra and background actor. (Courtesy of Phil Nardozzi.)

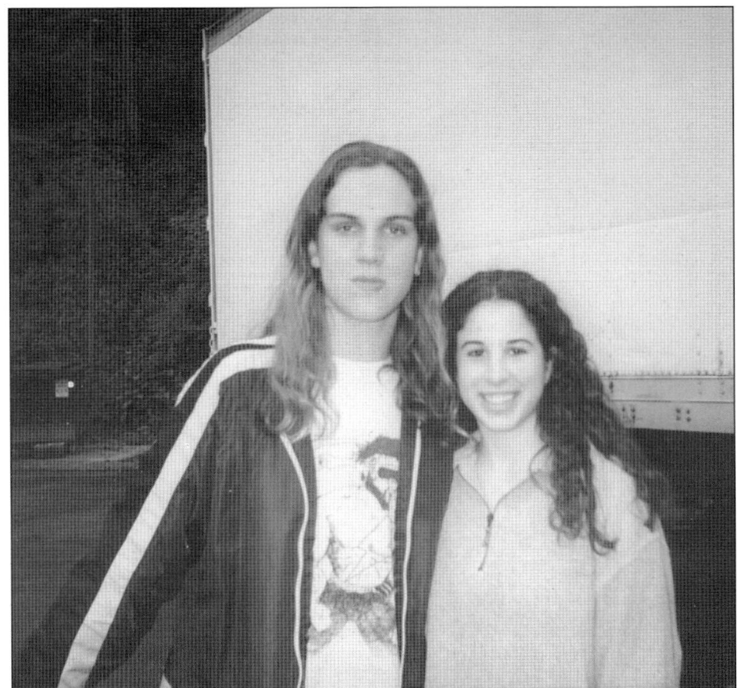

Pittsburgher Vicki Tallon poses with actor Jason Mewes while he was in town making *Dogma*. In *Dogma*, Mewes played the well-known Jay character from the duo Jay and Silent Bob. Mewes returned to Pittsburgh in early 2008 with his friend Kevin Smith to make *Zack and Miri Make a Porno*, playing the character Lester. (Courtesy of Vicki Tallon.)

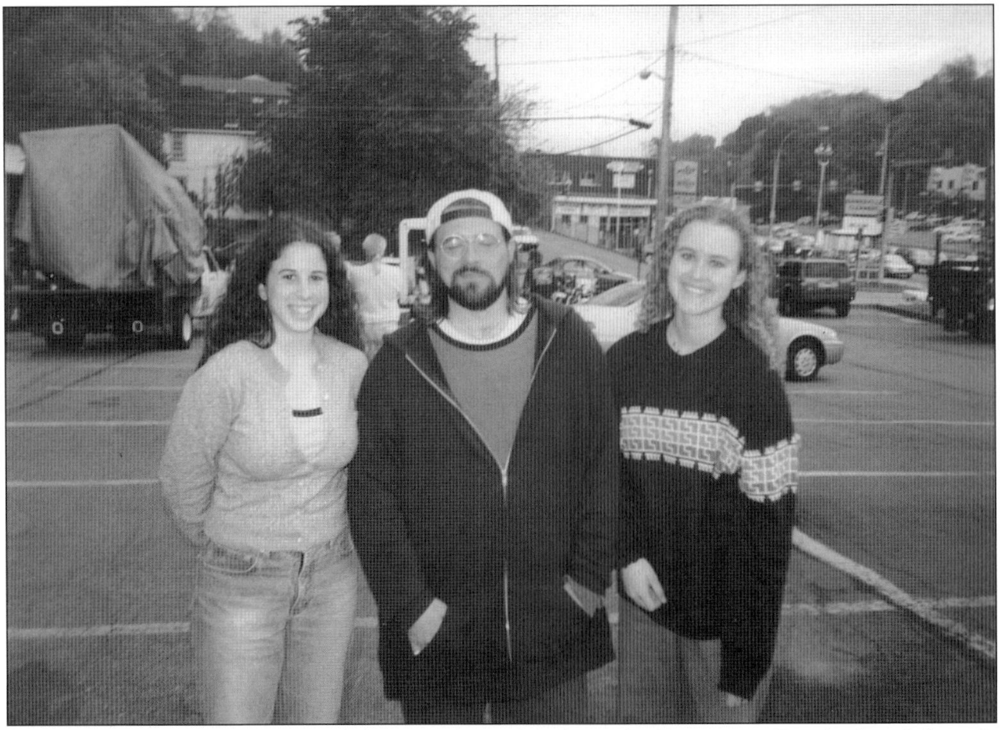

Vicki Tallon poses with actor and director Kevin Smith on the *Dogma* set. Smith played the role of Silent Bob in *Dogma*. He returned to Pittsburgh nearly a decade later to make *Zack and Miri Make a Porno*. Moviemaking aside, Smith has returned to Pittsburgh several times, promoting his work. (Courtesy of Vicki Tallon.)

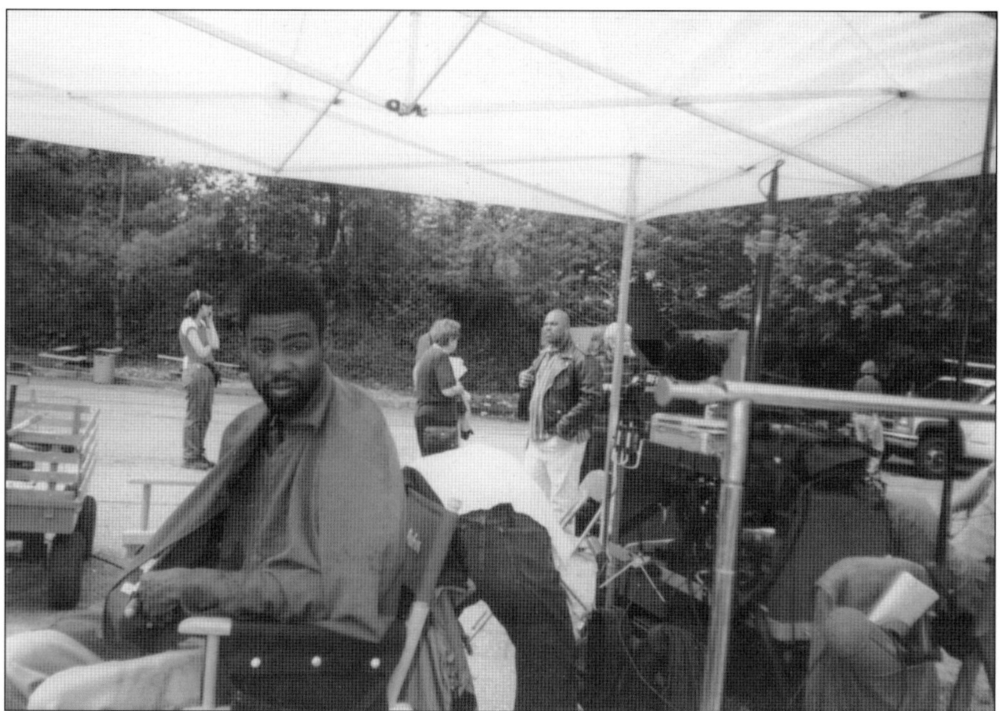

Actor Chris Rock poses behind the scenes of *Dogma*. This was the only time Rock worked on a movie in Pittsburgh. (Courtesy of Vicki Tallon.)

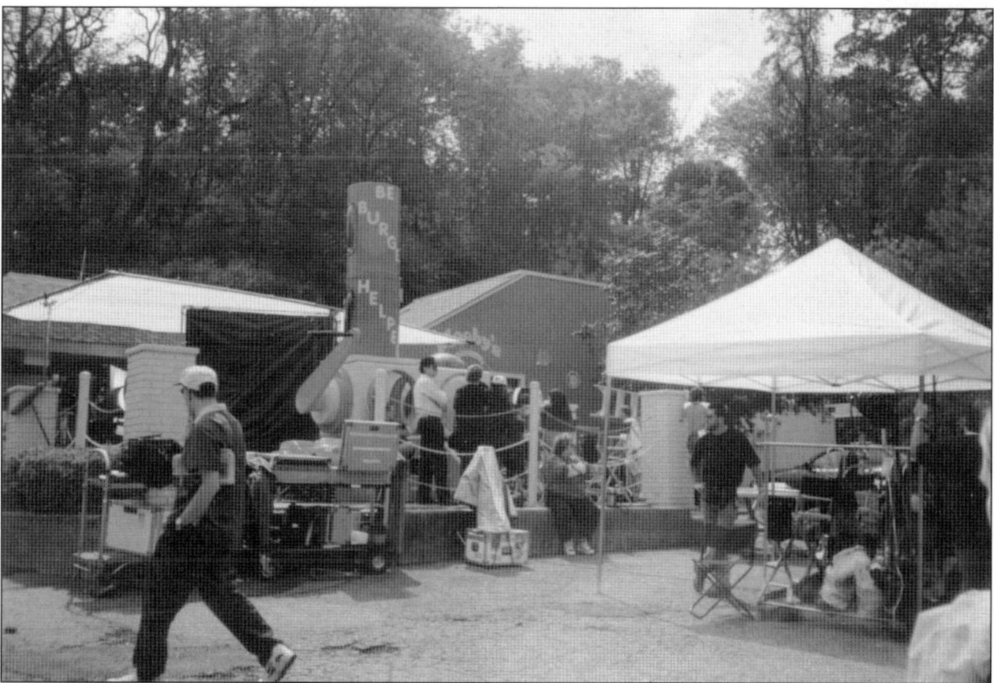

The crew of *Dogma* works behind he scenes. This was the constructed set of Mooby's restaurant, which was formerly a Burger King located on Banksville Road just south of Pittsburgh. (Courtesy of Vicki Tallon.)

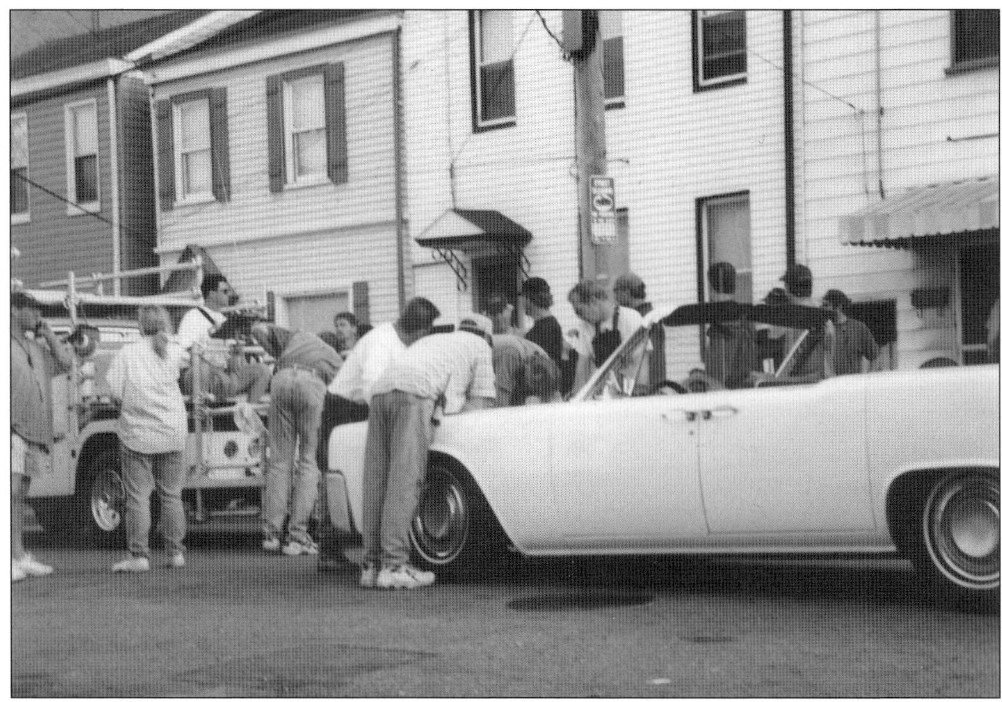

Local crew members work on a special prop car behind the scenes of the 1998 *Inspector Gadget* production. The production only spent a few weeks in Pittsburgh.

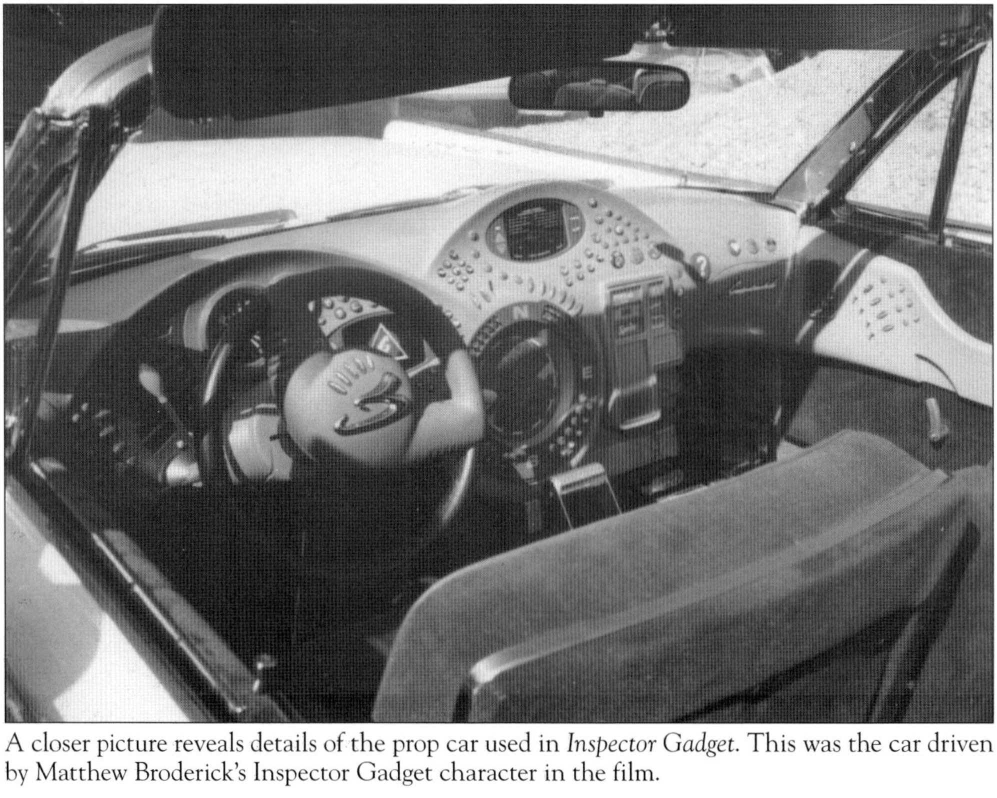

A closer picture reveals details of the prop car used in *Inspector Gadget*. This was the car driven by Matthew Broderick's Inspector Gadget character in the film.

This van was equipped with special modifications to film *Inspector Gadget*. Film crews often have to improvise on the set, using their creativity and ingenuity in order to film a specific shot.

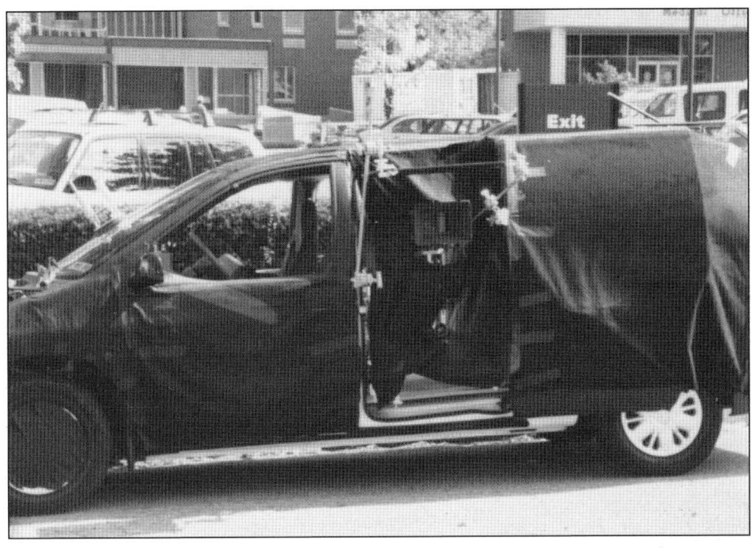

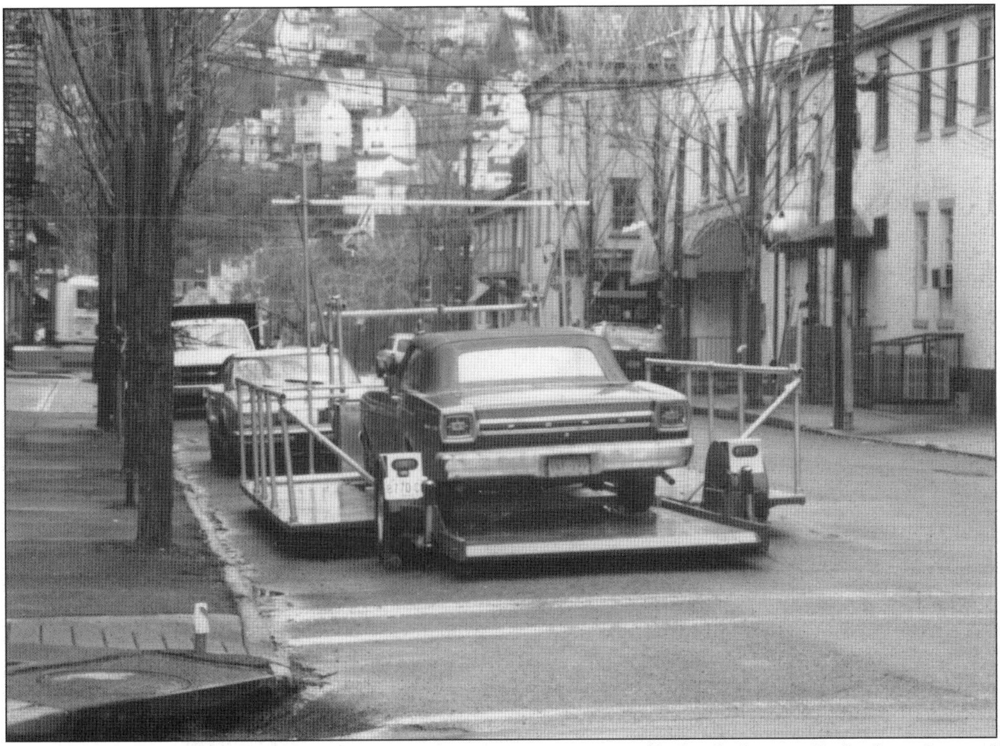

When car rides are filmed for movies, the vehicles are typically loaded on a flatbed trailer and pulled while the film crew is set up on the rest of the trailer around the vehicle. This car was used in the 1999 *Wonder Boys* production in Pittsburgh.

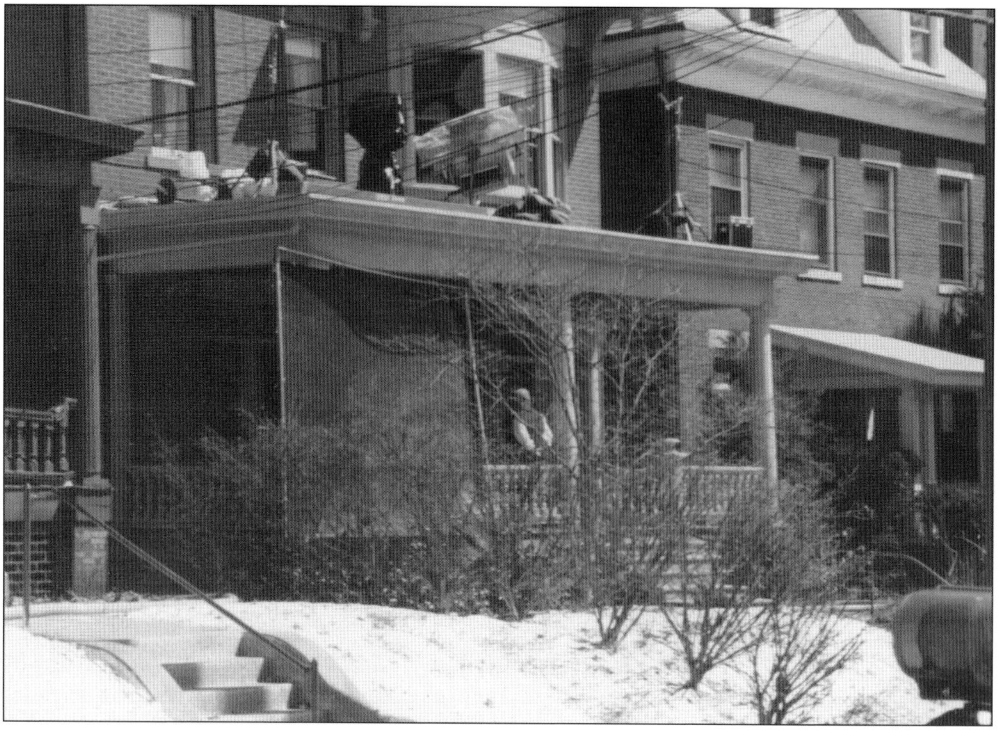

Production equipment rests on the roof and around a house that serves as a set for *Wonder Boys*. Typically, productions use a private residence for several days. The family or occupants of the home are usually relocated to a local hotel and are allowed to return to the house to get their belongings. Their hotel stay is paid for by the production company, and they are even provided monetary compensation. The terms of the contract are between the homeowner and the studio.

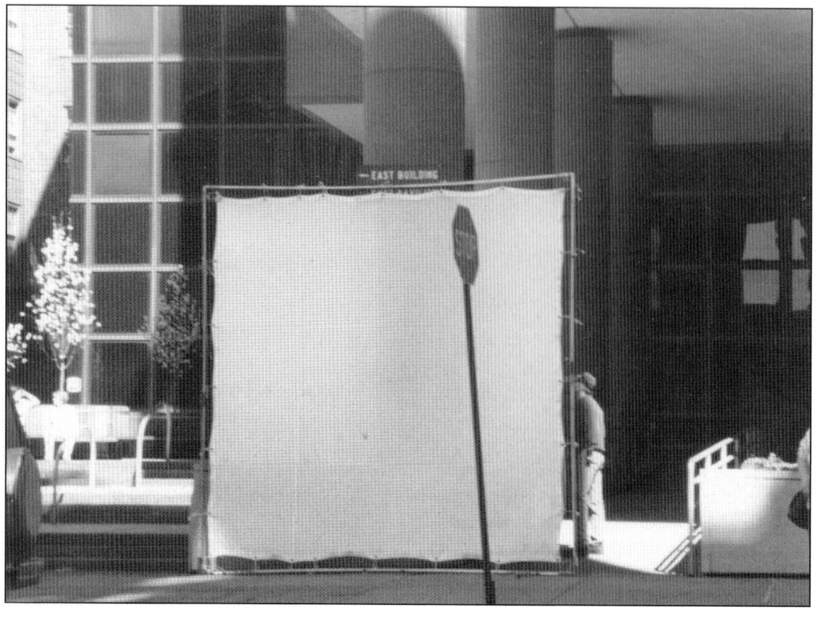

Light screens are typically seen on movie sets, with a primary function to help diffuse or reflect light. This light screen is being used for the movie *Wonder Boys*.

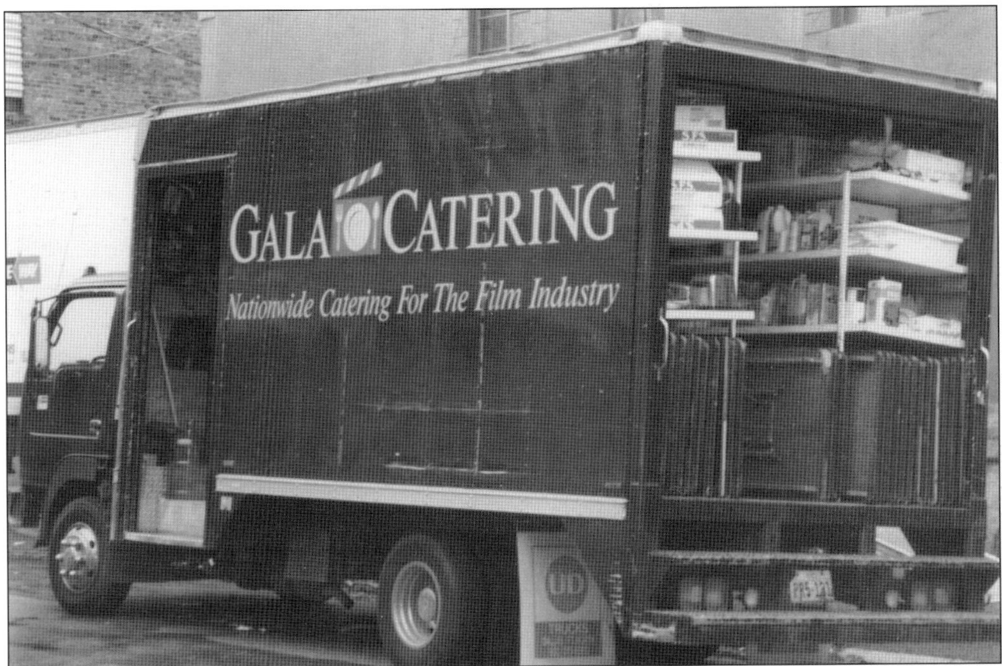

This catering truck was used for the *Wonder Boys* production. Catering for location filmmaking comes from a variety of different companies and local businesses.

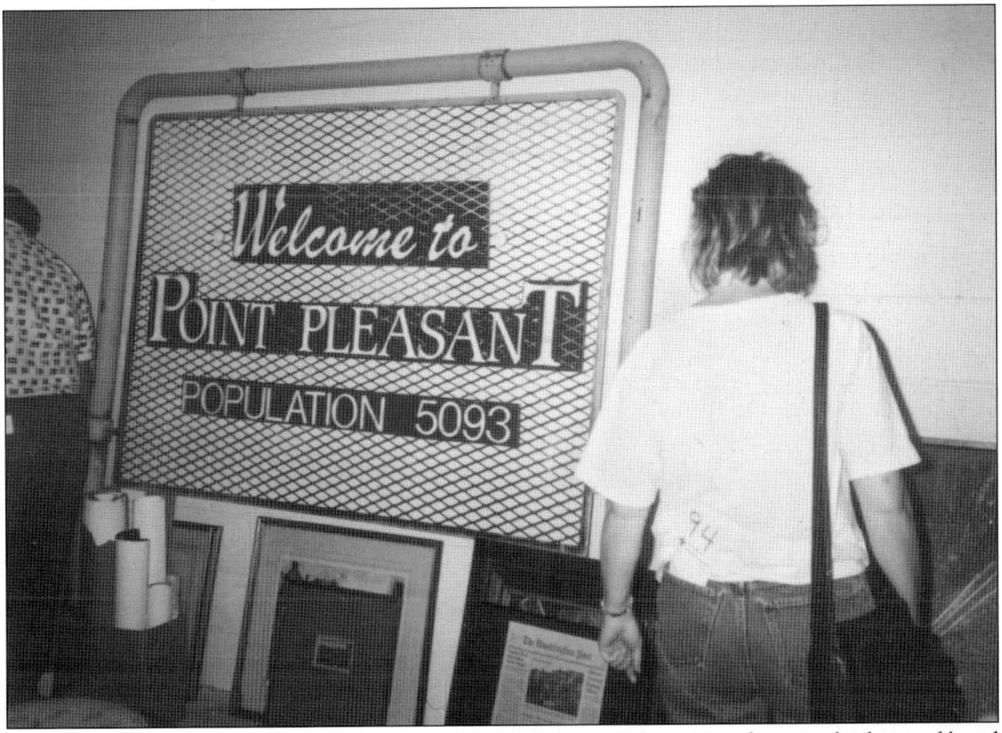

Props rest against a wall for the 2001 production of *The Mothman Prophecies*, which was filmed in and around Pittsburgh. The Point Pleasant scenes were filmed primarily in Kittanning, Pennsylvania, with a few miscellaneous shots filmed elsewhere.

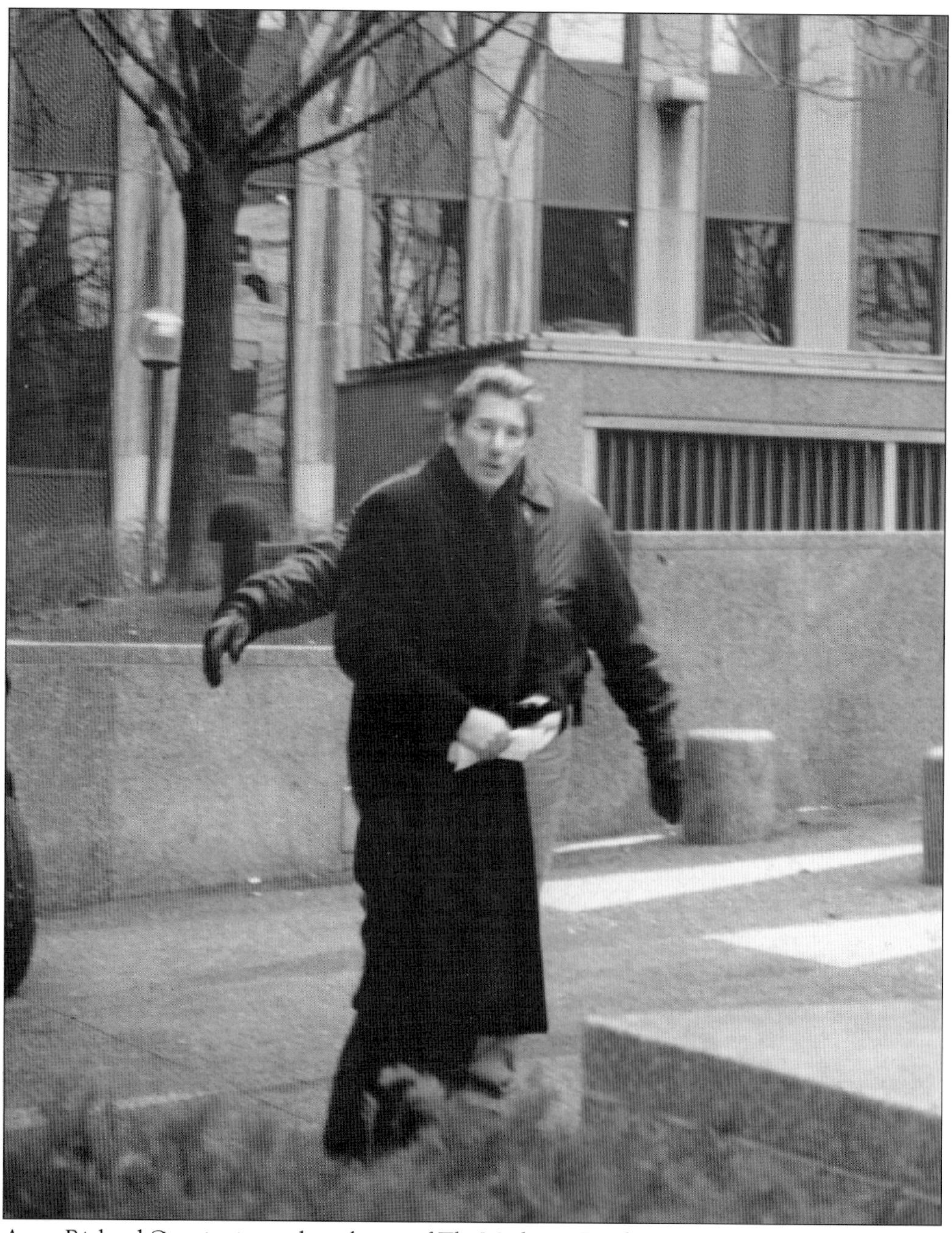

Actor Richard Gere is pictured on the set of *The Mothman Prophecies*. Currently, this is the only production Gere has worked on in Pittsburgh.

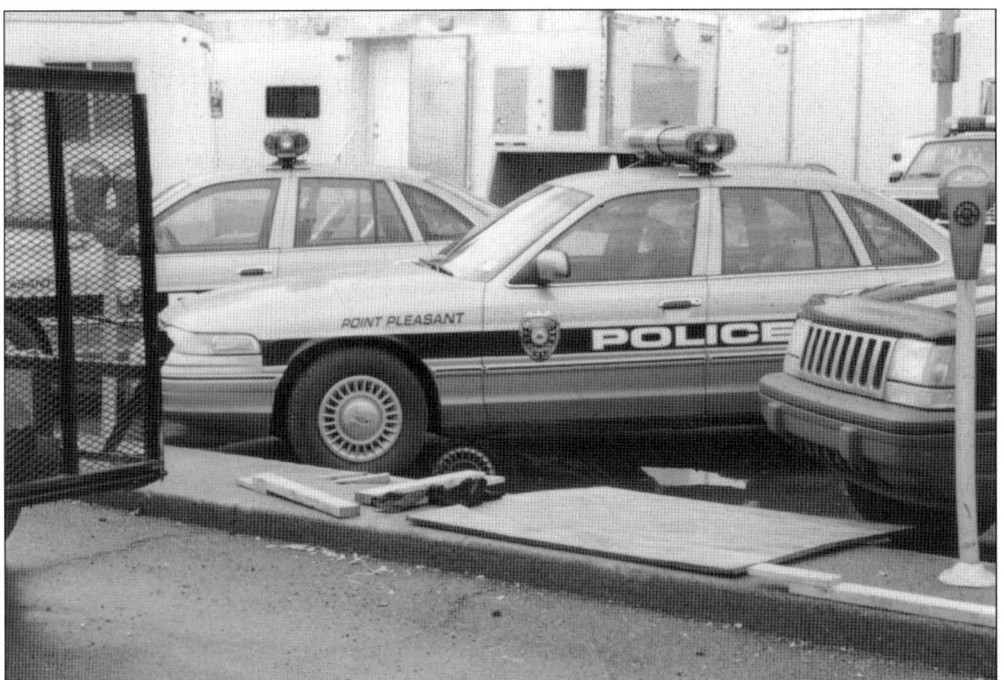

A Point Pleasant prop police car is parked near the production of *The Mothman Prophecies*. These police cars were primarily used in Kittanning, Pennsylvania.

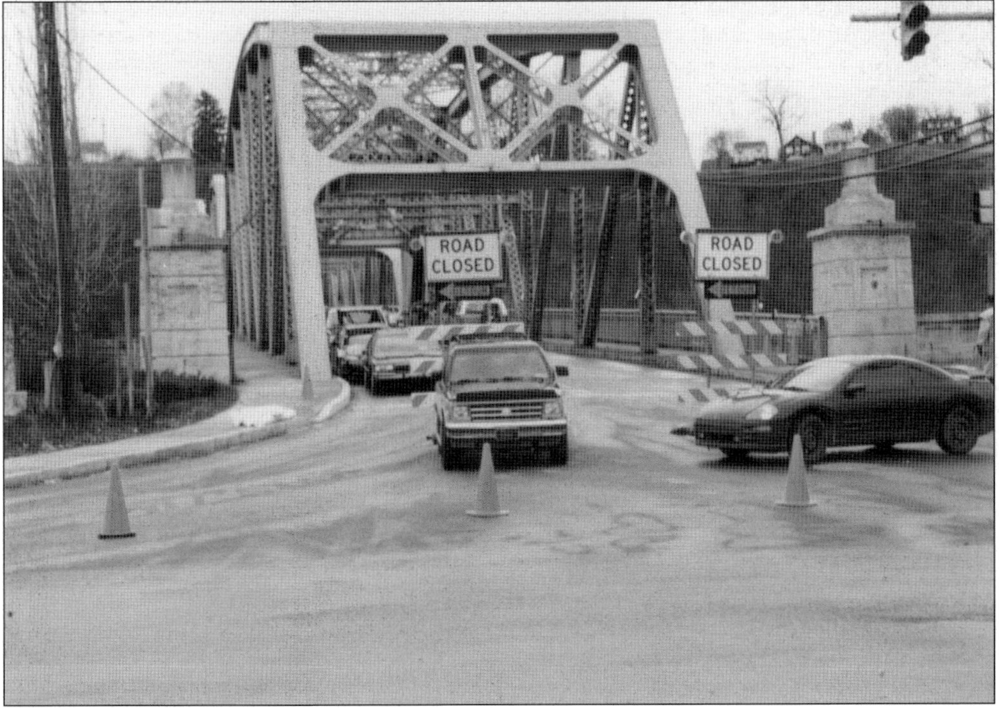

The Kittanning Bridge was used for the big finale of *The Mothman Prophecies*. The bridge is closed and crowded with prop cars as the production waits to film the scene at night. Traffic was rerouted for a few days while the film production used the bridge.

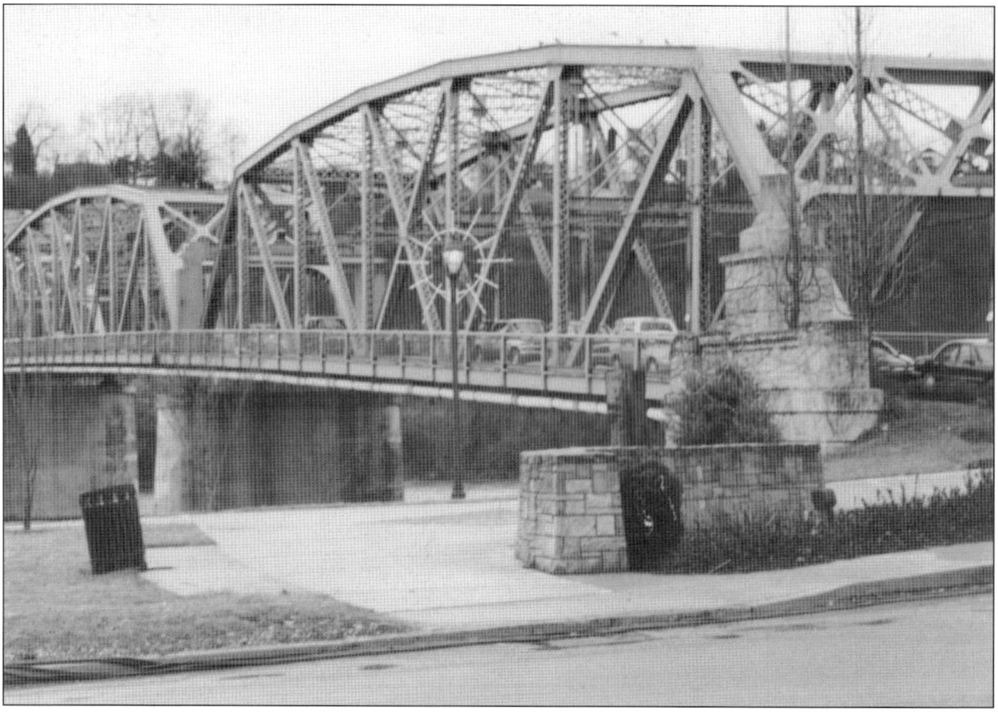

Another angle of the closed Kittanning Bridge reveals more prop cars used for *The Mothman Prophecies*. Sometimes, the vehicles being used in movies are recruited through a casting agency.

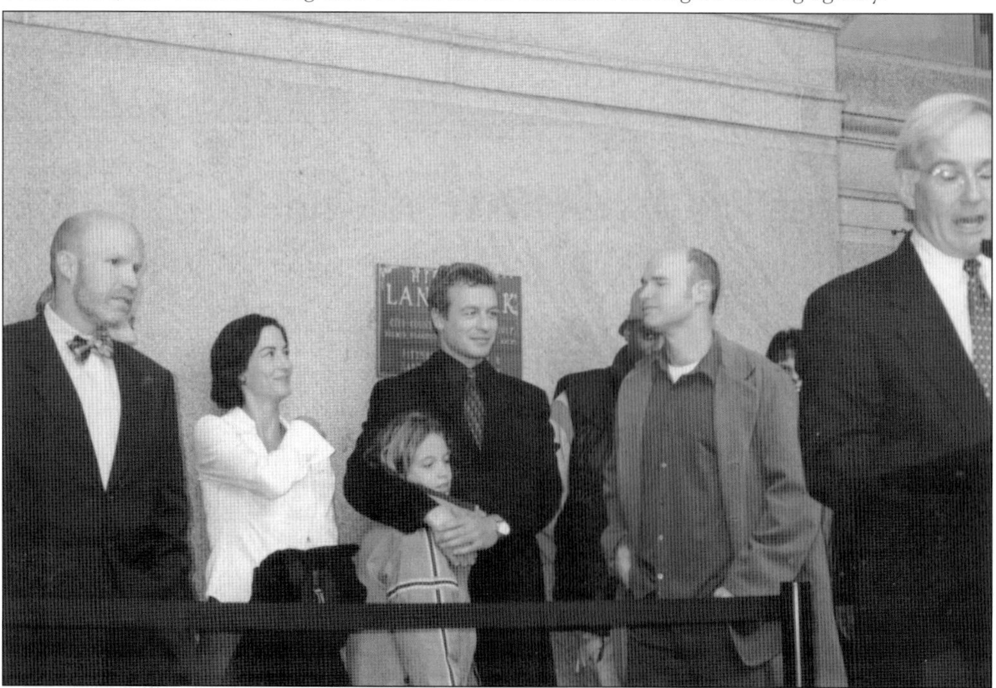

Simon Baker and his daughter appear at a press conference for *The Guardian* on October 7, 2002. Despite the publicity, the production didn't film much in Pittsburgh, opting for other locations instead.

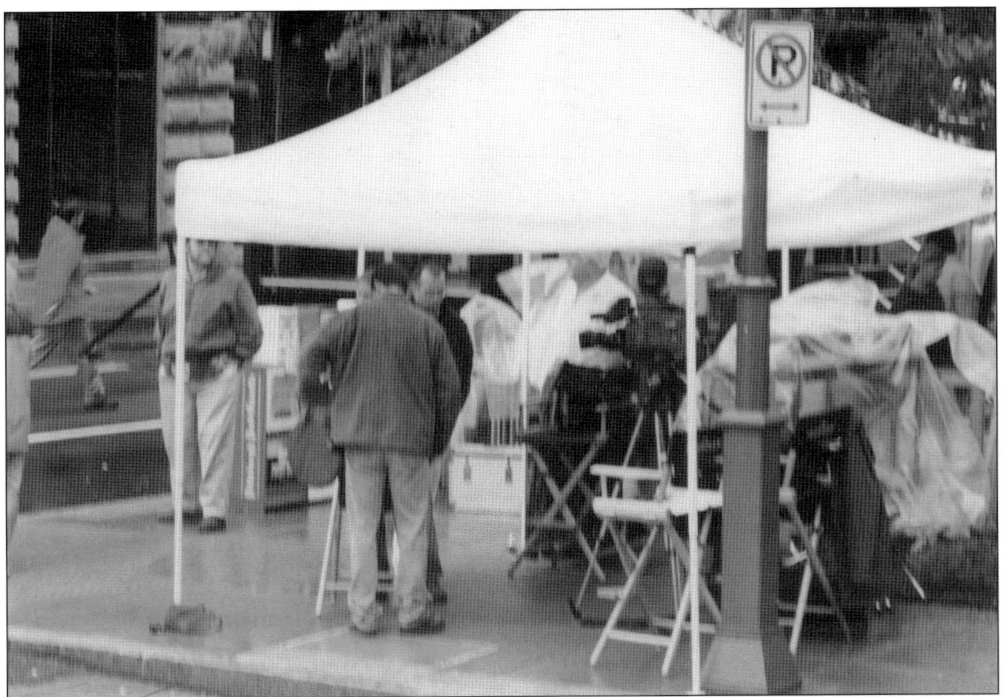

The Guardian production crew works in Pittsburgh. Given the short amount of time the production spent filming in the city, behind-the-scene photographs in Pittsburgh are rare for *The Guardian*.

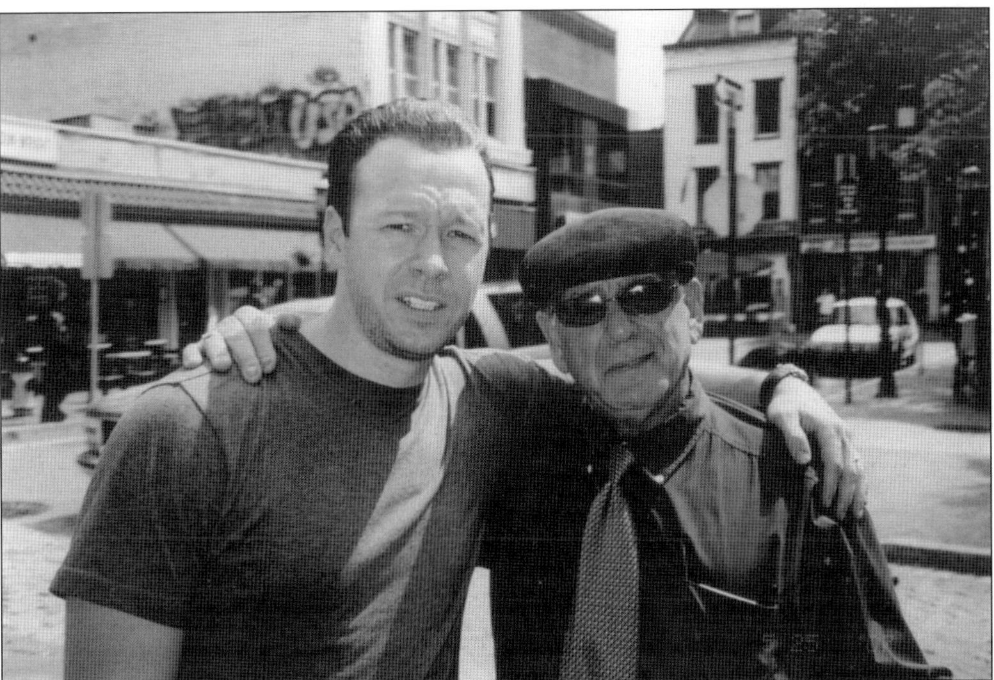

Actor Donnie Wahlberg and Pittsburgh background actor Tony Amen pose on the set of *The Kill Point* in 2007. The show aired as a miniseries on Spike TV and, despite good ratings, was cancelled.

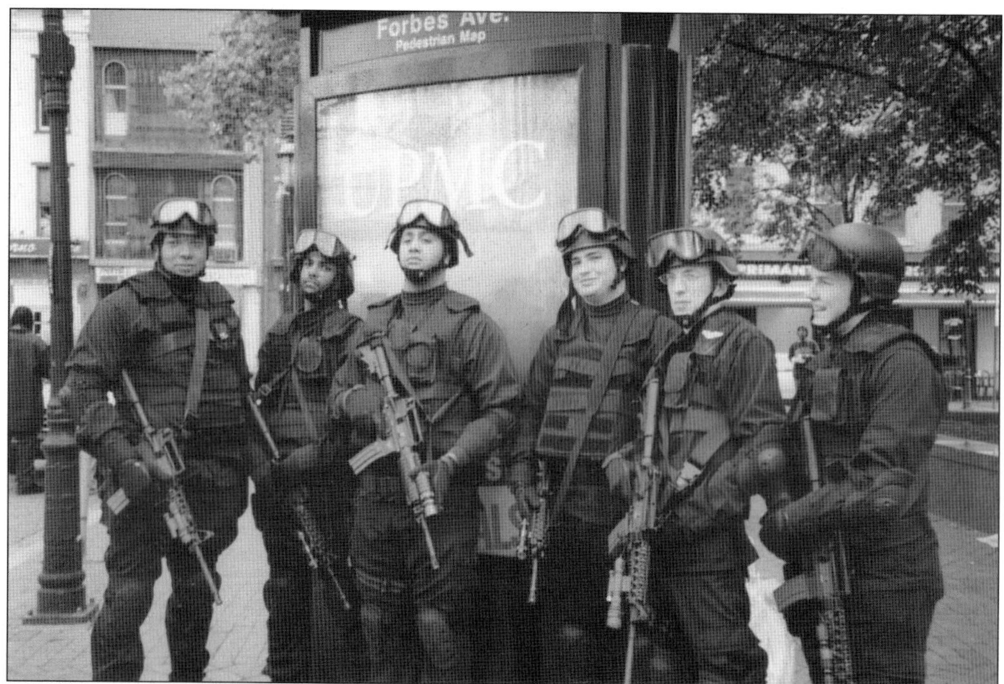

Local background actors pose in uniform while making *The Kill Point*. Extras such as these usually have to go through wardrobe fitting and a visit to the props department to collect—in this case—guns, radios, and other appropriate equipment.

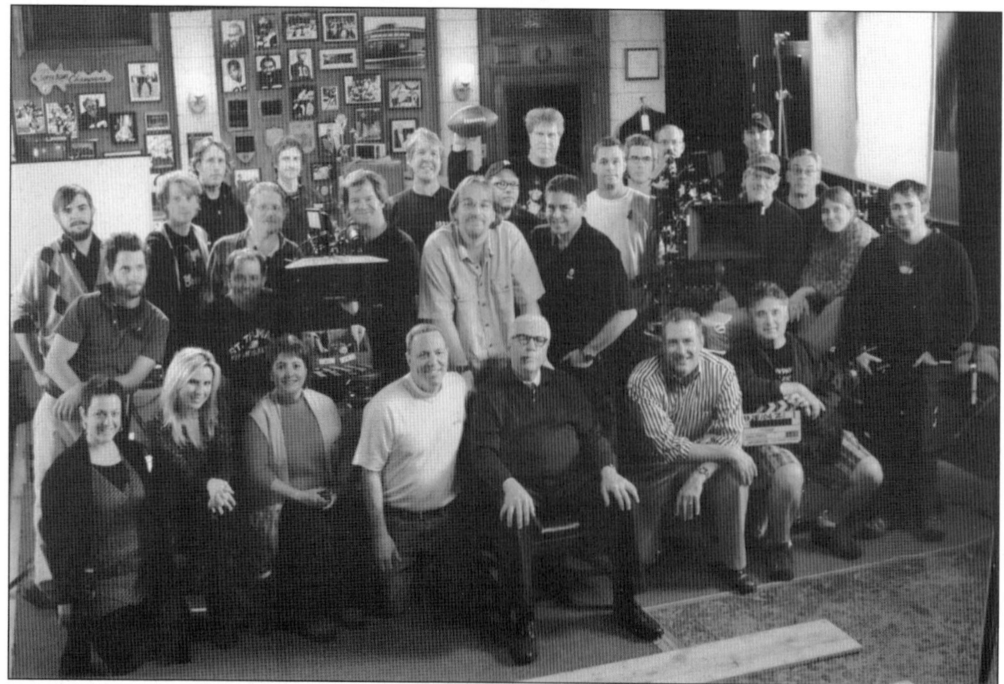

The cast and crew pose on the set of *The Chief* in November 2009. This film is based on the monologue play *The Chief* and is being sold through home video. The image includes director Steve Parys and veteran actor Tom Atkins. (Courtesy of Steve Parys.)

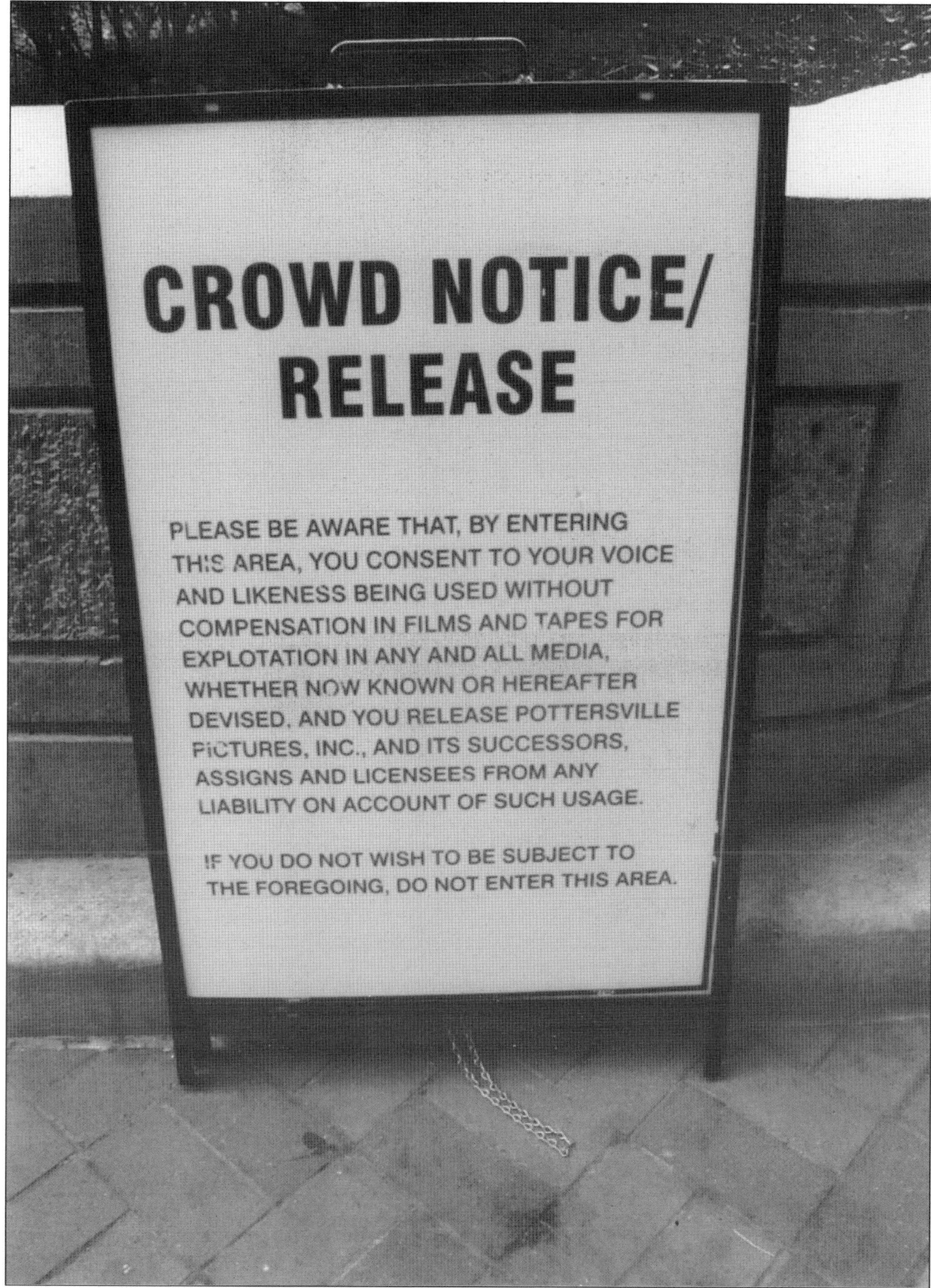

This crowd sign was positioned near the set of *Love and Other Drugs* in 2009. Signs such as these can usually be seen around areas of public filming. There have been instances where personnel have substituted for signs. (Courtesy of Denise Merriman.)

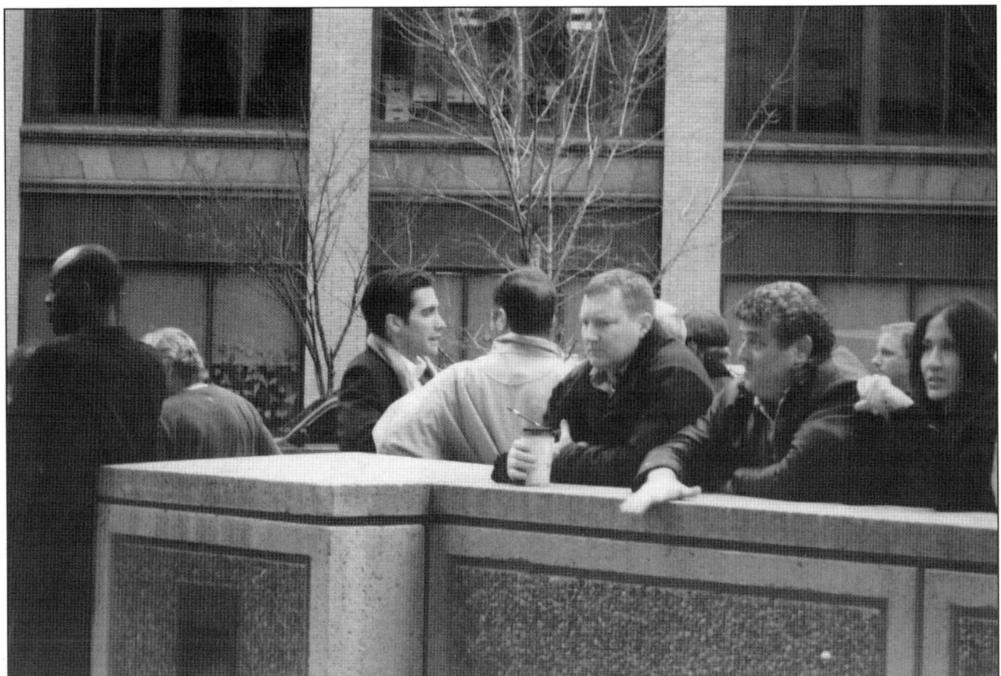

Jake Gyllenhaal (center left) and members of the crew stand around between takes on *Love and Other Drugs* in Pittsburgh. Gyllenhaal enjoyed his time in Pittsburgh and even got a Pittsburgh Steelers tattoo, which he revealed to the world on Jimmy Kimmel. (Courtesy of Denise Merriman.)

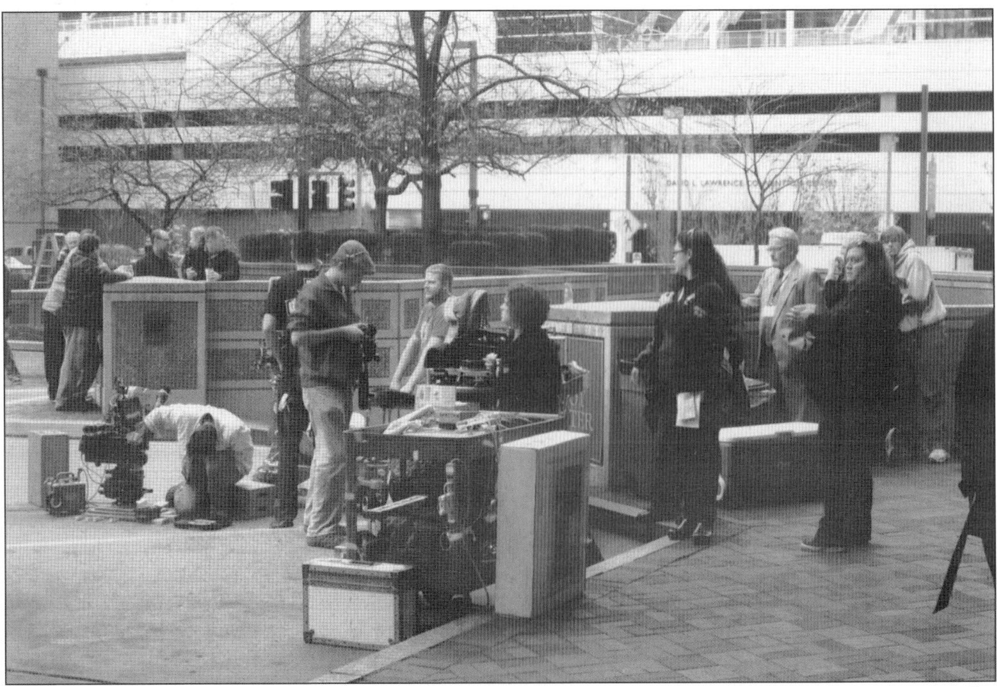

Crew members work on *Love and Other Drugs* outside the Westin Convention Center near the intersection of Penn Avenue and 10th Street in downtown Pittsburgh. The David L. Lawrence Convention Center can be seen in the background. (Courtesy of Denise Merriman.)

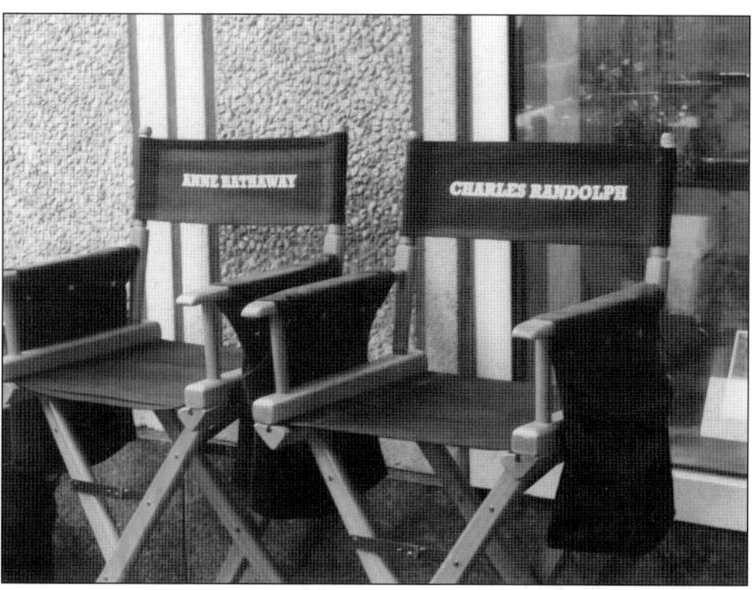

Seen here are the actor chairs for Anne Hathaway and Charles Randolph on the set of *Love and Other Drugs*. Hathaway returned to Pittsburgh soon after *Love and Other Drugs* when she played Catwoman in *The Dark Knight Rises*. (Courtesy of Denise Merriman.)

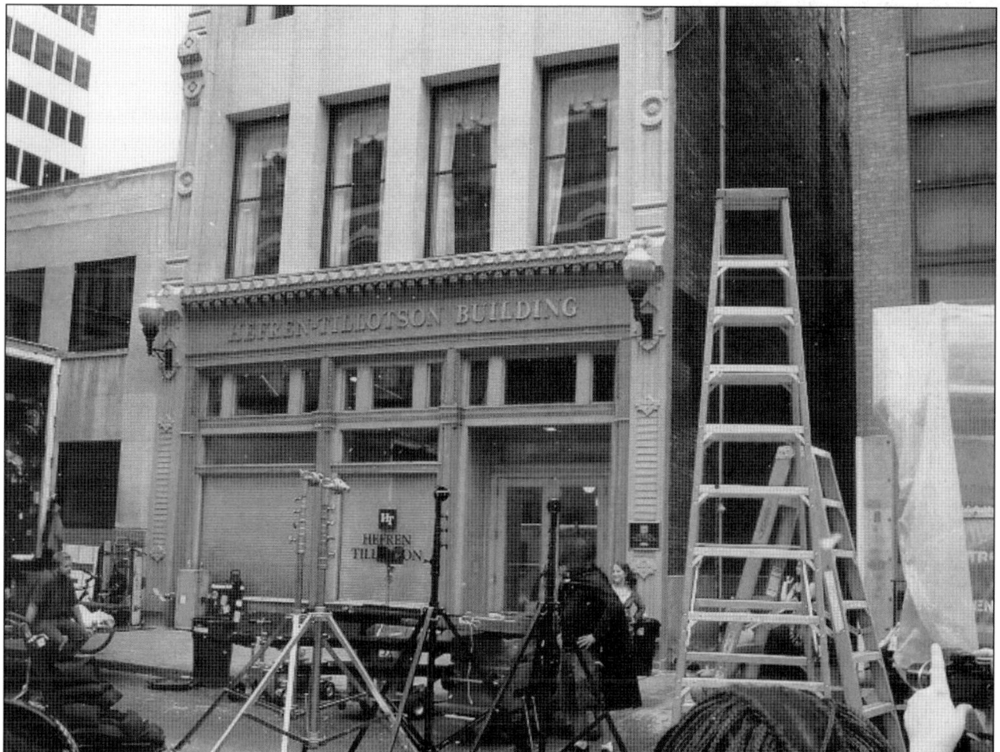

A few members of *The Dark Knight Rises* crew, as well as some of the production equipment, are pictured here. Production materials for location film and television productions sometimes come from local businesses. These local businesses may provide paint, lumber, and other necessary materials. (Courtesy of Bochy Fu.)

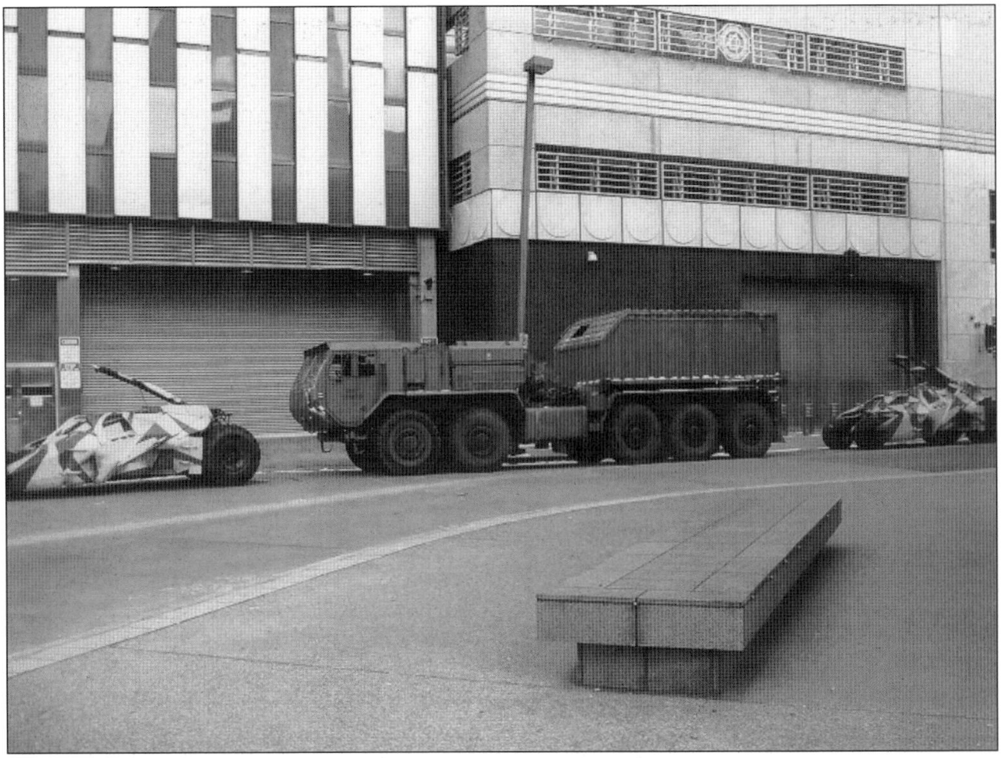

The Tumbler prop cars and a prop truck for *The Dark Knight Rises* are parked on the side of the street in 2011. These vehicles were prominently featured in the last half of the film, with the truck housing an atomic bomb and the Tumblers protecting the truck. (Courtesy of Bochy Fu.)

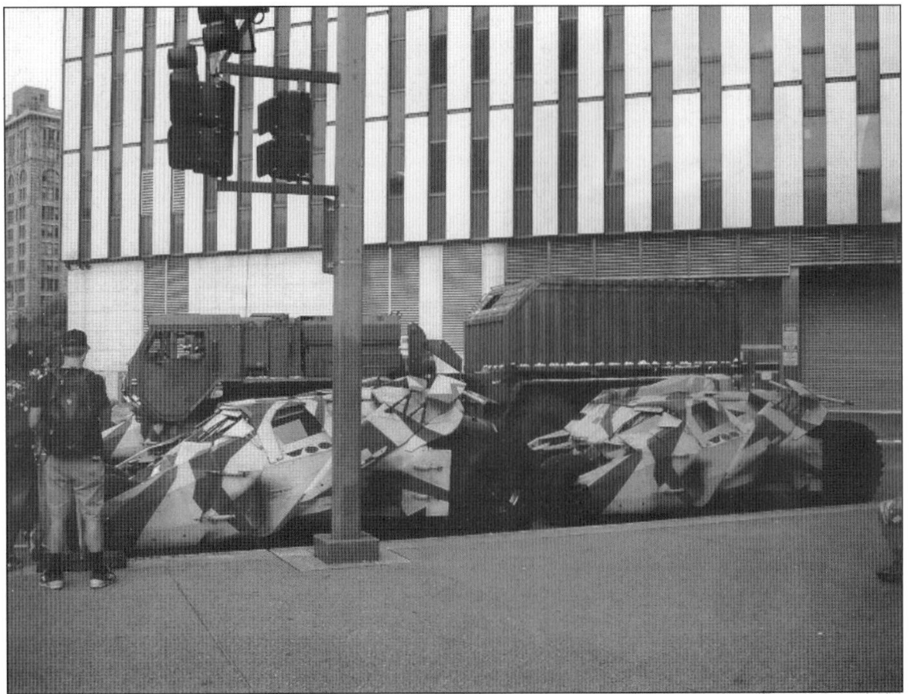

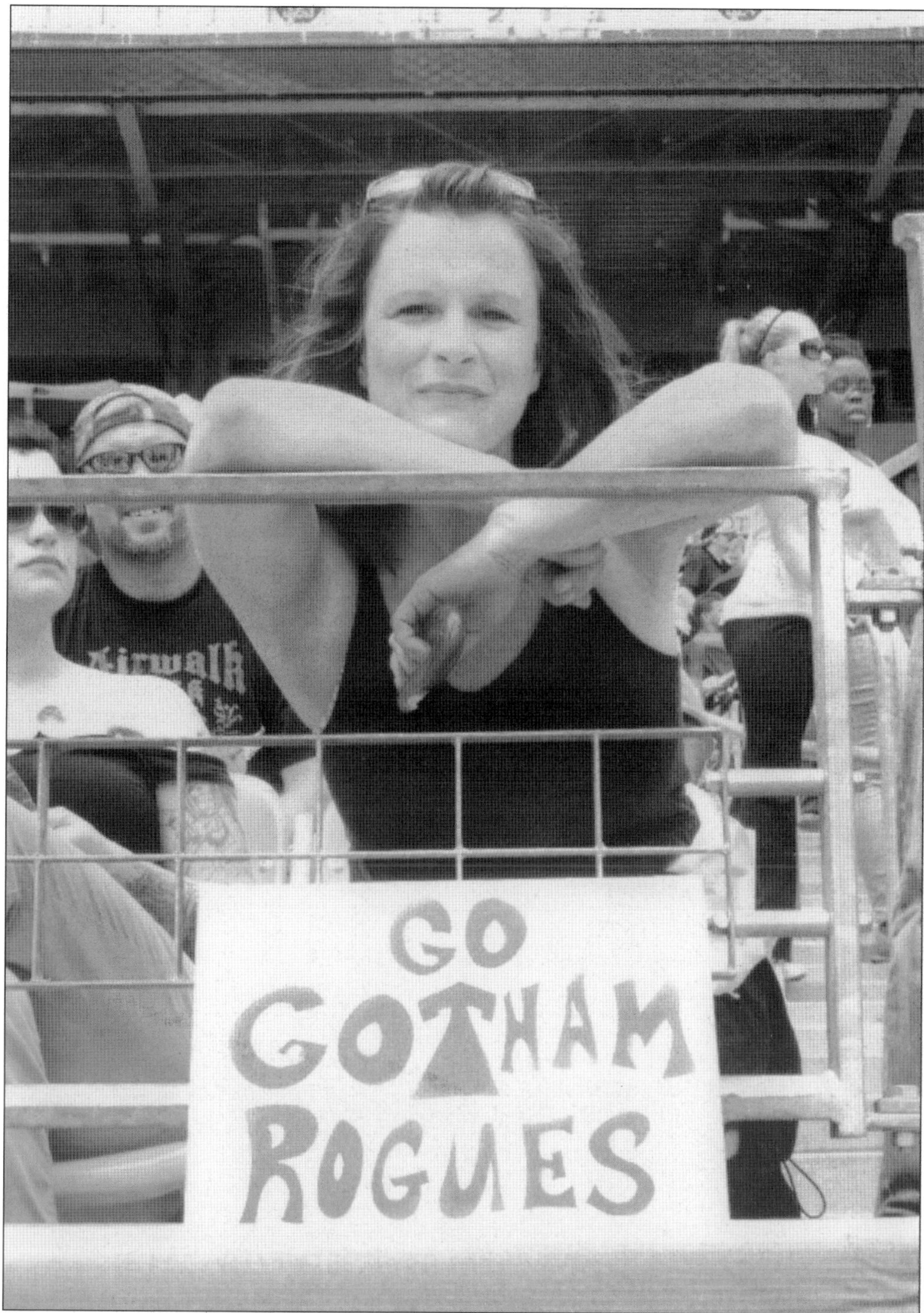

Coleen Angel poses for a camera phone picture at Heinz Field in August 2011 for *The Dark Knight Rises*. Angel, like thousands of other Pittsburghers, was an extra playing the part of a Gotham Rogues fan. In the film, the Gotham Rogues was the name of the Gotham City football team. (Courtesy of Coleen Angel.)

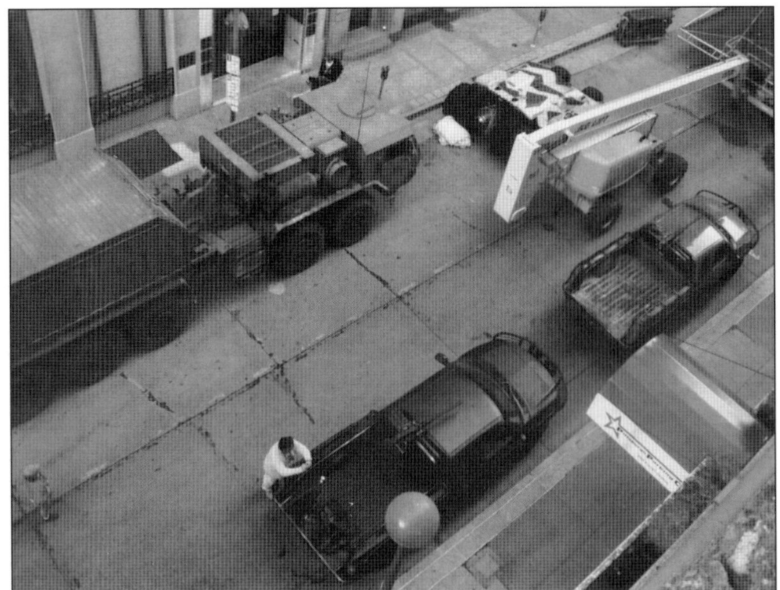

A Tumbler prop car and prop truck are parked on a Pittsburgh street. The scenes featuring these vehicles were filmed in the city of Pittsburgh during the final days of the shoot in the middle of August. (Courtesy of Denise Merriman.)

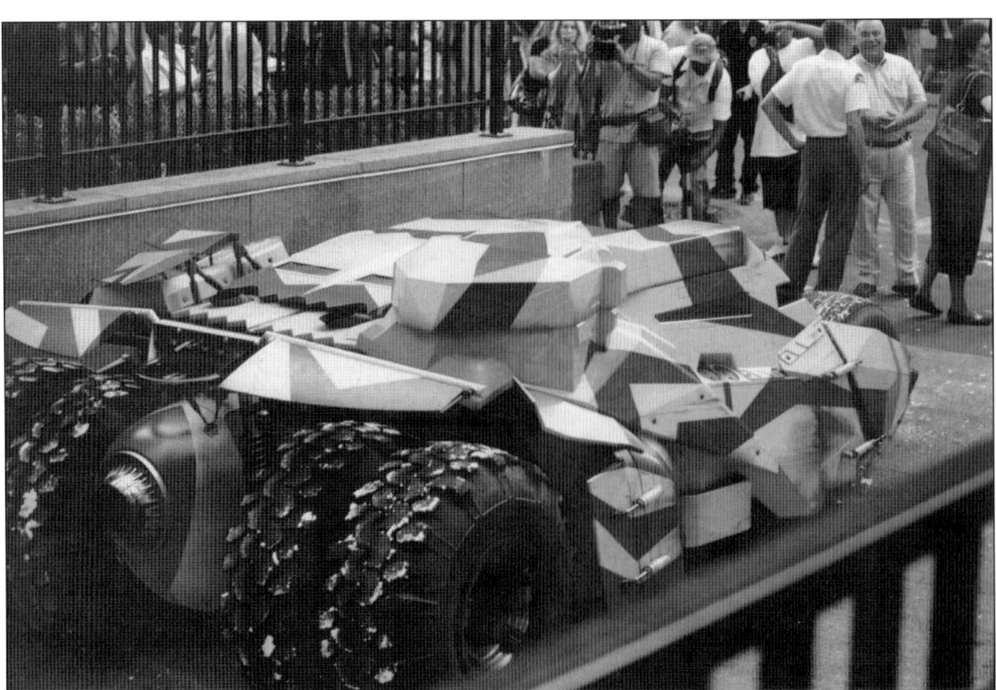

Fans and media take pictures of the Tumbler prop car for *The Dark Knight Rises*. This was the final installment in Christopher Nolan's Batman trilogy, one of the most successful comic book adaptation franchises of all time, and locals were very excited to be able to get a glimpse of the iconic vehicles, actors, and actresses. (Courtesy of Denise Merriman.)

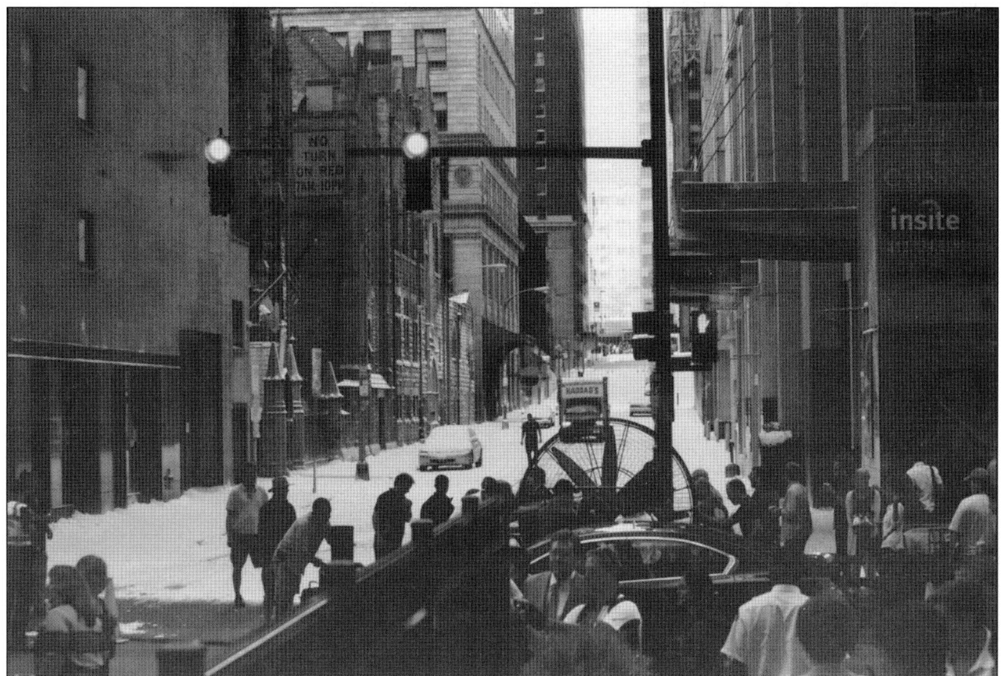

The crew of *The Dark Knight Rises* works on a winter scene shot in Pittsburgh. For many of the actors, actresses, and extras, it was a challenge filming a winter scene in the middle of the summer. (Courtesy of Denise Merriman.)

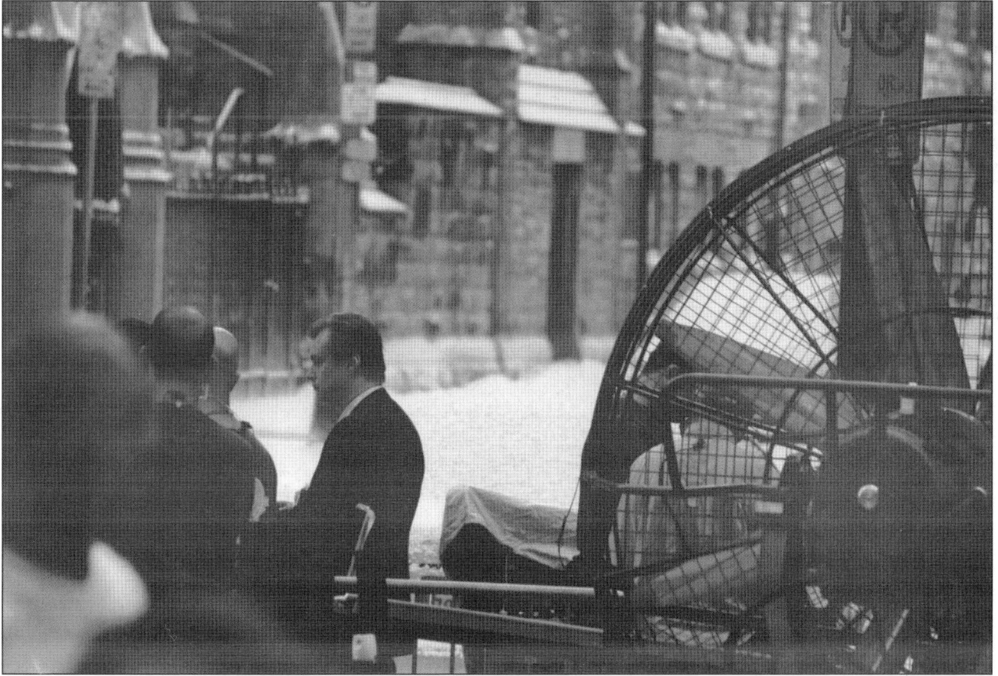

Director Christopher Nolan works on *The Dark Knight Rises* in downtown Pittsburgh during the final days of the shoot. (Courtesy of Denise Merriman.)